F

HOW AND WHY

EVERYONE

CAN ENJOY

MATERIAL AND

SPIRITUAL WEALTH

IN OUR

ABUNDANT WORLD

A FIRESIDE BOOK

Published by Simon & Schuster

GOD
WANTS
YOU
TO BE
RICH

PAUL ZANE PILZER

FIRESIDE
Rockefeller Center
1230 Avenue of the Americas
New York, NY 10020

First Fireside Edition 1997

FIRESIDE and colophon are registered trademarks
of Simon & Schuster Inc.

Designed by Karolina Harris

Manufactured in the United States of America

1   2   3   4   5   6   7   8   9   10

Library of Congress Cataloging-in-Publication Data
Pilzer, Paul Zane.
God wants you to be rich / Paul Zane Pilzer.
p.   cm.
Includes bibliographical references and index.
1. Economics.   2. Economics—Religious aspects.   I. Title.
HB71.P616   1995
330—dc20   95-20457
CIP
ISBN 0-684-80767-X
0-684-82532-5 (Pbk.)

To my tsadik, Charles Jay Pilzer

CONTENTS

Illustrative Articles

Chapter 3

Chapter 8

Appendix

Notes

Acknowledgments

Index

1

GOD WANTS YOU

TO BE RICH

"Professor Pilzer!" the woman exclaimed, following me into the elevator after my speech. "I must tell you how much your work has changed my life!"

"In what way?" I asked.

"All my life I wanted to be rich," she replied. "But I always believed that I could only succeed in business at the expense of someone else, and as a good Christian I could never do that. Reading your book and hearing you speak has shown me how wrong I was!"

The woman explained that two years ago, at age fifty-five, she had gone into her own business, and that she was now making three times more money than she had earned after working thirty-two years for someone else.

"How does your new financial success relate to your religious beliefs?" I inquired.

"That's the real tragedy of my life," she replied. "For fifty-five years, I believed that God didn't want me to have money, that the economy was always heading downhill, and that the only way to climb the ladder to success was by stepping on someone else. But I was wrong! Now I realize that these views were just excuses for my lack of initiative, and that one of the things God wants me to do most as a good Christian is to be rich. That's why he created a world where the more successful I am, the more wealth there is for everyone else to share."

Every major religion has an explanation of how God created the universe. What is important, however, is not *how* it was done, but *why*. As an economist and businessperson, I have devoted my life to explaining *how* people can become rich. I realize now that I have failed to reach certain people because I have incorrectly assumed that they already understood *why* they should become rich.

There is a widespread feeling today that there is something wrong with individual economic success. People who have become rich through great personal sacrifice sometimes feel guilty about their success—and often pass this guilt on to their children, with disastrous consequences. Even worse, people who fail to achieve success on their first try sometimes refuse to try again.

Most people believe they should achieve wealth primarily for their own material comfort or that of their families. This is far too narrow a view. God does want each of us to be rich in every possible way—health, love, and peace of mind, as well as material possessions. God wants this, however, not just for our own sake, but for the sake of all humankind. The reason, as we shall see throughout this book, is that an increase in wealth for an individual almost always represents an even larger increase in wealth for society at large. This is especially true in our modern economy, where the largest individual financial rewards are increasingly reserved for those people making the greatest positive impact on our society.

In ancient times people didn't spend much time wondering about how to improve their lives. People generally believed that their lives were predestined. A person was not supposed to try to change his or her fate, let alone even ponder whether such a fate was predestined in the first place. It was each person's obligation to follow the will of God—or the gods—whatever that will might be.

Until roughly the fourth century B.C., it was commonly believed in parts of the world that the mysterious lights in the sky were gods wandering about the heavens. In fact, the word "planet" comes from the Greek word for "wanderer." This illustrates what most people thought about their daily lives. The gods (planets) wandered about in the heavens, and their wanderings caused the crops to grow, the rain to fall, and the tragedies and joys of human existence.

The Greek philosopher Aristotle was one of the first people to refute this belief. Aristotle believed that there was an order to things that people could understand and use to control their lives. In 340 B.C., Aristotle devised one of the first modern theories of the universe, asserting that the planets and every other object in the heavens were in fact spheres that revolved in fixed paths around a stationary earth.

The Aristotelian view of the world, and the order to the seasons and our lives that it created, was refined by Ptolemy about 450 years later into a mathematical calendar. And this view, though wrong in its fundamental assumption that the earth, rather than the sun, was at the center of our solar system, became the bedrock of civilization for the next eighteen hundred years.

Looking back, we can see that its endurance was hardly surprising, for it accorded with the evidence of one's senses. After all, from your vantage point on earth, it certainly looks as if everything revolves around you.

But the Aristotelian-Ptolemaic calendar was not accurate, because it incorrectly placed the earth at the center of the universe. Every hundred years or so it would snow in Rome in July, and the pope would set the calendar back about six months. This led to a great quest among astronomers to discover a working model of the universe that could accurately track the months and predict the beginning of the seasons.

It wasn't until the early sixteenth century that the Polish astronomer Nicolaus Copernicus succeeded in this quest. By manipulating mathematical equations, Copernicus determined that the sun was at the center of the solar system, and that the heavenly bodies—including the earth—revolved around it. This model was later refined by the Italian astronomer Galileo, who, using his newly invented telescope, was able to confirm Copernicus's hypothesis.

We can easily see how astronomers before Copernicus were misled. For centuries they labored in vain trying to perfect the calendar and predict the seasons in order to increase agricultural and economic output. But the very definition of their science—the study of how the spheres in the heavens revolved around the stationary earth—precluded astronomers from discovering the true nature of the universe.

In our time, the science of economics has been hindered by the same sort of tunnel vision. Today the very definition of economics—"the study of how people choose to employ scarce resources"[1]—

precludes economists from discovering an accurate theory of economics and hinders economic success.

Most economists have agreed on one basic premise—*a society's wealth is determined by its supply of physical resources (land, oil, gas, minerals, and so forth)*. Underlying this premise has been another, even more basic (in fact, *so* basic that it is rarely mentioned)—*the world contains a limited amount of these physical resources*.

The incorrect supposition that we live in a world of scarce resources has done more than preclude most individuals from achieving economic success. Over the centuries, this zero-sum-game view of the world has been responsible for wars, revolutions, political strategies, and human suffering of unfathomable proportions.

Since 1975, when I entered the Wharton Graduate School, I have belonged to a small group of economists who believe that the world does *not* contain a limited amount of physical resources. Quite the contrary, I believe that the world is a virtual cornucopia of physical resources. I developed my belief into a theory of economics, which was first published as *Unlimited Wealth—The Theory and Practice of Economic Alchemy* (Crown Publishers, 1991).

Many notable people found truth in my theory. The late Sam Walton, founder of Wal-Mart, praised *Unlimited Wealth* for having put into writing beliefs to which he attributed his own success. My views were disseminated via national television appearances and in numerous publications. And businesspeople worldwide applauded *Unlimited Wealth* for establishing a practical, decision-making framework based on a cornucopian theory of economics.

Yet, both as a writer and as a teacher, I had failed. *Unlimited Wealth* was highly praised by those who were already successful or who were on their way to success. But it was largely ignored by those who could benefit from it the most. I felt like a clergyman preaching to the choir. The people who really needed to hear my sermon were not attending my church.

Unlimited Wealth explained in scientific terms, through deductive logic, why we live in a world of unlimited physical resources. It explained how, over the short term, advancing technology continually increases the supply of our existing physical resources and how, over the long term, advancing technology constantly changes our very definition of "physical resources" as new ones are discovered. But, in promulgating a scientific explanation for our economic lives, *Unlimited Wealth* failed to directly confront a theological belief that prevents most people from understanding, and thus achieving, unlimited wealth.

Today, this mistaken view of the world continues to take its toll on most Jews, Christians, and Moslems, who collectively make up more than 75 percent of the world's population. The erroneous economic belief in scarcity leads directly to the mistaken theological belief that *God does not want us to be rich*. After all, in a world of scarce physical resources, a person could achieve personal wealth only by taking wealth from another—something that a truly benevolent, loving God would never allow.

Throughout history, God's teachings have often been distorted, as people were taught the mistaken belief that there is something wrong with being economically rich. For example, Jesus states three times in the New Testament:

> It is easier for a camel to go through the eye of a needle, than for a rich man to enter into the kingdom of God.
> —MATTHEW 19:24 (King James Version)[2]

These words, incorrectly taken out of the context in which they were said, have been used for two millennia to criticize the accumulation of economic wealth. However, Jesus did not mean that there was something wrong with being rich. Jesus said these words to explain what God expects of a person in order to gain admission to heaven—and the special, even higher, obligation to help others that God expects of those who have achieved economic success.[3]

Interestingly, the very next chapter in the New Testament explains the obligation of the unemployed, or "not yet rich," to take the first step toward taking care of themselves. A householder approaches several idle laborers and inquires, "Why stand ye here all the day idle?" The laborers explain, "Because no man hath hired us." The householder then explains that if they would go into the fields on their own and "do whatsoever is right," then they, too, will receive their just rewards. The formerly unemployed workers are then handsomely rewarded for taking the initiative and starting to work on their own.[4]

God wants us to show compassion and understanding toward the unemployed or the poor not *because* they are poor, but because poor people, with help from those who are already successful, can become rich. And when the poor become rich, all will benefit, because in our modern economy *new unemployment is the first sign of economic growth.*

Most of the unemployment we are experiencing today is the result of new technology—a machine replaces a worker, or better methodology enables one person to perform a job that used to require two. As technology advances, individual jobs are eliminated; but the gross national product remains unchanged—society still receives the products or services from the eliminated jobs, which are now performed by a machine or by fewer workers using a better method. When the displaced worker finds a new job, the output of that job adds to the gross national product, and society experiences an increase in real wealth.

Unemployment resulting from this type of displacement always creates new wealth for society, although sadly not always for the same displaced worker. The wages of the displaced worker are transferred to the owners of the machine that replaced him, to his employer, and to the remaining workers who utilize the better method. These immediate beneficiaries of the displacement then use their increased remuneration to purchase new products and services, often products and services that were created just in response to their increased ability to afford them. Today, as explained in Chapter 4, "Economic Alchemy," virtually 95 percent of our economy is involved in producing new and innovative products and services that did not exist fifty years ago.

From an economic standpoint, this is how our society has progressed since the beginning of civilization. The only thing new about this process today is the speed with which it is occurring, as changes that used to take place over millennia or centuries now take place in decades or even a few years. This increased speed underlies most of our employment problems today, as individuals must deal with changes over a single lifetime rather than over several generations.

In 1930, there were approximately 30 million farmers in the United States, barely producing enough food to feed a population of approximately 100 million people. Technological breakthroughs in agriculture over the next fifty years made farming so efficient that by 1980 approximately 3 million farmers were producing enough food for a population of more than 300 million. This represents a 3000 percent increase in productivity per farmer! The farmers who were displaced during this period were lucky. They had fifty years to grow old, retire, and watch their children develop new careers as carburetor mechanics or vinyl record manufacturers—careers that were then on the cutting edge of new technologies. Their children, however, who left the family farm to pursue these new careers weren't nearly as fortunate.

In 1980, approximately three hundred thousand people in the United States were employed in the manufacture and repair of mechanical carburetors. In just five short years, however, virtually all of these jobs disappeared as automakers replaced $300 mechanical carburetors with much more efficient $25 computerized electronic fuel injectors.

In 1985, approximately one hundred thousand people in the United States were employed in the manufacture of vinyl records. At the time, virtually every American had at least one record player and a vinyl record collection. No one would have believed that all these jobs would be lost virtually overnight as consumers abandoned their lifelong record collections in favor of a new technology. But that's exactly what happened when the digital compact disc took hold in 1985 and captured virtually the entire vinyl record industry by 1990.

As we will examine more closely in Chapter 5, "What's Happening to Our Jobs," just as only a few of the farmers in the 1930s made the switch to making carburetors or vinyl records, only a few of their displaced children in the 1980s made the switch to making computerized fuel injectors or digital compact discs. Unlike their children, however, the farmers had ten times the number of years to adjust to these dramatic changes.

As a society, with retraining we always have jobs for workers displaced by technology. This is because, by definition, such displacement always represents a transfer of their wages to some other group —a group that then has an increased propensity, and a greater financial ability, to consume more products and services. But, as we will examine more closely in Chapter 8, "Government," we now need an affirmative program to deal with this displacement, because vocational changes that used to take place over several generations now take place several times over a single lifetime.

What guarantees that the immediate beneficiaries of technological displacement will always want to purchase new products and services with their increased remuneration? The answer is the very thing that caused the displacement in the first place—increasing technology. The technology that causes displacement also creates *unlimited demand* by lowering the price of existing products and services and by creating new products and services for people to consume. Unlimited wealth comes from fulfilling this unlimited demand with a potentially unlimited supply of retrained displaced workers.

This process entails one great risk, both for individuals temporarily displaced by technology and for society at large. That risk is our potential failure to understand that unemployment caused by technological displacement is the opportunity for personal and economic growth, rather than the beginning of permanent economic decline. Individuals who fail to realize this are doomed to economic failure, and societies that make this mistake are in danger of total collapse (see, in Chapter 8, "The Greatest Challenge of Our Century").

In 1960, manufacturing was the bedrock of America's economic power, employing approximately 40 percent of all U.S. workers. Suppose I told you, in 1960, that 50 percent of the country's manufacturing jobs—20 percent of all U.S. employment—would be eliminated by 1980 because of advancing technology. Suppose I also told you not to worry about the country's economic power because by 1980 the remaining manufacturing employees would be producing more than five times the 1960 level of output. And suppose I further told you not to worry about overall unemployment because the food service industry alone would absorb all of the displaced manufacturing workers, as the amount of meals U.S. consumers ate out of their homes would rise from 5 percent in 1960 to 50 percent in 1980.

If you had been familiar with the restaurant industry in 1960, you wouldn't have believed my predictions for at least four seemingly valid reasons:

First, you would have argued in 1960, only the very wealthy could afford to eat half their meals out of the home—to which I would have responded that advancing technology would lower production costs so much that by 1980 it would be less expensive to eat out than dine at home.

Second, you would have argued in 1960, there weren't enough restaurants in America to seat that many people at mealtimes—to which I would have responded that over the next twenty years, tens of thousands of suburban shopping centers would be built to house hundreds of thousands of new dining establishments.

Third, you would have argued in 1960, people would be bored eating out so much, since, back then, there were only two basic types of cuisine available ("food" and "French")—to which I would have responded that by 1980 there would be restaurants serving cuisines that I couldn't describe to you in 1960 because some of them would be from countries that weren't even independently named countries yet.

Fourth, even if you accepted my incredible predictions about lower costs, increased number of dining establishments, and unlimited varieties of cuisine, you would have argued that people just didn't have the time to eat out so often—to which I would have responded that by 1980 there would be a whole new category of restaurants defined not by their price, location, or country of origin, but by the speed of their service; establishments that we would call "fast food" restaurants.

The incredible displacement of employees in the manufacturing sector from 1960 to 1980, and the even more incredible growth of employment in just the restaurant industry during the same period, is indicative of what is happening today throughout our entire economy at an ever-increasing pace. Moreover, most of the economic growth about to happen in the next two decades will be in sectors of our economy that may not even exist today.

For example, one of the fastest growing sectors of the economy today is the U.S. personal computer industry, which after only fifteen years enjoys sales of approximately $150 billion—$80 billion in software and $70 billion in hardware. Compare this to the U.S. automobile industry—after more than seventy years, car sales of the Big Three U.S. manufacturers are only approximately the same $150 billion.

Similarly, in the late 1970s, consumers started buying VCRs to record television programs while they were away from home. Today, sales of VCRs are approximately $2 billion. But sales and rentals of prerecorded video cassettes—an industry not even *envisioned* by the original VCR manufacturers—are approximately $18 billion! Ironically, some U.S. demagogues complain that Asian manufacturers stole the $2 billion VCR hardware business from the U.S. companies that invented the machine. This complaint falls on deaf ears in Asia, where parents feel compelled to spend for their children multiple times this amount on U.S.-produced VCR movies—most of them in English and many of them promoting distasteful (to them) cultural values.

In order to comprehend how our economy functions today, we need to have a scientific understanding of how it functioned yesterday. But in order to *use* this understanding to shape our future, we need to have a religious faith in *why* our economy works—a faith based on the belief that God wants us to be rich. This faith is important because the greatest economic opportunities of tomorrow, almost by definition, are in sectors of our economy that may not even exist today.

Before understanding *why* and *how* God wants you to be rich, I want to stress the importance of empathizing with the situations discussed in this book and drawing analogies between these situations and your own life experiences.

At the start of each semester at New York University, I ask the class why they are taking my course. A few bold students readily admit that they are there to learn how to become rich. I then pose the following question to the class.

"Do any of you have a younger brother or sister who has dated someone who you knew was going to break their heart?" I ask rhetorically. "You call them over and say, 'Sis, he's bad news'—and of course your sister immediately ends the relationship and thanks you for sharing your wisdom." My students laugh as I explain how we are often powerless to teach others even what we have learned through painful personal experience. Often the only way to truly learn something is to experience it for yourself. In light of this, the best we can do is let our younger sibling know that we will always be there for them and will always love them unconditionally, no matter what choice they make.

Unfortunately, I explain to my students, despite the experiences that I and their other business mentors have had in the business world, there is often little we can really teach them—true learning often requires firsthand experience. But the more you can empathize with other people's past experiences and draw analogies with your current experiences, the faster and less painfully you will be able to learn new things for yourself.[5]

This book is composed of two interleaved parts. The first part is the main text, which is divided into the nine chapters shown on the Contents page. The second part consists of thirty-eight articles illustrating the concepts discussed in the main text. You can read these articles in the order they are presented throughout the main text, or you can simply select them by their descriptive titles on the Contents page.

The nine chapters of this book and their descriptive articles progress from the abstract to the practical. Chapter 2 ("The Covenant") explains the contract that underlies our entire modern economy—God's promise to Abraham that one day all his children would understand the concepts of unlimited wealth. Chapter 3 ("Searching for Camelot") examines the development of traditional (e.g., scarcity) economic thinking and answers the question: If everything is so good, how come so many people think everything is so bad? And Chapter 4 ("Economic Alchemy") summarizes a decision-making theory of business based on the economics of abundance rather than the economics of scarcity.

Taking a more practical approach, and using the information in the first few chapters as a base, Chapter 5 ("What's Happening to Our Jobs") explains what is happening to our careers today. Chapter 6 ("The Workplace of the Twenty-first Century") takes this information to the next stage, explaining what we will need in the future and what each of us can do now to prepare for it.

As a former executive with Citibank and as a technologist on the information superhighway, I have always been fascinated by the concept of money—the abstract invention we use to record our prosperity and store our wealth. Chapter 7 ("Money") examines historically where money and savings come from, and explains how both are becoming obsolete in the new technological order.

Since the Israelites first asked the prophet Samuel to anoint them a king, the optimum form of government has been a continual subject of debate. Chapter 8 ("Government") explains how the U.S. Constitution laid the foundation for U.S. economic success, and proposes innovative solutions for contemporary problems in education, crime, and unemployment.

As you read this book, stop at the end of each chapter and descriptive article and ask yourself whether the information just presented makes sense. If so, why does it make sense? What have you experienced in your life that illustrates how it works, and what can you do to apply the information to your current economic situation? And for those readers who become upset thinking that they should have made a different choice in the past, remember that the only way to truly learn something is to experience it for yourself—and that, like the perfect older sibling, God loves us unconditionally and will always be there for us, regardless of the choices we have made.

Now, let's get started understanding *why* and *how* God wants you to be rich.

2

THE COVENANT

That in blessing I will bless thee, and in multiplying I will multiply thy
seed as the stars of the heaven, and as the sand which is upon the
seashore; and thy seed shall possess the gate of his enemies; And in thy
seed shall all the nations of the earth be blessed; because thou hast
obeyed my voice.

—GENESIS 22:17-18

In the Book of Genesis, God puts Abraham's faith to the ultimate test
by asking him to sacrifice his beloved son, Isaac. Abraham, willing to
obey God's directive, binds the boy and raises his knife to slay him.
When God sees this, he instructs Abraham not to kill the boy and
rewards him for his faith by restating the covenant. In this covenant,
God promises to make Abraham's descendants as numerous as the
sands of the seashore and the stars in the heavens.[1] The covenant first
appears earlier in the Bible, when God changes Abraham's name from
"Abram," which means "father," to "Abraham," which means "father
of many nations."[2]

Today, this story is interpreted by some Christians as the promise
made to "their father" that the entire world will one day be Christian.
It is interpreted by some Jews as the promise made to "their father"
that the entire world will one day be Jewish. And it is interpreted by
some Moslems as the promise made to "their father" that the entire
world will one day be Moslem.

Is this what God had in mind when he made the covenant with
Abraham? In our society, when a dispute arises over the meaning of a
contract or covenant, a court seeks to determine the intent of the

parties who made the agreement. Let's examine what God and Abraham may have intended when they made this covenant.

According to the Christian, Jewish and Moslem scriptures, Abraham was a nomad from Ur of Chaldees who became a farmer in Canaan. Nomads take food from the land until they have exhausted the supply, at which point they move on to different land with more food. By contrast, farmers plant seeds and grow a continual supply of food on the same piece of land. Farming is predicated on the concept of land ownership, because people would not spend time cultivating land that they did not expect to occupy at the time of harvest.

Several hundred years ago, European explorers purchased land from Native Americans, who, as nomads, had no concept of land ownership. Imagine a Native American chief advising his tribe that he has sold land to a visiting white man—land from which the tribe had already removed the game and edible plant life and thus was planning to move on from anyway. The tribe might jokingly suggest that next time the clever chief offer to sell the white man the sun, moon, and stars as well, for Native Americans could no sooner imagine owning land than they could imagine owning the celestial bodies.

Similarly, imagine Abraham, a nomad-turned-farmer, confronting a nomadic Egyptian or Phoenician who stumbled across the food growing in Abraham's fields.

"Excuse me," Abraham might have said to the nomadic stranger, "what are you doing on this land?"

"Oh," replies the stranger, "I'm harvesting this food to take back to my people."

"But you don't understand," says Abraham. "This is our food. This is our land. My people and I planted this food last spring to harvest this fall."

"Silly man," says the stranger. "Everyone knows that God owns land, not man. God makes food, not man. You have as much claim to this land and the food on it as you do to the sky and the planets."

Nomads, accustomed to moving to new lands for the express purpose of taking what the land had to offer, had no respect for the claim of the farmers to the produce of land that the farmers had cultivated. In contrast, Abraham realized how prosperous all of God's children could be if everyone strove to create and improve his own property or wealth, instead of forcibly trying to take property from someone else.

In the chapter immediately following the sacrifice of Isaac, Abraham becomes the first person in the Bible to recognize land as individual property that can be improved, purchased, and sold. Abraham purchases for four hundred shekels of silver the field of Ephron together with the trees on the land and the cave of Machpelah as a burying place for his wife Sarah. The discussion over the price, the exacting legal description of the property, and the public announcing of the acquisition before those who entered the city (Hebron) contain the basic elements of all present-day contracts for the sale of real property.[3]

Today, from an economic standpoint, there is no limit to the amount of available wealth if everyone on earth were to follow the way of Abraham. Traditional economists sought wealth by hoarding as much of a given resource as possible (oil, gold, and so forth), much as the nomads did. They depended exclusively on wealth that God had already put on earth, consuming what they found, then moving on to find more. Of course, they could accumulate additional wealth only by taking from someone else. By contrast, today's economic alchemists seek wealth by utilizing advancing technology to create more resources than currently exist, much as the farmers did by growing crops on cultivated land. They increase their own wealth—and therefore the overall wealth of society—by improving the productivity of their God-given property.

The concept of real and intellectual property ownership, as originally conceived in the laws of Abraham, is the foundation of our modern technological economy. When people who improve their lot (literally as well as figuratively) are allowed to keep the rewards, total prosperity has no limit. As explained in Chapter 4, "Economic Alchemy," there is no limit to our God-given ability to increase the quantity of our physical resources through advancing technology. This has been particularly evident during our lifetimes in the rapid economic growth of Japan and other Asian nations (Taiwan, Singapore, and Korea)—countries with high population densities and seemingly limited physical resources.

The covenant was not a promise by God that one day every human being would be Christian, Jewish, or Moslem. Rather, the covenant was God's promise that one day all of his children would respect one another's private property, thus giving all the opportunity to become rich. If Abraham were alive today, he would see that God has kept his agreement. The laws of Abraham relating to property ownership are codified in every major religion; and following the fall of Communism in the early 1990s, these laws are becoming the common and statutory laws in virtually every nation on earth.

Abraham might be perplexed to learn that some Christians, Jews, and Moslems have mistakenly interpreted the covenant as a sign that everybody would one day be Christian, Jewish, or Moslem. There were no "Jews" until approximately a thousand years later, when Moses was given the Ten Commandments at Mount Sinai. There were no "Christians" until twenty-five hundred years later, when Jesus Christ died on the cross in Jerusalem. And there were no "Moslems" until thirty-one hundred years later, when Mohammed began preaching Islam in Mecca.

Abraham might have difficulty today understanding the differences between these three religions. From the standpoint of his teachings, they are all basically the same except for their interpretation of creation: Most Moslems believe that God created the earth in six days and rested on Friday. Most Jews believe that God created the earth in six days and rested on Saturday. And some Christians believe that God created the earth in six days and rested on Sunday. (Of course, as an astute businessman, Abraham might appreciate the fact that his children observe the Sabbath on different days, since the economy couldn't function if everyone took off at the same time.)

Some religions maintain that we are entering an age when the Messiah, a deliverer of worldwide prosperity to all, will soon appear. One might ask what the Messiah will do to distribute such worldwide prosperity when he gets here. Will he simply hand over great wealth to all of God's children and depart? Or, like a loving father, will he instead give us tools to work with, tools that will enable us to achieve and maintain great wealth ourselves?

Today, every one of us is capable, with God's help, of achieving unlimited wealth. Thanks to the now universal application of his ultimate tool, the laws of Abraham, the blessings of the Messiah promised to our ancestors are finally within our grasp. What remains is for each of us to learn how to use what God has given us.

• • •

The most important economic concept underlying our modern economy is the concept of unlimited wealth. Here's an exercise I use to teach this all-important concept to students in grade school.

I tell the class to pretend that they are shipwrecked on a desert island with no provisions. In order to survive, they must organize a society and divide themselves into work groups according to specific chores—building shelters, making weapons, gathering food, and so forth.

I consistently find that, at first, the students want to democratically rotate the various chores throughout their new island society. However, they quickly learn that the society fares far better if each person specializes and works full-time at a particular task. The person who builds shelters on Monday can usually accomplish the same task in less time on Tuesday, and in even less time on Wednesday, as skills and knowledge requisite to the task are developed. Moreover, repetition of the task often leads to the development of tools that help complete the task better and in even less time.

The students soon realize that as they develop proficiency at their particular chores, the chores can be performed by fewer and fewer people. Soon all of the necessary tasks (shelter, weapons, food) are performed by a fraction of the people originally required to handle them. This frees some members of the society to explore new pursuits, perhaps producing new products and tools, or even providing entertainment. Before long, the society's members become so efficient at producing their particular product or service that a new need arises—distribution—and soon some people are engaged full-time just distributing the products that everyone else is creating.

The students quickly come to understand the two principles underlying our modern economy that Abraham discovered three thousand years ago. First, there is no limit to the amount of a single good or service an individual can produce by making use of the advancing technology that results from increasing specialization. Second, the total wealth of society is limited only by the number of individuals available to trade with for their specialized produce.[4]

The more each of us specializes in one particular task, the greater our individual, specialized produce. The greater and more specialized our produce, the more we desire to trade and share with other individuals for their specialized produce, and the greater the total economic produce of our society. The greater the economic produce of our society, the more we need other societies to trade with and share their specialized economic output. And the more societies with whom we thus trade and share, the greater the total global wealth. Only a true God could have created an economy based on such simple, but powerful and loving, concepts.

As explained in Chapter 8, "Government," these concepts are incorporated into the Constitution of the United States.

In the late 1700s, the term "state" meant an independent sovereign nation. The Constitution allowed each state to rule itself with one very powerful exception: No state was allowed to make any law or rule that infringed upon the rights of its citizens to freely trade with the citizens of any other state. Nowhere in the course of human history have the laws of Abraham been so excellently codified in a secular document.

When we teach the constitutional origins of the United States, we usually stress that our forefathers formulated the Constitution because it was a morally correct thing to do. We must not ignore, however, the fact that the invisible hand of God was guiding our forefathers not just morally, but economically as well—ensuring that what was morally correct would also serve to allow everyone to enjoy the greatest possible slice of the future American economic pie.

Once we understand the powerful economic concepts underlying the laws of Abraham, we might rightly ask why it has taken us so long to discover them. A partial answer can be found in a very popular movie that has touched people's hearts for three generations, *The Wizard of Oz*.

As the movie begins, a storm sends Dorothy's house crashing down on top of the Wicked Witch of the West, killing her instantly. Then the Good Witch of the North appears and gives Dorothy the magic slippers of the deceased Wicked Witch. Throughout the movie, Dorothy has learning experiences as she helps her new friends obtain what they believe they need to succeed: intelligence for the Scarecrow, courage for the Lion, and a heart for the Tin Man. At the end, the Wizard's balloon accidentally floats off, leaving Dorothy behind, forlorn at having lost the opportunity to return to her family in Kansas.

At this point, the Good Witch of the North appears again and tells Dorothy that she has always had the ability to return to Kansas— simply by clicking the heels of her magic slippers together three times. Dorothy rightly asks why she wasn't told about the power of the magic slippers when she first received them. The Good Witch explains that the magic slippers (like most things in life) work only for those who have faith in their own abilities to accomplish their goals. Dorothy was able to help her friends obtain what they wanted most by getting them to believe in their own abilities. Until she accomplished this, Dorothy didn't have faith in her abilities to achieve her own goals.

This is what God now expects of us after five millennia of what we have called "civilization." As Dorothy was given the magic slippers, God gave us the laws of Abraham—a tool with which to begin developing the technology to take care of ourselves. Then he guided us through hundreds of painful learning experiences—from plagues in biblical times to modern world wars and civil wars—to develop faith in our ability to use technology for the purpose for which it was intended.

The ancient alchemists sought to obtain great wealth for all of God's children by discovering the secret of turning base metals into gold. Ironically, if they had succeeded in their quest, gold would have become worthless and their efforts would have been for naught. However, their attempts to make gold laid the foundation for modern science and technology, which today has given us the ability to achieve their dream for every man, woman, and child on earth.

Today we live in the kind of world dreamed of by these ancient alchemists—a world where our material wealth is determined almost entirely by what we desire to create for ourselves. Today, for those of us who understand the covenant underlying our alchemic economy, the only economic limit to our dreams is the size of the dream itself.

> You've got to have a dream,
> for if you don't have a dream,
> then how you gonna make your dreams come true?[5]

· · ·

In theory, the covenant underlying our alchemic economy is so simple a schoolchild can understand it. In practice, however, many of us who have already achieved its objective—more wealth than we can consume in our lifetimes—are incapable of teaching to others what we have supposedly learned.

In the 1967 movie *The Graduate,* Dustin Hoffman was offered a confident, one-word solution to the quest for economic success— "plastics." How many of us today could provide our children with a similarly confident directive upon their graduation?

It seemed so simple in the past. The recipe for success was to go to school, choose an occupation or a company, and work hard in that field or for that company for the rest of your life. Looking back on just the past ten years, we can see that this former recipe for success has become a recipe for disaster!

Whether in helping us plan our future as individuals, or in finding ways to take care of the increasing number of poor in our society, virtually the only thing that our so-called experts on economic success —our economists—can agree upon is that they can no longer agree on almost anything. Economists have taken to qualifying their predictions and prescriptions with phrases such as "on the other hand," a state of affairs that once led President Truman to remark that what the United States needed was a good one-handed economist.

The science of economics today has advanced only to where the science of medicine was at the beginning of the nineteenth century. In the early 1800s, doctors could administer the few medicines that existed, and by way of trial and error could observe which medicines cured which diseases. But even when a medicine worked, doctors didn't know *why* it worked. The underlying theories that explain bacterial infections, and the inoculations and antibiotics that these theories would produce, had not yet been discovered. Without a knowledge of these underlying theories, doctors were unable to learn and grow from their experiences, and only a select few people could afford what little medical care existed. Once these theories had been developed, good medical care became widespread. In fact, the ensuing decades brought cures for many of the diseases—smallpox, typhoid, polio—that had been the scourge of mankind for millennia.

When it comes to searching for a working economic theory that we can apply to our individual lives as well as to societal problems, there is much to be learned from the study of medical history. The people responsible for these great medical breakthroughs—men and women like Louis Pasteur, Marie Curie, Jonas Salk, and Paul Ehrlich—never doubted for a moment that there was a solution. Their faith in God caused them to believe that there were cures for these diseases and that it was their responsibility and their destiny to discover them.

By contrast, most of the people responsible for the greatest break-throughs in the science we now call economics, and many prac-titioners of the science today, do not harbor such lofty notions about the ultimate outcome of their work. Traditional economists believed that all of the world's resources existed in a fixed, limited supply and that the best they could hope to discover or achieve was a better or fairer way of distributing these scarce resources amongst ourselves. No wonder economics is often called "the dismal science"!

This economic view of the world conflicts directly with the teach-ings of all great religions. No world religion expounds, and no reli-gious person today would accept, the notion that a true and just God created a world where one person's gain must be another person's loss.

It is in this light that we begin our quest for economic success—a quest consistent with our belief that God, our Father, did not put us on earth to profit at the expense of one another. Implicit within this belief is our understanding that, like a loving father, God would not simply hand over to us, his children, everything that we desired. Rather, he would give us the tools that we require to succeed, and allow us to discover for ourselves how to use them.

Albert Einstein said that God does not play dice with the universe. Although God may not reveal it during our individual lifetimes, he has a master plan for each of us and for our society. And in order for each of us to achieve financial success, he requires that we become active participants in his plan. This may be illustrated by the humorous story of a modern-day Joseph—a very pious individual seeking to become rich.

For nearly fifty years, Joseph was one of God's best servants. He kept the Sabbath. He was devoted to his family. He gave part of his meager weekly salary to charity. And every week, on Sabbath, he turned toward God and asked whether this was the week when it was his turn to win the lottery. Now, at age sixty-five, facing seemingly insurmountable financial problems, Joseph began to question his years of unwavering faith.

"God," he exclaimed one day during his Sabbath prayers, "unless I get a sign by tomorrow morning telling me exactly what you want me to do this week to finally win the lottery, we're through. No more Sabbath, no more devotion to my family, no more charity."

That night, an exasperated God appeared to Joseph in his dream: "Joseph," God said, "give me a chance—buy a ticket!"

God may not actually want us to buy a lottery ticket. After all, unlike the economic world we live in, the lottery really is a zero-sum game. However, Joseph's story does correctly illustrate what God expects from each of us in order for us to achieve financial success. He expects us to take the first step—to buy a ticket. And, in our economic world —the world God promised to Abraham in the covenant, a world in which the quantity of our own wealth is directly proportional to the number of people with whom we share the rewards of our increased specialization—the particular ticket may be different for each of us.

This is our quest—to discover, as individuals, which ticket God wants us to purchase in order to become rich and take better care of the people we love.

3

THE SEARCH FOR

CAMELOT

To a man like my father, it was inconceivable that God would allow
people to multiply in the billions and yet deny them the ability to feed
and shelter themselves. Yet, like a loving father, God would not simply
hand over to his children everything they needed. Rather, He would
give them the necessary tools and allow them to discover how to use
the tools to take care of themselves."
—UNLIMITED WEALTH, 1991 [1]

The great Christian theologian Saint Augustine (A.D. 354–430) was
once asked what God did before he created the universe. Augustine's
reply: He was busy preparing hell for the people who would ask such
questions.

Today, most of us do ask—and encourage our children to ask—
such questions. For today, even though we do not have all the answers, we are surer than ever before that there are answers—and that
it is our God-given destiny as human beings to discover them.

And yet, in the one area where most of us spend the majority of our
waking hours—economics, earning our livelihoods—few of us feel
that we have found the answers we seek.

Some of us have seen our economic aspirations frustrated. And
most of us, even though we intellectually know how much better off
we are each year on a material basis, feel like Alice in Wonderland,

trapped in the Red Queen's race—having to run faster and faster merely to stay in the same place.

Why is it that in economics, the one area in which so many of us want to succeed, so few of us seem to have found the answers we seek? The reason is that, until now, the science of economics has been falsely based on the wrong presupposition, of scarcity. The very definition most economists use to define their science is "the study of society's allocation and distribution of scarce resources."[2]

This dismal definition of economics is not just limited to economists. Economics, as a defined field of study, is less than one hundred years old—the Nobel Prize for economics was created only in 1969.[3] But in various forms, the perception of the world as a spaceship hurtling through space with a limited supply of fuel has plagued humankind since the dawn of time.

The End of the World (Again)

From approximately the thirteenth century until the beginning of the Industrial Revolution, a significant part of the world's economy rested on the whaling industry. The blubber was used to produce whale oil for lighting and heating homes; the spermaceti was used to make candles and lubricants; and the whalebones were used for numerous applications ranging from artistic carvings to the flexible stays in women's corsets.

In fact, the economies of some of the earliest settlements in the United States were built entirely on the whaling business.

When America itself was less than one hundred years old, it had already, thanks to Yankee ingenuity, come to dominate this six-hundred-year-old industry—by 1850 the U.S. whaling fleet numbered approximately 700 of the world's largest 950 whaling vessels. While the ships of other countries caught whales and brought them back whole to their home ports for processing, ingenious Yankee whaling ships were entire floating factories in themselves—processing the raw whales into their useful products before they returned home.[4] This allowed them to bring back cargoes of much greater value and stay out longer at sea.

The world's first major energy crisis struck in the middle of the nineteenth century, when the worldwide supply of whales dwindled, mostly as a result of the Yankee efficiency in harvesting them. In 1859, over ten thousand whales were harvested from the North Atlantic alone; this caused a worldwide shortage in whale products on both sides of the ocean.

But in 1859, just as the doomsayers were predicting the end of their economies, due to the shortage of whale products, another burst of Yankee ingenuity came onto the scene with a lower-cost substitute for virtually all whale-based products. Col. Edwin L. Drake drilled the world's first successful oil well in Titusville, Pennsylvania, on August 27, 1859, ushering in the modern petroleum age.[5]

In England, which dominated much of the world's economy during the nineteenth century, the internal economy was primarily dependent on coal production. Coal, which was used both as a source of energy and as a principal ingredient in steelmaking, formed the backbone of British industrial power.

"The Coal Panic," as the newspapers called it, struck in 1865, when William Stanley Jevons wrote a book predicting the end of the British industrial era, due to the exhaustion of Britain's coal supplies by 1900.

Although Jevons (1814–1891) was born into a well-to-do prominent English family, he had considerable trouble in his personal life before he came to write his book in 1865. His mother died in 1845, his eldest brother became mentally ill in 1847, and his father, a Liverpool iron merchant, went bankrupt in 1848. This failure of the family finances led him to quit college, where he studied chemistry and mathematics, and accept a post in Australia until 1859 when he returned to England to finish college.[6]

In 1865 he published *The Coal Question: An Inquiry Concerning the Progress of the Nation, and the Probable Exhaustion of our Coal Mines,* a book not unlike the doomsayer books that appeared during our recent energy crisis in the 1970s. Utilizing his knowledge of chemistry and mathematics, Jevons had graphs and parabolic curves showing that at the then-current 3.5 percent annual rate of increase in coal consumption, "The conclusion is inevitable that our present happy progressive condition is a thing of limited duration."[7]

Jevons was a true pessimist in suggesting a possible escape from this difficulty. He was skeptical of finding substitutes for coal, and he discounted the possibility of reducing consumption through more efficient use. "Cutting costs would," he argued, "simply stimulate industrial expansion and so ultimately lead to increased demand for coal."[8]

He predicted the demise of prosperity and ended his book with the statement, in italics: *"We have to make the momentous choice between brief greatness and longer continued mediocrity."*[9] His only positive suggestion was to reduce the national debt in order to partially compensate posterity for the extravagance of the current generation.

Jevon's book made him nationally famous and led to the appointment of a royal commission on coal. This commission, which did not report until 1871, produced reassuring estimates of coal reserves, and the public forgot its fears.

Meanwhile, the rapidly developing petroleum industry displaced coal in the economy long before Jevon's prediction of coal famine by the end of the century could have occurred.

Jevons abandoned the subject of coal shortages and began work on a link between periods of economic activity and the then-recently discovered astronomical phenomenon of solar sunspot cycles.[10]

*J*evons was but one in a long line of people who made themselves famous by predicting the end of prosperity due to a coming shortage of some material resource. If fact, many of the founding fathers of economics were primarily known as economic doomsayers in their own time.

Thomas Malthus (1766–1834), a clergyman who pioneered both economics and demography, argued that as the wealth of the working class increased, so too would its birthrate, increasing the number of people who must share the wealth and dooming the society to live forever at a subsistence level. Malthus regarded war, famine, and pestilence as "positive" checks on population growth.

This pessimistic view of population growth was shared by his friend the great classical economist David Ricardo (1772–1823). Ricardo asserted that the wealth of a nation was determined by its available farmland and that an inevitable scarcity of land would eventually put an end to economic growth.

Today we know that these and hundreds of other famous doomsayers throughout history were wrong. Dead wrong. Despite large areas today of worldwide poverty—which, we will see later on, is due mostly to politics and economic policies rather than material shortages —the only thing that has grown faster than the population of our beloved earth has been the ability of our planet to support everyone on it.

Since 1750 the gross world product has increased more than seventeen hundred times, while world population has increased only six times. The 38 million people counted in the British census of 1901 were far better off than the 12 million counted in the census of 1801 at the time of Malthus and Ricardo.[11] More recently, world grain production since World War Two tripled, while the world's population only doubled. From 1972 to 1986, the real prices (adjusted for inflation) of our major food staples—rice, corn, sugar, beets, and soybeans —halved, on account of massive oversupply in world markets.[12] And in the world's poorest countries, from 1961 to 1980 food output rose 3.1 percent per year—or roughly doubled—well ahead of even their soaring populations. (India and China became self-sufficient in grain production during this period.)[13]

When we review the professional lives of Jevons, Malthus, Ricardo, and other famous economists of the nineteenth century—with the benefit of twenty/twenty hindsight—a pattern emerges that contains an important lesson for us today. Despite the fact that they lived at a time when technological advances during their lifetimes exceeded those of perhaps the previous five hundred years, they failed to realize that the rate of technological advance itself would continue to accelerate—that progress would not merely continue, but that the rate of progress would grow along with progress itself.

These economists lived at the same time Charles Darwin was developing his theory of natural selection and survival of the fittest species. But in applying Darwinian theories to humankind, these economists failed to comprehend the God-given ability of human beings, unlike any other species, to continually increase their supply of available resources through the application of technology. And thus they failed to see that, for at least the basic needs of their nineteenth-century world, technology would cause the supply of goods and services to outstrip the demand for them, not the other way around—leading to an increase, rather than a decrease, in the general lifestyle.

As we review the personal lives of Jevons, Malthus, Ricardo, Marx, and other famous doomsayers of the nineteenth century—also with the benefit of twenty/twenty hindsight—another pattern emerges. While they were all clearly great thinkers and pioneered the study of what we now call economics, we would probably not even know their names today were it not for the alarm they each created by predicting the economic demise of their current era. While throughout history there have been prophets of gloom and prophets of boom, since the dawn of the Industrial Revolution the prophets of doom have received most of our attention.

Let's digress for a moment and examine why this is so. If you and I were walking down the street on a sunny day and passed a newspaper stand with a headline that read "Sunny Day Tomorrow," we would probably just smile and continue uninterrupted on our journey. If the headline read "Snowstorm Tomorrow," we might interrupt our walk to purchase and read the paper about tomorrow's storm. Similarly, if we were walking down the street on a snowy day, we would probably ignore a headline forecasting more snow but might stop to purchase a newspaper predicting sunshine.

This example may seem insignificant and a bit simplistic, but it illustrates a key point about human behavior: We generally pay attention only when someone or something predicts a change in our existing situation. Throughout history there have been prophets predicting good and bad times, but the ones predicting a change in the status quo almost always received most of the attention. At times of political or economic turmoil, people generally listened to prophets predicting peace and prosperity. And more significantly for us today —when most of us enjoy political stability and relative plenty—we have a natural tendency to be more interested in news of economic adversity than news of continued prosperity.

Why Do We Have So Much Bad News?

> I admit that I do not feel toward freedom of the press that
> complete and instantaneous love which one accords to
> things by their nature supremely good. I love it more from
> considering the evils it prevents than on account of the
> good it does.
> —DEMOCRACY IN AMERICA, Alexis de Tocqueville, 1835 [14]

We live today in a mass media environment where the companies that deliver the news to us—television stations, newspapers, radio stations, magazines, and so forth—are commercially dependent on maintaining our interest. And today, maintaining our interest means giving us a continual barrage of bad news.

In an increasingly complex world, fewer and fewer journalists understand the dramatic changes our economy undergoes each day, let alone the statistics—unemployment, gross national product, trade deficits—that accompany these changes. Yet most news directors and aspiring anchorpeople seem to know that bad news for the economy means good news for their nightly ratings and for their careers.

The material lifestyle of almost every American has steadily risen since the end of the Second World War. Little of this is evident in our mass media, which, whether preparing for the nightly news or tomorrow's headlines, must continually weigh maintaining our interest against a balanced reporting of the day's economic events.

For example, since 1960, every time the federal government releases statistics on the median price of a new house, we are treated to a barrage of how the average American no longer can afford a detached single-family home. Meanwhile, the media conveniently neglect to mention that the median-size home Americans supposedly can no longer afford is more than twice the size of the median-size home they supposedly could afford back in 1960, let alone the fact that it includes air-conditioning, dishwasher, and countless other features that make it perhaps four times more valuable to its new occupant.[15]

In reality, the average price of a new home, when adjusted just for consumer purchasing power and physical size—let alone technological improvements—has fallen steadily during the past thirty years. This is supported by the fact that during the 1960–1990 period, the number of owner-occupied housing units increased from 33 million to 59 million homes, well in excess of the growth in the general population.[16]

In the early 1990s, when the price of existing homes—which had risen far above their replacement values in the inflationary 1980s—began coming down to more realistic and affordable levels, the media sensationalized this price adjustment as a sure sign of a coming depression. They failed to point out that the sale of a home at a lower than expected price is merely a transfer of wealth from a home owner to a home buyer. Every unhappy home seller made for a very happy home buyer.

The unprecedented rise in home prices during the 1980s was an unfair transfer of wealth from our younger citizens (home buyers) to our older citizens (home owners). Recent housing price adjustments merely reflect a return of some of these unearned gains to the next generation.

This misreporting of the economic effect of home price declines is almost insignificant when it comes to the misunderstanding by the media of important economic issues like unemployment, trade deficits, and gross national product (GNP).

One of the largest components in the GNP is based on the value of all the homes in America. When home prices fall, it is negatively reported as a dramatic drop in GNP, when, as long as there remains a buyer for the home at *some* price, it is merely a transfer in wealth from home owners to home buyers.

On unemployment, we regularly see heartbreaking reports of people unemployed because of the closing of local plants. There is never any follow-up on what happens to these unfortunate individuals—reporting that would show that one-third find new jobs with a 20 percent or more increase in salary.[17]

On trade deficits, we regularly hear that Japanese cars account for 3.7 million of the approximately 10 million vehicles sold in the United States. We never hear that more than 2.2 million, or 61 percent, of these "Japanese" vehicles are manufactured in the United States (employing over 15 percent of all U.S. auto-workers).[18]

On GNP, we regularly hear meaningless statistics quoted about the rise or fall in GNP without any relationship to what really matters—the purchasing power of the American consumer. For example, when General Motors manufactures a 1995 $10,000 automobile with all the features of a $15,000 1991 model, the consumer enjoys a $5,000 increase in lifestyle, while the media reports a $5,000 drop in GNP.

Our mass media, because of their misunderstanding of what's really going on in our economy, fail to report the economic information that matters most to ordinary Americans—what is really happening to their jobs, to the economic future of their country, and, most important, to their lifestyles. However, at least for the major television networks, this lack of understanding certainly doesn't hinder them from grossly overreporting bad news.

A university study of how television covers economic affairs—during periods when GNP was both rising and falling—found that when GNP was rising, the number of stories devoted to the economy dropped 26 percent. More significant, the number of stories reporting the key economic indicators dropped 64 percent. For every 10 stories reporting an announced numerical decrease in GNP, there were only 3.4 stories reporting a later corresponding increase.

As the sponsor of the study observed, newscasters can't seem to find a GNP figure that they like. "If the number is strong, they warn of an overheated economy and inflation; if it's weak, they worry about recession." [19]

*B*ut the negative reporting of economic news by the media is almost nothing compared to the misinformation created by the bad-news industry—independent organizations and individuals who make their living solely by reporting, and in some cases manufacturing, bad news. This industry can be broken down into three major groups—businesses, political organizations, and individuals—with considerable overlap between them as they work together whenever it suits their mutual interests.

Why Do Businesses Sometimes Report Bad News?
GM Learns the Japanese Drive on the Wrong Side of the Road

Businesses have numerous reasons for manufacturing bad news —not the least of them being getting more business.

For example, approximately two decades ago we realized that we were seriously polluting our environment—that our rivers, groundwater, topsoil, and many other resources would become scarce if we didn't come to grips with what we were doing to them. During the next twenty years we reversed the tide of environmental pollution and—while much remains to be done —we are on track toward leaving our children a cleaner and healthier planet than we received from our parents.

In the 1990s we will spend $500 billion on cleaning up existing polluted sites, most of it with major *Fortune* 500 companies in the environmental cleanup industry—an industry that is already much bigger than many of the industries it is cleaning up after.

The reason we receive so little good news about the progress we have made in cleaning up our environment is that these cleanup businesses, which provide a significant part of the money that supports environmental action groups, have vested interests in sponsoring only organizations that promote environmental hysteria, which in turn promotes more environmental cleanup business. The largest public company in the cleanup business, Waste Management Inc., boasts in its annual report that it "generously donates" more than $350,000 a year to such organizations.

Notwithstanding the promotion by business of bad news that indirectly promotes their businesses, the main reason companies manufacture bad news about the general economy is to cover up their own managerial failures. Every time a business fails to meet the expectations of its shareholders, it seems to publish a report about the generally dismal state of its industry, rather than the more than likely truth about the generally dismal inadequacy of its current management to deal with changes in the marketplace.

The best example of this can be found throughout the top management of our automobile industry, who continually blame free trade and our political system for their shortcomings in selling U.S. automobiles in Japan.

In early 1992, during a visit by President Bush to Japan, on which he was accompanied by the chairman of General Motors, the GM executive went for a photo opportunity to a GM dealership in Tokyo. The press had a field day when they, along with the chairman of GM, discovered that the GM cars for sale in Japan had their steering wheels on the wrong (left) side of the vehicle —the Japanese, like the English, drive on the right side of the road. No wonder GM couldn't sell any cars in Japan; they hadn't even extended the Japanese the courtesy of making cars suited for their market!

*B*ad-news sponsorship by business is relatively insignificant compared to the amount of bad news generated by politicians and political organizations seeking our votes and our dollars. In a multiple-party democracy, the objective of the party not in power is to get elected— often by damming the truth in good economic times. These distortions of the truth—by their inherent pessimistic nature and newsworthy presentation formats—almost always receive more media coverage than the true facts.

But the greatest original source of bad news, particularly when it comes to news about the general economy, comes from individuals sometimes frustrated by their own inadequacies in either supporting their families or getting their message across to the public. These individuals—sometimes academics or journalists surrounded by successful students and businesspeople—never seem to let truth stand in the way when it comes to making their own personal break to fame or economic freedom.

Dr. Doom

In 1985, Dr. Ravi Batra was an obscure professor at Southern Methodist University in Dallas, Texas, who had self-published a book on economic cycles and the unfair disparity between the social classes in our capitalist society.

In this book, originally titled *Regular Cycles of Money, Inflation, Regulation, and Depressions,* Dr. Batra put forth his thesis that because of unfair income distribution in a capitalist society, a major economic depression occurs every thirty years. He also mentioned that because we didn't have the economic depression predicted by his theory in the 1960s, unless we quickly began redistributing the wealth in America, we were scheduled to have an extra-serious depression in the 1990s.

I should point out here that, unlike most of the business press, I believe that Dr. Batra is a serious scholar and I have enjoyed his work on economic cycles — although I disagree with virtually all economic-cycle theories.[20]

However, notwithstanding my professional respect for Dr. Batra's work, I feel that he is a socialist, or probably a Marxist, who truly believes in his cause and will use economics and any other tool at his disposal to promote his beliefs. These beliefs include immediately confiscating the accumulated wealth of the rich and imposing federal maximum ceilings on individual earnings.

Before self-publishing his book on economic cycles in 1984, Dr. Batra had sent it to Lester Thurow at MIT, one of the most respected and influential economists in the country. Thurow agreed to help out the young Batra by writing a brief introduction to the book.

In 1987 Simon & Schuster, smelling a market for a sensationalist book to coincide with the stock market crash of October 19, 1987, purchased the rights to Batra's book on monetary cycles under the condition that it be rewritten and retitled *The Great Depression of 1990.*

Thurow was furious and fought to have his name removed

from the new book. However, upon finding out that such a fight would only give more attention to Batra's work, Thurow figured, "No harm done. Who the hell is going to read it?"[21]

Fortunately for Simon & Schuster and Dr. Batra, but unfortunately for us, Thurow was wrong. Despite Thurow's protests that he had written the introduction for a different book, Simon & Schuster billed Thurow's name as prominently as Batra's on the cover, and the book sold more than a million copies.

Thurow is not worried about his reputation. What frightens him most is the thought that someone might actually follow Batra's advice. As Thurow told *Fortune* magazine soon after the book became a best-seller, "The fear haunts me that ten years from now I'll be walking down the streets of New York and some bum will look up at me and say, 'Because of you and the Batra book . . . now here I am in the gutter.' "

After the initial success of *The Great Depression of 1990,* Batra rushed out a sequel entitled *Surviving the Great Depression of the 1990s.* Although both of these books were totally discredited by the business press and the few economists who agreed to comment on them, together they sold over 2 million copies.

When Nobel Laureate Milton Friedman was asked about Batra's books, he replied: "I have no interest in reading fiction."[22]

Interestingly, Friedman's comment foreshadowed Batra's next method to tap the mother lode he had discovered of people wanting bad economic news. He has written his first novel, in which all his predictions—and their socialist solutions—come true. The novel has everything from jobless rioters attacking the homes of the rich to the government eventually owning the shares of public companies and turning them over to the employees.

Dr. Batra, along with other individuals, politicians, and businesses who falsely promote bad news, has been successful because we have been receptive to the idea that things could be getting worse. For most of us today, the roots of this receptiveness lie in what happened during the worst decade of American attitudes since the Great Depression—the 1970s.

• • •

Throughout the 1970s, pessimism was the order of the day. The world, it was said, was running out of everything. Unless radical action was taken immediately—action that included massive conservation efforts and a wholesale lowering of Western standards of living—humankind was doomed. This mistaken view of the world in the 1970s was primarily the result of two events—the appearance on the Johnny Carson show in 1968 of one of the most popular bad-news demagogues in history, and a study published in 1972 that *Time* magazine called "the first vision of the apocalypse ever prepared by a computer." [23]

The "Ecologist"

Of all of the charlatans who make their living preying upon our fears by promoting bad news, perhaps no one has done more damage to the truth than the self-called ecologist, Paul Ehrlich. [24]

In the 1960s Ehrlich, then a California college professor, began giving lectures on the problems of overpopulation. Ehrlich, who had already put his Malthusian principles into practice by limiting his family to one child and having a vasectomy in 1963, caught the attention of Ballantine Books, which helped him package his message into a book before the 1968 presidential election. [25]

That book, *The Population Bomb*, began:

"The battle to feed all of humanity is over. In the 1970s . . . hundreds of millions of people are going to starve to death . . . nothing can prevent a substantial increase in the world death rate . . . (America's) vast agricultural surpluses are gone."

Six years later he wrote another book, *The End of Affluence*, in which he raised the predicted death toll to "a billion or more people starving to death." In this book he said that "before 1985 mankind will enter into a genuine age of scarcity" in which the accessible supplies of many key minerals will be nearing completion. . . . One general prediction can be made with confidence: the cost of feeding yourself and your family will continue to increase. There will be minor fluctuations in food prices, but the overall trend will be up.

Many such words are often written by individuals seeking personal attention or attempting to gain support for one political cause or another—but fortunately, even our sensation-seeking news media has some sense of public responsibility and ignores them.

In this case we weren't so lucky.

In 1968 Paul Ehrlich was interviewed by Johnny Carson for one hour in a nationwide television appearance on *The Tonight Show.* The show received more than five thousand letters about Ehrlich's appearance, and his book became an overnight bestseller—eventually selling more than three million copies.

Ehrlich become the darling of the gloom-and-doom set and, unfortunately for us all, the best-known ecologist in the United States. This is truly unfortunate, because while most serious ecologists are concerned about improving the quality of life on our planet for more and more humans to enjoy it, Ehrlich's warped view of ecology means having fewer and fewer humans on the planet.

In the weeks leading up to Earth Day on April 22, 1990, Ehrlich appeared on *The Today Show* and other programs to promote his books. These appearances culminated in his address at a big Earth Day rally in Washington, where "the crowd of more than 200,000 applauded heartily after Ehrlich told them that population growth could produce a world in which their grandchildren would endure food riots in the streets of America."[26]

Looking back to when Ehrlich began publishing his predictions in 1968, we find that virtually every one of his predictions has been proven wrong. Unfortunately, many people did die of starvation, but mostly from specific geological or political events rather than from overpopulation or widespread shortages of food.

In fact, since Ehrlich's dire prediction of 1 billion or more people starving to death, world population has grown by 2 billion people, to about 5.5 billion. (In 1969 Ehrlich said: "By 1985, enough millions will have died to reduce the earth's population to some arbitrarily acceptable level, like 1.5 billion people.")[27]

And while we still have a long way to go in improving the lot of most of the world's people—particularly outside of the developed Western nations—the average planet Earth inhabitant today is considerably healthier, wealthier, and better fed than in 1968.

When it comes to discrediting such charlatans as Ehrlich or Batra, things now change so fast in our economy that we have seen with our own eyes the fallacy in their arguments. Then why is it that so many people today still believe that we are running out of resources, that we need to limit or even retreat from our aspirations to take care of everyone on earth?

The answer to this question lies in an enormously influential— and utterly downbeat—study published in 1972, which shaped, and continues to shape, the thinking of many of the journalists and policymakers in power today.

The Club of Rome

The study *The Limits to Growth* was issued in 1972 by the Club of Rome, a collection of distinguished industrialists, scientists, economists, sociologists, and government officials from twenty-five countries.[28]

The Club of Rome had commissioned the experts three years earlier to peer down the road a bit and report back on humankind's economic and environmental prospects. Using some of the most sophisticated computer modeling techniques then available, these experts produced a 197-page report that came to a genuinely shocking conclusion.

What their computer models told them was that, with the

world's population growing at a rate of about 2 percent a year and industrial output rising by 7 percent annually, the world's physical resources would be exhausted sometime in the next few decades—a calamity, they said, that could wind up wiping out most of humanity before the year 2100.

More specifically, *The Limits to Growth* predicted that the world would run out of gold by 1981, mercury by 1985, tin by 1987, zinc by 1990, petroleum by 1992, and copper, lead, and natural gas by 1993.[29]

The study's impact was phenomenal. For as long as anyone could remember, economic growth had been regarded as the solution to all of humankind's woes; now, suddenly, it seemed to be the problem. Thinking big was deemed archaic, if not downright antisocial.

To be sure, not everyone was persuaded by *The Limits to Growth* that the sky was falling. But most such doubts were washed away the following year when Arab oil producers responded to the 1973 Yom Kippur War in the Middle East—first by unilaterally raising prices and then by cutting off deliveries to the West.

Though the actual embargo didn't last very long, the price hikes stuck—in the process, establishing the Organization of Petroleum Exporting Countries (OPEC) as a force to be reckoned with. They also marked what at the time seemed to be the end of the era of cheap and abundant energy—an era that most people took to be synonymous with prosperity and growth.

What followed over the next few years seemed to prove the doomsayers right. Between 1973 and 1981, soaring energy prices pitched the United States headlong into its worst recession in four decades. Economic growth sputtered to a halt, unemployment mounted, and inflation soared, seemingly out of control. Long lines became commonplace at gas stations, with frustrated motorists often coming to blows. Electrical brownouts became a regular feature of urban summers. With heating oil deliveries uncertain, nervous New England home owners turned down their thermostats in winter.

The future looked grim indeed. The government even printed up millions of gasoline ration cards. As David Rockefeller observed in 1975, there seemed no getting around the fact that there were now "constraints on the rate of economic growth, constraints that were not apparent in the preceding twenty years."[30]

In short, it looked as if the world we had known—the world of expansion and prosperity, of thinking big and rising expectations—was coming to an end. In its place, a new image came to dominate our thinking: that of the earth as a fragile spaceship with a rapidly declining store of supplies and fuel. And the consensus was that we had better get used to it.

"The idea of sitting still until this thing blows over is just a bunch of nonsense," declared the president of Booz, Allen & Hamilton, Inc., one of the nation's largest management consulting firms, in 1975. "It ain't gonna blow over. You can bet that for the next generation we're going to have to live with the conditions we've seen over the last decade."[31]

But then a strange thing happened. The world didn't come to an end.

The world's energy reserves, which the Club of Rome predicted would run out, actually *rose* by more than 50 percent during the next 20 years—and as a result of enhanced recovery methods, they may soon be increased an additional 200 percent! Technological advances like the electronic fuel injector replacing the carburetor caused a virtual doubling of automobile fuel economy. The same experts predicting a twenty-year supply of oil in 1972 now acknowledge that our current supplies may last ninety years or more.

The price of oil, which approached $40 a barrel at the end of the 1970s, fell to $15 dollars a barrel—actually less than $7 a barrel when adjusted for inflation—right in the middle of a major war in the Middle East.[32]

The price of basic agricultural products halved or actually fell by 75 percent when adjusted for inflation—although most consumers spent part of this savings at the supermarket by trading up to more packaged and processed foods. And the same increases in supply and decreases in price proved true for most other commodities.

In 1970, worldwide natural gas reserves were estimated to total some 1,500 trillion cubic feet. By 1987, that estimate had been revised upward to nearly 4,000 trillion cubic feet.

Similarly, global reserves of copper more than doubled (from 279 million to 570 million tons) between 1970 and 1987. Over the same period, silver reserves climbed more than 60 percent (from 6.7 billion to 10.8 billion troy ounces), gold reserves rose by 50 percent (from 1 billion to 1.52 billion troy ounces), and bauxite reserves were up more than 35 percent (from 17 billion to 23 billion metric tons).[33]

And the only thing changing faster than the increase in supply of these supposedly scarce resources has been their falling prices —which are as much the result of the increased efficiency with which we use them as of our better methods of finding and extracting them.

Between 1980 and 1985 alone, prices in the International Monetary Fund's thirty-product commodity index dropped fully 74 percent. Throughout the 1980s and early 1990s, the cost of such raw materials as bauxite, coal, cocoa beans, coffee, copper, cotton, hides, iron ore, lead, manganese, nickel, oil, potash, rice, rubber, silver, soybeans, sugar, tin, and wheat collapsed—many falling to their lowest level in half a century.

And the outlook for the foreseeable future is for more of the same. Indeed, the downward trend has been so dramatic that the U.S. Office of Technology Assessment has concluded that America's "future has probably never been less constrained by the cost of natural resources."[34]

*F*ortunately for all of us who need to make decisions based on real facts rather than on what the media requires to keep our attention, there is a hero in the story of how the economic truth has been distorted over the years.

His name is Julian Simon.

Apart from his work as an economist, Simon is a successful businessperson who, in the 1960s, became expert in mail order marketing and wrote the definitive book on the subject—a book that has since sold more than two hundred thousand copies. However, over the past few years Dr. Simon's fame in economics has eclipsed his notoriety as an expert in mail order marketing as people have come to recognize this man for his true genius.

Julian Simon
The Ultimate Resource

Julian Simon was traditionally educated as an economist at the University of Chicago in the early 1960s and started out as a Malthusian. Then, in 1963, he came across a work called *Scarcity and Growth,* written by Harold J. Barnett and Chandler Morse.[35]

In this book, the authors tracked the price of natural resources back to 1870 and found that virtually everything had fallen. The average worker's buying power per hour of work had steadily increased—things were getting better, not worse. This book provided Julian Simon the inspiration to further develop the "boomster view of history."[36]

To be fair, there are other economists throughout the world who, despite their classical educations, have not buried their heads in the sand with a my-mind-is-made-up-don't-confuse-me-with-the-facts attitude. Among them are Charles Maurice and Charles W. Smithson, who have looked back at ten thousand years of resource crises and seen a pattern of innovation in response to material shortages. But none of them have so eloquently stated the case, or carried the torch as high, as Julian Simon has since writing the definitive work on the subject in 1981.

"Natural Resources are not finite. Yes, you read correctly," Simon wrote in his 1981 book on what has been happening since the dawn of history to our supposedly scarce supply of natural resources. That book, still required reading for anyone today interested in understanding what's really going on in our economy, is wonderfully titled *The Ultimate Resource*[37] in reference to the uniquely human God-given ability to create, rather than merely use, natural resources.

Simon, never one to rest on his laurels, has gone on to become the leading cornucopian economist of all time. His most recent work, *Population Matters,* expertly refutes each of the arguments against increased population, empirically demonstrating the positive relationship between population and economic growth.

In *Population Matters* Simon notes that American fathers work the equivalent of two to five weeks a year extra for each additional child, more than offsetting the mother's temporary withdrawal from the workforce.[38] Singapore, Hong Kong, Japan, and Taiwan all experienced astronomical population and economic growth during the past few decades, while sparsely populated Argentina has stagnated for at least twenty-five years.

As Simon notes, "The ultimate resource is people—skilled, spirited and hopeful people."[39]

Simon first revealed his optimistic view of our world in a 1980 *Science* magazine article entitled "Resources, Population, Environment: An Oversupply of Bad News." Responding to the article in a rebuttal, ecological doomsayer Paul Ehrlich attacked the magazine itself for publishing Simon's then-nonconforming economic views, writing: "Could the editors have found someone to review Simon's manuscript who had to take off his shoes to count to 20?"[40]

Ehrlich later gave a speech advocating the idea of having the government set quotas on the amount of resources that could be used each year. In this speech, Ehrlich referred to Simon's book, saying, "The ultimate resource—the one thing we'll never run out of is imbeciles."[41]

But the last laugh has already been had by Julian Simon.

In 1980, convinced of the righteousness of his position, Simon issued an open challenge to all Malthusians to bet that the future price of any natural resource at any future date would be reduced. Ehrlich announced "that 'he would accept Simon's offer before other greedy people jump in.' "[42]

A bet between them was placed in October 1980 on the October 1990 combined price of five metals—chrome, copper, nickel, tin, and tungsten. The price of a certain quantity of these metals was $1000 in 1980: Simon agreed to pay Ehrlich the amount to which they increased over the next decade and Ehrlich agreed to pay Simon the amount to which they decreased.

The bet was settled ten years later, in October 1990. Ehrlich, who had never met Simon in all the years that he had berated him—Ehrlich refused to debate, saying that Simon is a "fringe character"—simply sent Simon a check for $576.07 with a sheet of his calculations. The price for the combined basket of metals had fallen to 57.6 percent of the 1980 price. If inflation were taken into effect, the price for the metals had really fallen to less than 30 percent of the 1980 price.

According to an excellent cover story by John Tierney in the Sunday *New York Times Magazine*—which finally gave Simon's great work the recognition it deserved—Simon sent Ehrlich a thank-you note offering to "raise the wager to as much as $20,000, pinned to any other resources and to any other year in the future."[43]

In the 1960s, when the Nobel Prize for economics was added to the list of other Nobel Prizes, it was generally believed that the science of economics had evolved to the point where there was a working theory of economics. And the theory that economists thought could finally explain what was going on in the economy was Keynesian economics.

John Maynard Keynes (1883–1946) was and remains undoubtedly the most influential economist of all time. Even in the depths of the Great Depression, Keynes was able to see that advancing technology would lower the cost of producing goods and services so much that one day every person would be able to afford everything that they (then) desired.

It has been said that one can learn more from studying the mistakes of our greatest minds than from studying where they were correct. In this regard, Keynes was brilliant in correctly being able to foresee the end of scarcity due to the advance of technology, but Keynes was mistaken in his inability to see that this same advancing technology would lead to a continual ever-increasing demand for new products and services.

John Maynard Keynes
The Defunct Economist

In 1936 a great man wrote:

> The ideas of economists . . . are more powerful than is commonly understood. Indeed, the world is ruled by little else. Practical men, who believe themselves to be quite exempt from any intellectual influences, are usually the slaves of some defunct economist.[44]

Today, a misunderstanding about human behavior made by that same great man lies at the foundation of many of our social and economic problems.

The man was John Maynard Keynes, the most influential economist of the twentieth century. In 1936, Keynes published *The General Theory of Employment, Interest, and Money,* which still stands today as the authoritative work in explaining the way many aspects of our economy function.

However, in the *General Theory* Keynes also put forth the notion that the economy does not naturally tend toward full employment by itself. Keynes believed that the government should take affirmative actions—like cutting taxes and making public expenditures even when such actions created deficits—to bring the economy up to full employment.[45]

Such a policy may not seem unusual today—indeed it has been embraced by the Democratic Party in the United States and most western European governments—but it was radical thinking when Keynes wrote it. Economists back then believed that the economy tends toward full employment by itself—and that any government interference could only make a bad situation much worse.

Keynes's view that government intervention was necessary to reach full employment was based on his landmark theory of oversaving. This theory states that as people become richer, they spend smaller and smaller proportions of their income.[46] To Keynes, people are far more strongly motivated to satisfy their "immediate primary needs"—food, clothing, and shelter—than to purchase any luxuries they can afford after these basic requirements have been met.[47]

Looking ahead beyond the economic crisis of the 1930s, Keynes foresaw the day when most Americans would have a car and a four-bedroom, one-bathroom house. He once warned President Roosevelt that when most people had fulfilled the American dream, they would lose part of their incentive to work. These productive Americans, Keynes felt, would shift from spending their increasing incomes to saving it, until the economy would grind to a halt—a victim, as it were, of its own success.

Therefore, he argued, the government should adopt policies—like deficit spending, progressive taxation, and the manipulation of interest rates—designed to keep the most productive people in our society working harder and from hoarding too much of their income as their affluence increased.

Today we know that while Keynes's theory that increasing affluence breeds complacency and oversaving (rather than increased consumption) seems logical, it is wrong. Indeed, the very opposite of what Keynes predicted has come to pass.

Upscale consumer demand is insatiable. The more we earn, the more we spend; the more we spend, the more we get; the more we get, the more we want; and the more we want, the harder we seem to be willing to work to earn more money to get it. If any segment of our society has lost the incentive to work, it is the very poor, whom we seem unable to help get over the hurdle of purchasing their *first* car or their *first* house—the purchase that leads to the never-ending cycle of unlimited consumer demand.

Looking back at the time when Keynes developed his landmark theory of oversaving, it is easy to see where he went wrong. During the 1930s, an insufficiency of consumer demand was the root cause of the continued depression—nothing the government could do seemed to be able to get the consumer spending again. And Keynes was convinced that without such measures as higher and higher income tax rates on increasing personal income, doom was inevitable again.

In so many areas where we have seemingly insurmountable social problems, the roots of these problems can be traced back to government programs that were based, at the time they were implemented, on this gross misunderstanding of human behavior by one of the greatest thinkers of the twentieth century.

For example, just one of Keynes's suggestions for government employment programs in 1939 led to the United States building massive public housing projects throughout the nation. This had the unintended cruel effect of isolating the most unfortunate people in our society from the role models their children sorely needed to escape their predicament (see, in Chapter 8, "What's Wrong with Public Education").

Perhaps more than any other single event, this government program of housing large groups of poor people together in public housing projects led to the multigenerational welfare state we have today—breaking for many people the rags-to-riches cycle that had become a trademark of the American experience.

In the private sector as well, many of our current problems originated with the high progressive personal income tax rates that Keynes prescribed to keep the economy moving—rates that eventually rose to as high as 91 percent on marginal person income.[48]

These high personal income tax rates had a perverse effect on certain developing sectors of our economy, because corporations sought to reward their employees with nontaxable perks such as health care and pension plans, rather than simply pay them wage increases and let the free market determine the best product and delivery systems for these emerging sectors of our economy[49] (see, in Chapter 6, "Health Care"). High income tax rates also led to the development of an underground, or "black market," economy, which today exceeds in size the amount spent on all U.S. public education[50] (see, in Chapter 7, "How to Hit Criminals Where It Hurts the Most").

And yet, these and so many more of our social and economic problems can be solved when we understand that their roots lie in one mistake made by one of the greatest thinkers of our time. Ironically, when it comes to solving our social problems, much of our political thinking is enslaved by some of the *defunct* ideas of John Maynard Keynes.

*M*ost people think that Keynes had a greater impact during his time than he actually did. Many of the government programs of the 1930s and 1940s that are attributed to Keynes's recommendations were actually part of a larger phenomenon—active government involvement in the economy—that merely used the *General Theory* after the fact to justify their continued existence. (The actual New Deal programs of the 1930s preceded the *General Theory* by several years.)

John Fitzgerald Kennedy's Search for Camelot

The major impact Keynes had in his time was on the next generation of economists—many of whom were undergoing their educations during the Great Depression. As Paul Samuelson, who in 1936 was a twenty-year-old graduate student at Harvard, put it: "The *General Theory* caught most economists under the age of 35 with the unexpected virulence of a disease first attacking and decimating an isolated tribe of south sea islanders."[51]

Samuelson, who later became the first American to win the Nobel Prize in economics, made Keynes's radical ideas commonplace. Samuelson incorporated Keynes's ideas as mainstream views in his 1948 college textbook *Economics*—a book that has provided the introduction to economics to tens of millions of college students.[52]

In 1960, one of Samuelson's disciples—John Fitzgerald Kennedy—was elected president of the United States. Indeed, the very foundation of Kennedy's campaign was based on the policies recommended by John Maynard Keynes.

The Kennedy administration believed that by utilizing tax cuts and government expenditures they could fine-tune the economy at will—balancing an acceptable rate of unemployment against an acceptable rate of inflation and economic growth.

And for a while it seemed as if Kennedy and his all-Keynesian group of economic advisors, including Paul Samuelson, couldn't fail. Even after the president was assassinated, his handpicked group of Keynesians—bolstered and kept in power by the performance of the economy in the 1960s—didn't doubt that they finally knew the answers.

Their euphoria reached its peak when *Time* magazine devoted its year-end, December 31, 1965, issue to how Keynes's theories, some twenty years after his death, had finally given government policy makers the tools they needed to forever end economic downturns and produce "phenomenal economic growth and achieve remarkably stable prices."[53]

But this euphoria was short-lived. The greatest period of inflation in U.S history began in 1967 and lasted straight through the recessions of 1974, 1981, and 1991—each the largest economic downturn in the United States since the Great Depression. During the past three decades the United States has experienced simultaneous periods of high unemployment, recession, and inflation —something seemingly impossible under Keynesian theory. As stated in the book *Who Killed John Maynard Keynes?* by W. Carl Biven:

> At the very peak of success the Age of Keynes became a part of history. Those who observe today belligerent disagreement among economists about the basic model of how the economy works may now look back in nostalgia at the consensus and heady confidence that prevailed in the first part of the 1960s, in the place that "for one brief shining moment was known as Camelot."

*T*he decade of the 1970s proved the worst for both economists and government policy makers as two successive incumbent administrations were voted out of office—mostly because of the inexplicably poor performance of the economy. By the end of the decade a new economic indicator had been created to explain the U.S. economy, the "misery index," which consisted of the sum of the inflation and the unemployment rates.

By 1980 the only thing that most economists could agree on with certainty was that they couldn't agree on anything with certainty.

Reflecting on this almost universal view among economists that they no longer had the answers, a leading U.S. economic writer has called for rescinding the recently created Nobel Prize in economics, stating that

> Nobel Prizes are supposed to be given for work that confers "the greatest benefit on mankind," as Nobel put it in his will. The prize for economics flunks this test. . . . Probably the only people left who think economics deserves a Nobel Prize are economists. It confirms their conceit that they're doing "science" rather than the less tidy task of observing the world and trying to make sense of it.[54]

The next group of economists and government policy makers who felt they had the answers were the so-called *supply-side economists* who emerged in the late 1970s and were embraced in the conservative presidential candidacy of Ronald Reagan.

Ronald Reagan's Search for Camelot

The basic assertion of the supply-side school is that at some high percentage rate of income taxation, say 50 to 70 percent, the economy slows down because there is not enough individual incentive to work. When government lowers such a high rate of income taxation, people begin working harder and earning more money—raising total governmental receipts even though people are being taxed at a lower rate on their income.

For example, assume that a certain group of workers earn $2 million a year in total gross income and pay 50 percent of their wages in income taxes to the government. A supply-side economist might say that if the income tax rate was lowered to 40 percent, the workers would work harder and earn more money —raising their total gross income to $3 million. Government receipts from such a lowering of the tax rate would thus actually rise $200,000 a year, rather than fall, because the government would collect 40 percent, or $1.2 million a year, of their higher $3 million in gross income.

EARNED INCOME AND INCOME TAX RECEIPTS		
Income Tax Rate	50%	40%
Earned Income	$2,000	$3,000
Income Tax Paid	$1,000	$1,200

In 1980 the top federal income tax rates on personal and corporate income were respectively 70 and 48 percent a year—about twice what they are today. The supply-siders were confident that reducing these high income tax rates would not cause federal revenue to decrease. This confidence was critical because, as conservatives allied with Ronald Reagan's 1980 candidacy, they felt that deficits—government spending in excess of government receipts—were even worse than high income tax rates.

In 1981, urged on by newly elected president Ronald Reagan, the U.S. Congress passed the Economic Recovery Tax Act (ERTA), which dramatically lowered individual and corporate income tax rates.

Many traditional economists warned then that Reagan's Economic Recovery Tax Act would lead to an economic collapse; they expected federal deficits to balloon because government receipts would fall when the lower tax rates were applied to (what they thought would be) a relatively stagnant gross national product (GNP).

However, late in 1982, the GNP began a meteoric rise that initially outstripped even the most optimistic projections of the supply-siders. Not surprisingly, the supply-siders took full credit for the boom, and in 1984 Reagan was re-elected by the greatest landslide in U.S. history. This time the Republicans, rather than the Democrats, as in the 1960s, thought that they had discovered Camelot.

However, despite the meteoric rise in GNP, the federal deficit took off. This occurred primarily for two reasons. First, the expected corresponding increase in federal receipts didn't fully materialize until later on—primarily due to "leakages" in the way taxes were collected, some of which were corrected by the Tax

Reform Act of 1986.[55] But, second and most important, no one expected the massive $207 billion increase in the two largest areas of federal expenditures—national defense and Social Security.[56]

The following table illustrates what happened.[57]

GROSS NATIONAL PRODUCT VERSUS
FEDERAL RECEIPTS AND SPENDING
1981–1988

Year	Gross national product (billions)	Federal receipts (billions)	Federal receipts (% of GNP)	Federal spending (billions)	Federal deficit (billions)
1981	$3,053	$599	19.6%	$ 678	$ 79
1982	$3,166	$618	19.5%	$ 746	$128
1983	$3,406	$601	17.6%	$ 808	$208
1984	$3,722	$667	17.9%	$ 852	$185
1985	$4,015	$734	18.3%	$ 946	$212
1986	$4,240	$769	18.1%	$ 990	$221
1987	$4,527	$854	18.9%	$1,005	$151
1988	$4,792	$909	19.0%	$1,056	$147

Around 1984, following the then-largest federal deficit in the history of the United States, the supply-siders were starting to worry. Most of them began predicting that unless the spiraling budget deficit could somehow be checked, the nation would face severe inflation, escalating interest rates, and economic stagnation.

In a 1986 popular book by one of their own, former director of the Office of Management and Budget David Stockman predicted that unless the federal deficits were quickly eliminated, inflation and interest rates would soon exceed 20 percent, GNP would begin to decline, and the country would plunge into an economic downturn that would rival the Great Depression.

The economy, however, paid no heed to such warnings. From 1985 through 1988 and beyond, the budget deficit continued to increase, nearly doubling the national debt. Yet, despite dire predictions to the contrary, GNP continued its meteoric rise, inflation fell to its lowest level since the 1960s, and interest rates declined almost two-thirds to their lowest real levels since the Second World War. Clearly, something was going on that not even the supply-siders—the ones who supposedly had the answers—could explain.

During the presidential campaign of 1992, President George Bush and the Republican Party campaigned as the team that had found Camelot. As evidenced by the election of President Clinton, even though the recession of 1991 was ending in 1992, the American public was not ready to accept that the supply-siders had caused something they couldn't even begin to explain.

Sadly, there is another story hidden in the total economic figures of the 1980s. The average GNP per person in America did rise from $12,982 per year in 1981 to $20,705 in 1989, but these numbers belie the fact that much of this rise in average national wealth did not trickle down to many of the more needy members in our society.

Politicians are still debating the extent to which the rich got richer and the poor got poorer during the Reagan years, but few, if any, deny that at least to some extent, the riches of the Reagan years were unevenly distributed.

What the supply-siders and their political foes in Congress didn't understand was that the rising disparity between the rich and the poor during the 1980s and today has very little to do with Ronald Reagan, tax cuts, or supply-side economics.

It has almost entirely to do with who is, and who is not, able to deal with technological change. For today, changes that used to take place in fifty years take place in five or ten—eclipsing the lives, the careers, and the incomes of those among us who cannot effectively cope with it.

One of the things that did occur during the 1980s put to rest any lingering doubts that Keynes's landmark theory of oversaving might be correct. In 1981, personal income tax rates were lowered (for the highest brackets) from 70 percent to 50 percent, and then in 1986 they were lowered again, from 50 percent to 28 percent. If Keynes's theory of oversaving was correct, consumers should have saved rather than spent a large amount of this tax cut, and the proportion of personal income devoted to savings (rather than consumption) should have increased—the original reason the personal tax rates were raised so high in the first place was to keep affluent consumers from hoarding their increasing incomes.

Exactly the opposite took place. Personal savings as a proportion of personal income halved in the 1980s as consumers spent both the amount of their tax cuts and an additional 50 percent of the amount that they used to save.[58] Clearly, as will be explained further in Chapter 4, "Economic Alchemy," rising affluence breeds increasing rates of consumption, not increasing rates of savings.

What Really Happened During the 1980s

A hint to the answer of what happened to the U.S. economy during the 1980s—as well as the answer to what we are mostly experiencing today—lies in a close examination of the type of tax cuts that the Reagan Revolution's 1981 Economic Recovery Tax Act (ERTA) granted to businesses.

The majority of the business tax cuts were, in effect, government subsidies for the purchase of new machinery and equipment. These subsidies, which often amounted to 58 percent of the cost of new machinery, coerced American industry to retool their plants—whether they thought they needed to or not. In some cases, thanks to the investment tax credits and accelerated depreciation, a business could actually save more in taxes by purchasing a new machine than the machine itself cost.[59]

And fortunately, and coincidentally, another revolution—this one having to do with machinery and equipment rather than with less government and lower tax rates—had begun thirty-five years earlier and was ready to explode onto the American scene in 1981.

In 1946 the first electronic computer, known as ENIAC, was

developed at the University of Pennsylvania. Over the next thirty-five years, even though computers became progressively more powerful and easier to use, their use remained generally restricted to the sterile and carefully guarded data processing centers of universities, government agencies, and large corporations.

By 1981, however, the computer had evolved to the point where it was ready to burst out into the wider world—onto the factory floor, inside the automobile, into the office, and onto the supermarket checkout counter. During the 1970s companies had incorporated the computer into the design of thousands of products—manufacturing equipment, electronic fuel injectors, computerized word processors, bar-code-scanning cash registers—and were awaiting the turnaround of the economy to launch them.

And thus, when manufacturers, distributors, retailers, and service companies began calling on their equipment suppliers to ask what was new in 1981, their suppliers had a lot to offer. This accelerated implementation of the computer into American society, boosted by the financial incentives contained in ERTA, caused the *real* revolution—in American productivity—to take off. And a close examination reveals that what happened in 1981 was only the beginning.

Here's what happened to the total economy during the 1980s. In manufacturing, total U.S. employment fell 6 percent, while U.S. manufacturing sales rose 45 percent.[60] In the automobile industry, computerized fuel injection doubled gasoline mileage —destroying the OPEC cartel in the process and causing the price of oil to fall to its lowest level in twenty years. In America's office buildings, the personal computer increased information processing productivity as much as 500 percent—although much of this increase was absorbed by a corresponding increase in the quantity of information processed, which itself is leading to further increases in productivity throughout all sectors of the economy. And in our supermarkets, bar-code-scanning cash registers and other retailing innovations allowed the typical American family to purchase much healthier food and simultaneously see their weekly grocery bill decline by 10 percent.[61]

In total terms, these and thousands of other innovations caused

GNP to rise an incredible 72 percent (24 percent after adjusting for inflation)!

But sadly, many were left out of the Reagan Revolution or, more accurately stated, thrown out.

The reason many were left out of the economic revolution of the 1980s is that in order to participate you had to have a ticket —and the price of that ticket was having the ability to learn new things and the ability to change.

In order to work with computerized manufacturing equipment, you had to have the basic reading and math skills required to learn how to use it—as well as an employer willing to teach you. It didn't matter how good an auto mechanic you were repairing carburetors when the manufacturers stopped making them—the best mechanic went from being the one with the most experience repairing carburetors to the one most experienced at reading fuel injector repair manuals. In the office, the focus shifted from the person who knew how to accomplish an existing task the fastest to the person who knew how to learn new things the fastest. Even in the supermarket—the traditional labor force entry point for most teenage Americans—the most successful stock clerk went from being the person who stacked the shelves the highest to the person who could access the computer program for controlling the inventory.

Technological changes like these had been happening in society since time immemorial. So what was new about what happened in the 1980s?

What was new about what happened in the 1980s was that the speed with which these changes occurred accelerated to the point where dealing with the changes in business, rather than dealing with existing business itself, became the key to success for the individual and the organization. These types of changes used to take place so slowly that the rules of the game remained constant over an entire working career.

Now these changes seemed to redefine that career itself every five or ten years. In fact, by the end of the 1980s, more than 50 percent of Americans were changing their entire career every 6.5 years! [62]

It took fifty years for the United States to go from needing 30 million farmers to needing less than 3 million farmers (1930-1980). But it took only five years (1980-1985) to go from needing three hundred thousand people making and repairing mechanical carburetors to less than thirty thousand—when electronic fuel injectors took the automobile industry by storm. Or only five years (1985-1990) to go from needing one hundred thousand people making vinyl records to none—when digital CDs displaced vinyl records in the marketplace.

These and thousands of other changes are what happened to our economy in the 1980s, causing the incredible growth in our total economic wealth and an almost similarly incredible bifurcation between the haves and have-nots in our society.

*U*nderlying virtually all economic decision-making theories—classical, Keynesian, and supply-side—is the traditional concept of scarcity: that the world contains a relatively fixed supply of resources, and the responsibility of economists is to figure out the best way of allocating these resources among their possible uses. Of course, most economists inherently knew that advancing technology was constantly expanding the supply of existing resources—and defining new ones —but this knowledge didn't seem so important when their clients wanted to know what was going to happen *tomorrow,* not twenty or fifty years in the future.

But now the rate of change had accelerated—shrinking time itself in the process. Changes occurred so rapidly that the very supply of the *scarce* resources, upon which almost all economic decision making was based, were no longer scarce over even the shortest of time periods.

For example, how could anyone in 1980 have made an economic forecast about the future price of oil—based on the world's production capacity versus the existing demand—when automobile mileage was about to double in less than half a decade, halving gasoline consumption? How could anyone in 1980 have forecast the future price for fish—based on the capacity of the world's fishing fleets—when within a ten-year period the majority of the fish consumed in the United States would be grown inland in desert fish farms? And how could anyone in 1980 have made forecasts about the jobs available for a new generation entering the workplace when the majority of the occupations they would fill didn't even exist when they were born? No wonder our economic theories weren't able to stand up during this period of rapid technological change. The very foundation they were built on—scarcity—was collapsing.

Today most of us accept from our own observations that we are not running out of the resources that we once thought were scarce. Today most of us accept from our own observations that advancing technology and how we deal with it are the major determinants of success for both the individual and the organization. But when it comes to formulating a decision-making theory to explain what we see around us, we have been unsuccessful. We have been unsuccessful because we have tried to build upon our existing economic theories—virtually all of which are based on the obsolete concepts of scarcity and relative technological stability, rather than on abundance due to rapid technological change.

It is time to begin looking at our world in a new light—a light based on abundance due to rapid technological change. This light, in homage to the ancient alchemists who were the first to have the faith that such a light could exist, is the theory of economic alchemy.

And later on, after we have explained this new light, we shall examine again what happened in the 1980s and what is happening today. What we will see in this new light is that the economic problems we are experiencing—unemployment, health care, education, foreign competition—exist because we have been applying obsolete traditional economic theories to problems that require innovative, "alchemic" solutions.

4

ECONOMIC ALCHEMY

> Nature does not produce anything that is perfect in itself; man must
> bring everything to perfection. This work of bringing things to their
> perfection is called "alchemy." And he is an alchemist who carries
> what nature grows for the use of man to its destined end.
> —PARACELSUS, SIXTEENTH-CENTURY PHYSICIAN AND ALCHEMIST [1]

The ancient alchemists sought to discover the secret of turning base
metals into gold: how to create great value where little existed before.
They believed that by discovering how to make gold they could obtain
unlimited prosperity for all of God's children. And a close analysis of
their writings shows that their definition of prosperity included more
than just material wealth—for they believed that the secret to making
gold also contained the secret to great health, eternal life, and spiritual
fulfillment.

The alchemists' faith in the eventual success of their quest was
guided by their faith in a true and just God—for such a God could not
have created a world where the only way to get gold, or wealth,
would be to take it from someone else.

Most of the world's great scientists up until approximately the sixteenth century were alchemists, although today they are remembered
more for what they discovered while trying to make gold rather than
for the subject of their actual quest.

The thirteenth century's Roger Bacon, the Franciscan monk who
discovered gunpowder and refraction and laid the foundation for
mathematics as the basis for physical science, was actually an alchemist who also believed that gold dissolved in *aqua regia* was the elixir

of life—and that the discovery of how to make gold would lead to individual health along with great societal wealth.[2]

Up until the sixteenth century medical science believed that diseases were caused by an internal imbalance of bodily humors, or fluids, and that they would be cured by bloodletting and purging. Paracelsus (1493–1541), the greatest physician of his time, redefined the science of medicine by asserting that diseases were caused by agents external to the body that could be countered by chemical substances. However, in his day this great physician was better known as the greatest alchemist of all time. His medical and scientific discoveries resulted from his extensive travels in search of the philosopher's stone—widely believed to contain the long-lost secret to alchemic success.

After Paracelsus, the alchemists of Europe became divided into two groups: one that earnestly devoted themselves to the scientific discovery of new compounds and reactions, and one devoted to necromancy and fraud, from whom today most people's negative notion of alchemy is derived.[3]

And thus, while in our era the term "alchemy" is usually equated with false science or fraud, from an economic standpoint the alchemists were successful in their original quest in a manner that they could not have anticipated.

Consider this: If the ancient alchemists had succeeded in fabricating gold, gold would have become worthless, like lead, and their efforts would have been for naught. Yet through their attempts to make gold, they laid the foundation for modern science—pharmacy, medicine, metallurgy, physics, chemistry—which today has accomplished exactly what the alchemists hoped to achieve: the ability to create value and obtain unlimited prosperity for all.

Today we have achieved this ability through the most common, the most powerful, and the most consistently underestimated force in our lives—technology.

In the alchemic world in which we now live, a society's wealth is still a function of its physical resources, as traditional economics has long maintained. But unlike the outdated traditional economist, the alchemist of today recognizes that technology controls both the definition and the supply of physical resources. In fact, for the past few decades, it has been the *backlog* of unimplemented technological advances, rather than unused physical resources, that has been the determinant of real growth.

In calling economic alchemy a theory of economics it is important to note that economic alchemy technically lies outside of the science in which it is currently placed. Traditional economic theories define economics as the study of how to efficiently employ and distribute *scarce* resources or wealth. In contrast, economic alchemy is the study of how to efficiently employ and distribute *unlimited* resources or wealth, primarily through the advancement and application of technology. Instead of finding better ways to slice up the same old pie, in the alchemic world you concentrate on baking a new pie big enough for all to share.

There is nothing unique about a theory lying outside the definition of the science in which it is placed. In many areas where humankind has sought to improve its lot, the most limiting factor has often lain within the definition of what was being sought.

Most of our established business procedures—in marketing, management, and manufacturing, for example—were developed from economic theories based on scarcity and/or static technology. Today, thanks to the rapid advance of technology, many people now accept economic abundance based on what they have seen with their own eyes. And yet, many of these same people in business continue to practice methods that were developed from outdated economic concepts.

What is new about economic alchemy is the different behavior it suggests individuals take once they realize that many of their established business practices are based on outdated economic concepts.

For example, in retailing it once made sense to open more and more stores in order to increase total sales—whereas today it often makes more sense to concentrate on improving the sales per square foot of existing stores. Such a strategy wasn't technologically feasible until the recent availability of accurate, real-time information systems.

In management it once made sense to train new employees how to use the latest advanced equipment—whereas today it makes equal or even more sense to concentrate on designing customized equipment suitable to the skills of existing employees. This wasn't technologically feasible until the societal unit of technology shrunk from the $1 million mainframe computer to the $1000 personal computer or $25 microprocessor.

And in manufacturing it once made sense to develop exclusive technology and rely on patents to monopolize a marketplace—whereas today it makes far more sense to share or even give away new technology in order to take maximum advantage of having gotten there first.

This concept is illustrated by the failure of Sony's Beta format VCR in the 1970s and the subsequent success of Sony's 8mm VCR format in the 1990s.

How Sony Learned from Its Mistake

After Losing with Beta, Sony Wins with 8mm

When home videocassette recorders were first introduced in the mid-1970s, there were two competing formats, Sony's Betamax system and archrival Matsushita's VHS system. Sony was confident that the Beta format would prevail because of its clear technical superiority.

Matsushita, however, recognized that what it was selling wasn't electronic gadgetry but home entertainment—that as big as the direct market for VCRs seemed to be, it was only the tip of a much larger iceberg of potentially unlimited consumer demand for prerecorded tapes. And it was that tape market—which a conventional businessman might define as a subsidiary market—that would in fact shape the dynamics of the VCR market.

Thus, while Sony tried to prevent competing manufacturers from using its superior system, Matsushita went about aggressively licensing hundreds of other firms to produce its technologically inferior VHS machines. Before long, the sheer volume of VHS machines flooding the marketplace began to overwhelm the Beta. As a result, software manufacturers began offering a wider selection of tapes in the VHS format than in Beta. That gave consumers an even greater incentive to buy VHS rather than Beta machines—which, in turn, encouraged videotape distributors to tilt their product mix even more heavily in favor of VHS.

By 1987, VHS machines were accounting for more than 90 percent of the $5.25 billion U.S. market for VCRs. Sony finally threw in the towel early in 1988, announcing that it would begin manufacturing VHS machines.[4]

But by the end of the 1980s it was evident that Sony had what it takes to succeed into the next century—the ability to learn from their mistakes and the ability to change.

In the late 1980s, Sony introduced a new proprietary format for video recorders, the 8mm videotape, which it began using in making palm-sized video camcorders. Like its then-almost-obsolete Beta cousin, Sony's 8mm format was technologically superior to the existing camcorder VHS format being sold by Matsushita, known as VHS-C. The problem was that while Sony's 8mm format was a superior product in terms of picture quality and recording time, unlike Matsushita's VHS-C format, it could not be played on the existing 70 million VHS recorders in U.S. households.

So Sony took exactly the opposite tack it had taken with its Beta format. It licensed the 8mm format to all comers—VCR manufacturers, tape manufacturers, and other palm-sized-camcorder manufacturers. It even also began selling individual components of 8mm camcorders in order to make it easier for competitors to quickly enter into 8mm camcorder production.

As early as 1991 this new strategy for Sony had paid off. Eight-millimeter camcorders had captured over 50 percent of the 10-million-unit 1991 market for camcorders and over 60 percent of the market in gadget-crazy Japan, where many new electronic products are first launched.[5] And Sony was the largest individual manufacturer of 8mm camcorders, as well as the beneficiary of a royalty payment for each 8mm camcorder sold by one of its competitors.

Moreover, by 1991 there were nearly two thousand movie titles available in Sony's 8mm format, and Sony was marketing a portable video Walkman that played 8mm tapes on a color four-inch screen. Clearly, Sony has higher sights set for its 8mm format than just camcorders—it is out to displace the VHS tape as the standard format for all video recorders. Time will tell whether Sony is successful using the same strategy against its archrival Matsushita in the 1990s that Matsushita used to beat Sony in the 1970s.

*T*he lesson in this story is clear. The world market for any one product, process, or method today is too large for any manufacturer to completely satisfy. When a product is successful—that is, *demanded* by consumers—the manufacturer must profitably share technology with anyone who wants to participate or risk being displaced by a competitor who is willing to share—even a competitor with an inferior product.

My father often consoled me with the thought that we learn only by our mistakes. When we unknowingly do something right the first time, we haven't yet learned anything and may be setting ourselves up for a grave mistake in the future. This certainly happened to IBM in the 1980s when it succeeded with the open-architecture IBM PC but subsequently failed with the closed-architecture IBM PS/2.

How IBM Did Not Learn from Its Success

Accidental Success with the PC Failed to Translate to the PS/2

Everyone thought IBM was brilliant in the early 1980s when it entered the personal computer market, which up until then was effectively monopolized by Apple, which refused to share its unique proprietary technology.[6]

IBM adopted an open architecture for its IBM PC line that positively encouraged competing manufacturers not only to produce software and peripheral equipment for the IBM PC but even to build knockoffs (clones) of the machine itself. Most observers thought that IBM knew that the more IBM-compatible machines there were in the marketplace, the more IBM-compatible software would be written—and the more people would buy IBM machines.

Sure enough, despite Apple's superior technology, IBM-compatible personal computers became the industry standard. Apple was almost driven out of business and in the 1990s had to run up the white flag. Apple began building IBM-compatible processors into their machines and licensing their proprietary operating system technology to clone makers.

The successful strategy that IBM pursued with its original PC in the 1980s was radical back then for a corporation that had previously made its mark by developing proprietary technology, jealously guarding it, and selling every component of its systems —hardware, software, and accessories. By 1986, although IBM had started far behind in 1982, it had captured approximately 26 percent of the personal computer market, more than twice the market share of rival Apple.[7]

However, IBM's success with the original IBM PC may have been a fortuitous accident. In 1987, IBM returned to its former ways with PS/2—IBM's trade name for perhaps the greatest computer flop of our time.

In April 1987, IBM announced a new type of personal computer, called the PS/2, which used a Micro Channel architecture that was incompatible with the existing millions of PCs in the American workplace—even incompatible with IBM's own brand of PCs. Moreover, whereas the design of the original IBM PC was treated as common property, the new PS/2 machine's technology was secret, and its patents were rigorously defended. (PS/2 machines could run most of the existing software, but they could not accept the thousands of hardware accessories that customers used to customize their machines.)

IBM thought it could crush the IBM-clone and accessory makers by making their existing and future products obsolete. But in a stunning move the clone makers, led by Texas-based Compaq Computer, formed their own "gang of nine" and developed a new open-architecture standard offering the same features as IBM's Micro Channel design. But this standard, popularly known as EISA (for Extended Industry Standard Architecture), could utilize all existing IBM-compatible PC accessories and software.

By 1988, IBM's 26 percent of the personal computer market had fallen to 18 percent, and once-loyal IBM customers were abandoning IBM in droves for trying to monopolize a technology and for trying to make its customers' existing machines obsolete.[8]

Then, in late 1988, IBM unveiled a new model of the PS/2, the Model 30, that used—guess what—the old open-architecture design!

In fact, in an even bolder move to catch back up and remedy its mistake, in the early 1990s IBM virtually abandoned the Micro Channel architecture and began manufacturing IBM machines, and even IBM clones, under different brand names, that utilized the "gang of nine" EISA standard.

Moreover, in the 1990s IBM captured the portable PC market with a new line called IBM Thinkpads—notebooks featuring numerous proprietary IBM inventions such as a keyboard-based trackpoint pointing device instead of a mouse. In a testament to how much IBM had learned from its mistakes, IBM not only opened the market for third-party manufacturers to make peripherals for Thinkpads; it even began licensing the rights to use the trackpoint, the keyboard, and other proprietary IBM Thinkpad innovations to the original "gang of nine" for their notebook PCs.

*I*n trying to summarize the lessons behind these and hundreds of other examples, I have attempted to divide economic alchemy into six basic areas or laws. Before beginning an explanation of these six laws, I want to state that I do not believe that the theory of economic alchemy is altogether original or that it is necessarily correct.

Like all theories, economic alchemy is built on the foundation of those who have come before and contains much of their work. And like all theories, it seeks to better explain what people see around them, and it is only correct in the sense that it accomplishes this task better than the theories that have preceded it.

I hope for three things as you now read a brief summary of the theory of economic alchemy.

First, I hope you will find it correct—that is, that it better explains for you what you see every day and that it can assist you in predicting your future.

Second, I hope that it will stimulate you to examine many of your beliefs in light of the abundant world that God has given us, rather than in the darkness of scarcity that our fears and suspicions have often led us to accept in the past.

And third, I hope that it will assist you in developing your own theories that are more correct—that is, that better explain what we see every day and that better explain how we can shape, let alone predict, what's ahead in our future.

PRINCIPLES OF ECONOMIC ALCHEMY

The foundation of the theory of economic alchemy rests on three basic principles:

- Technology is the major determinant of wealth because it determines the nature and supply of physical resources.
- The advance of technology is determined mainly by our ability to process information.
- The backlog of unimplemented technological advances (the "technology gap") is the true predictor of economic growth for both the individual and society.

From these three principles we derive the six laws of economic alchemy and their related definitional terms—a summary of which is contained in an Appendix at the end of the book.

First Law of Economic Alchemy

The first law states:

By enabling us to make productive use of particular raw materials, technology determines what constitutes a physical resource.

This is perhaps the most startling, and the most obvious, part of the theory of economic alchemy. At every point in history there have always been resources by which the current society defined its wealth —tools or hunting implements in the time of our nomadic ancestors, land and livestock in the time of our agrarian great-grandparents, and oil and other energy resources throughout most of this century. And yet, while we even call our past ages by the critical resources of their time—the Stone Age, the Bronze Age, the Iron Age—these very resources that defined their wealth were almost entirely man-made creations.

Land wasn't a resource until human beings, applying technology, first learned how to farm it. Livestock wasn't a resource until humans developed the technology of hunting, dressing, and domesticating animals. And certainly oil—the black goo that (in ancient times) used to appear in pools and pollute the fresh water supply—wasn't a resource until humans developed the technology of refining and burning it.

We call this type of technology explained by the First Law of Economic Alchemy—the technology that enables us to define what constitutes a valuable physical resource in the first place—*definitional technology*.

Definitional technology used to be important only to historians and others interested in how our forefathers lived. This was because until recently the speed that definitional technology advanced was so slow that little changed over the lifetime of a single individual. The resources by which people defined their wealth were, for the most part, the same when they were born as when they died. Thus, most people spent their time accumulating existing already-defined resources rather than worrying about obtaining or defining new ones.

There were exceptions to this rule, most of them occurring during times of war or national emergency. The transition for the Greeks from the Bronze Age to the Iron Age accelerated during wartime—a disruption in the supply of tin (used to make bronze) caused the Greeks to begin using iron. The worldwide scarcity of whale oil during the 1850s accelerated the development of the petroleum industry (see, in Chapter 3, "The End of the World [Again]"). And today's rubber industry developed when the United States, facing a scarcity of Asian natural rubber during World War Two, undertook a massive program —second in scale only to the nuclear bomb project—to develop a substitute made from commonly available petroleum by-products.[9]

But for the most part, generations were born and died over the time it took for the various ages to give way to one another. Modes of

transportation, farming methods, medical practices, building techniques—these and other technologies that defined the time in which
one lived rarely changed noticeably within a single individual lifetime.

As a result, the ability of technology to define resources has been
taken for granted to such an extent that it was as if it didn't exist.
Even those who did notice definitional technology treated it—for
decision-making purposes—as a constant over their lifetimes.

Today, technology changes so fast that our most powerful resource
itself is our ability to define our physical resources. Since the beginning of this century, the majority of the world's personal fortunes have
been made by people working with products that didn't exist when
they were born.

While the definitional technology explained by the First Law of
Economic Alchemy is probably the most important type of technology
in determining our society's wealth, it is not the most important type
of technology affecting our daily decision-making process. Although
we live in a constantly changing world—indeed, in a world in which
the rate of change is constantly accelerating—not everything in our
world changes every day. There is at any given moment an existing
level of definitional technology—which is to say, an existing base of
currently defined physical resources—that for all practical purposes
we can and do consider to be the measure of what is available to us.

Today our resource base consists of such relatively familiar commodities as bauxite, copper, coal, iron, gold, natural gas, petroleum,
silicon, timber, tin, and uranium. A hundred years ago this list would
have looked very different (bauxite, silicon, and uranium would have
been absent, for example, while ivory and whale oil might have been
present). A decade from now it will be different again, no doubt in
ways that we cannot today imagine. Nonetheless, those of us who
must make decisions for today and tomorrow need to know: How can
we increase our supply of what we currently regard as valuable physical resources?

Reading history, one might quite understandably come to the conclusion that the best way—indeed, the only way—to increase one's
supply of currently defined valuable physical resources is to take them
from someone else. The notion that the resource pie was fixed and
that a larger slice for you inevitably meant a smaller slice for me has
always struck the vast majority of humanity as a matter of basic com-

mon sense. This notion, like the ancient Aristotelian notion that the sun revolves around the earth, seems consonant with the evidence of our senses. But this notion, like the ancient Aristotelian notion about the sun revolving around the earth, is wrong.

In fact, the resource base has never been fixed—and not simply because the nature of its components is always changing as definitional technology advances. The fact is, even in the context of a given set of previously defined physical resources, the supply of resources is always expanding.

It's not that vast new amounts of oil or gas or copper are somehow spontaneously being created deep in the bowels of the earth. The amount of these commodities is pretty much the same as it has always been—less, of course, what we've consumed over the millennia. But the *amount* of a resource is not the same as the *supply* of a resource. The amount of a resource is how much of it physically exists in the universe. The supply of a resource is how much is known to exist and is physically available for our use—a figure that is determined as much by how we use it as by the quantity we happen to have available.

Second Law of Economic Alchemy

This leads us to the second law:

Technology determines our supply of existing physical resources by determining both the efficiency with which we use resources and our ability to find, obtain, distribute, and store them.

What makes a physical resource a resource—as opposed, say, to just a pretty rock or an annoying black goo—is its usefulness. Take oil, for example. One of the things that make oil such a valuable physical resource is that we can refine it into gasoline and use it to power our cars. In this context, the most sensible way of measuring how much oil we have is not in terms of how many barrels it can fill up (filling up barrels, after all, isn't really what we want to do with the stuff) but in terms of how many miles of driving we can get out of it.

The actual amount of oil buried in the earth (the number of barrels or gallons) is irrelevant. What counts is how much good the oil we know we have will do us—in other words, the supply.

Clearly, a veritable ocean of oil won't do us any good if we don't know it's there. Nor will it do us any good if we can *find* it but can't get to it. Or if we can *obtain* it but can't move it to where we want it. Or, finally, if we can *distribute* it to where we want it but can't find a way to *store* it there until we need it.

Beyond these constraints, there's the additional question of how we actually use it. If I've got a car that gets ten miles to the gallon and you've got a car that gets twenty miles to the gallon, the same amount of gasoline will get you twice as far as it will get me. In other words, even though we may both have the same number of gallons of gas, your effective supply is twice as big as mine.

From this it should be clear that there are basically two ways to increase the supply of a previously defined physical resource: (1) We can improve our ability to *find, obtain, distribute,* and *store* it; and (2) we can improve the efficiency with which we use it.

The first set of abilities constitutes what we might call *supply technology*. The second set can be labeled *use technology*. Together, they constitute the general category of technology considered by the Second Law of Alchemy—*quantity technology,* or technology that determines the available quantity of existing physical resources.

Of the two kinds of quantity technologies, the technology of supply has the more straightforward impact on our resource base. Consider its effect on the supply of oil and natural gas over the past two or three decades. To begin with, advances in geology (our ability to *find* oil and gas) led to the discovery in 1968 of the huge oil field beneath Prudhoe Bay on Alaska's North Slope—as a result of which, estimates of total global oil reserves were revised upwards by nearly 10 billion barrels. On top of that, improvements in drilling techniques (our ability to *obtain* oil and gas) allowed gas producers, who had previously never delved deeper than five or ten thousand feet, to sink wells six miles or more into the earth's crust—which gave them access to huge reservoirs they'd never before been able to tap. In addition, the evolution of the supertanker and the advance of pipeline construction methods (our ability to *distribute* oil and gas) enabled new discoveries to be brought onstream almost as quickly as they could be made. And finally, the development of relatively safe above- and below-ground storage tanks (our ability to *store* oil and gas) gave us the ability to store heating oil in our homes and put a gas station on virtually every street corner.

In general, the four aspects of the technology of supply—the ability to *find, obtain, distribute,* and *store* a resource—constitute a kind of conceptual pipeline through which all physical resources must flow for them to be of any value to us. Our ability to clear up bottlenecks at any of those four points thus effectively increases our supply of a given resource.

In the case of oil and gas, the worst bottleneck we face today involves distribution. Over the past decade or two, we have become very good at finding, obtaining, and storing oil and gas. But as was illustrated by the horrendous *Exxon Valdez* spill that disfigured Alaska's Prince William Sound in 1989, our ability to transport oil safely still leaves much to be desired. As a result, we have (possibly with unconscious wisdom) let potentially huge supplies of oil and gas— such as the large, highly promising federal tracts in Alaska, off the California coast, and in the Gulf of Mexico—go unexplored.

This is true of most currently defined physical resources in the alchemic world. The biggest constraint on our supply of resources is not the difficulty of finding, obtaining, or storing resources, but the inability to distribute them efficiently to where they will do us the most good.

Perhaps nowhere has the frustration of this bottleneck been more glaringly illustrated than in famine-ravaged Ethiopia. Even when the northern provinces were stricken by drought in the 1980s, the country's main agricultural region—the south—continued to produce food in ample quantities. In 1985, a massive international relief effort— including the hugely popular Live-Aid concerts—was undertaken to alleviate the famine in the north, which resulted in more than five hundred thousand tons of grain being shipped to Ethiopia that year. However, very few hungry people got fed, because the grain wound up rotting in warehouses in the eastern Ethiopian port cities of Assab, Massawa, and Djibouti. As the relief workers discovered to their dismay, what Ethiopia needed wasn't more food but more trucks and better roads.

Moreover, this limitation—read opportunity—in the distribution sector applies to more than just the distribution of physical resources in the Third World. In almost every industry in America, and even more so in Japan and Europe, the greatest economic opportunity of the 1990s lies in distributing finished products. This is because we have yet to apply to distributing products many of the technological advances that we have already applied to manufacturing them.

Distribution—The Greatest Opportunity in the 1990s

Back in 1967, when the movie *The Graduate* summarized the key to wealth in a single word, the key to wealth for most people did lie in finding less expensive ways to make things.

Today, however, thanks to "plastics" and so many other better ways of making things, the key to wealth for most of us no longer lies in the manufacturing of existing products. In the 1990s, the greatest opportunities lie in the distribution sector of our economy. Here's why.

In the 1960s a manufactured product that sold for $300—for example, a camera or a television set—typically had a manufacturing cost of approximately $150 and a distribution cost of approximately $150. Distribution costs back then accounted for approximately 50 percent of retail prices.

In the 1990s the same product of similar quality typically retails for approximately $100 (although many people don't realize this because they have shifted to purchasing higher-quality products). This two-thirds price reduction for similar-quality items has occurred primarily because innovative manufacturing methods have lowered production costs all the way from $150 to approximately $20 or less. Distribution costs have also fallen, from $150 to approximately $80, to where they now account for approximately 80 percent of the price for a typical $100 retail product.

The reason that distribution costs have not fallen as much as manufacturing costs is that we have yet to apply to distribution many of the innovative methods that we have already applied to manufacturing.

Thus, in the 1960s it was possible to make a great deal of

TYPICAL RETAIL PRODUCT COST BREAKDOWN				
	1960s		1990s	
	$	%	$	%
Manufacturing Costs	$150	50%	$20	20%
Distribution Costs	$150	50%	$80	80%
Total Retail Price	$300	100%	$100	100%

money by lowering the cost of production. Back then even a 10 or 20 percent reduction in manufacturing costs could lower your retail price by $15 or $30. Great fortunes were made by those who found ways to lower manufacturing costs all the way from $150 to $20 or less, often by moving production facilities overseas.

However, in the 1990s, when manufacturing costs represent less than $20 of a typical $100 retail price, a 10 or 20 percent reduction in manufacturing costs might only represent a $2 to $4 retail price reduction on a $100 item.

In the 1990s, when distribution costs represent more than $80 of a typical $100 retail price, a 10 or 20 percent reduction in distribution costs might represent an $8 to $16 retail price reduction on a $100 item. A 50 percent or greater reduction in distribution costs—sometimes feasible by just eliminating one leg in the distribution chain between the factory and the consumer—might represent a $40 or even greater retail price reduction on a $100 item.

Primarily because of the role of increased distribution costs in our economy, many of the production facilities that moved overseas in the 1960s are now moving back to the United States. In 1991 approximately 2.2 million of the 3.7 million Japanese cars sold in America were made in America. In the latter half of the 1990s it is expected that most of the large television sets sold in America will be made in North America.

More important, in the past two decades the majority of great personal fortunes have been made by people who found better ways of distributing things rather than better ways of making things.

For example, by 1992 the richest man in America was a person who had started his company only in the 1960s and never *made* anything in his life—the late Sam Walton, founder of Wal-Mart. Or take the person who became a billionaire in the 1970s by founding an entire airline for moving products rather than people —Fred Smith of Federal Express. Or consider the person who became a billionaire in the 1980s by discovering better ways of moving other people's information between other people's computers—Ross Perot of EDS.

Prior to the past few decades, most of the great personal fortunes in American history—fortunes like those of the Astors (fur trading), the Rockefellers (oil), the Carnegies (steel), and the Fords (automobiles)—were built on the bedrock of natural resources and manufacturing. Today, as is evidenced by the financial difficulties of the richest families of just the past decade— the Hunts (oil and silver) or the Reichmans (real estate)—the key to wealth no longer lies in owning or making physical assets but in distributing them.

As the First and Second Laws of Alchemy indicate, our base of physical resources—and thus our wealth—is determined by the advance of technology. But then, we might ask, if it is technology that determines the definition of our physical resources, and if it is technology that determines the supply of already defined physical resources, how can we get more technology? What controls the advance of technology itself?

This question brings us to the most important realization of all— that of the Third Law of Alchemy. This law explains what determines the advance of technology—and hence the nature of the key to increasing our wealth.

Third Law of Economic Alchemy

The third law states:

The rate at which a society's technology advances is determined by the relative level of its ability to process information.

Scientific and technological advance does not—indeed, cannot—occur in isolation. It depends on the ability of scientists and engineers to keep up with the latest developments, to cross-pollinate, to learn from the experience of others. As Sir Isaac Newton once put it, "If I have seen further it is by standing on the shoulders of giants."[10] Without access to the work of Nicolaus Copernicus, Galileo Galilei might never have discovered (with his telescope) that the earth revolves around the sun. Without knowledge of the pioneering field equations of the nineteenth-century Scottish physicist James Clerk Maxwell, the twentieth-century Italian engineer Guglielmo Marconi would not have been able to invent the radio—nor German-born Albert Einstein develop his theory of relativity.

In short, the speed at which technology advances depends on how easily members of a society can access and share their acquired knowledge—that is, it depends on the level of *information-processing technology*.

In this model of how technology (and thus the supply of resources) advances, the written word—which was developed approximately seven thousand years ago—*caused* civilization, for now a farmer could pass on a new agricultural method to someone in a different place and time.[11] The printing press—developed by Gutenberg in the sixteenth century—*caused* the Industrial Revolution, for now a scientist or inventor could efficiently distribute his or her research throughout the world.[12] And the computer—which was invented in 1946 but has just started becoming widespread in our society—is *causing* a similar monumental economic expansion, which, in a much shorter time period, will make the advances of the Industrial Revolution itself pale by comparison.

And just as the greatest economic opportunities today lie in the distribution of finished products and physical resources, similar opportunities exist in the distribution of information. The widespread integration of computers in modern society has not only ignited an information explosion but also given us the means to manage the overwhelming fallout of that explosion. But we are still better at producing new information than we are at accessing and sharing it. Indeed, technology is advancing so rapidly on so many fronts that the main constraint on innovation today is not so much the capacity of engineers and entrepreneurs to come up with new ideas, but their ability to keep abreast of and integrate the latest developments from fields outside their own particular specialty.

This, then, is the way to increase the size of the pie. The more we can improve our ability to process information, the faster technology in general will advance. The faster technology in general advances, the greater its ability both to increase the effective supply of existing physical resources and to define entirely new ones—and the richer we will be.

For those readers who like to think in mathematical terms, this ability of technology to give us unlimited wealth can be stated:

$$W = PT^n$$

W stands for wealth, *P* for physical resources (that is, the traditional measures of wealth, such as land, labor, minerals, and water), *T* for technology, and *n* for the exponential effect of technological advances on themselves. (As is later explained by the Sixth Law of Economic Alchemy, technology has a multiplier effect on itself as each new technological advance becomes the foundation for another advance.)

This simple formula has enormous implications—not just in terms of improving our understanding of the economic basis of our society, but as the key to developing more effective strategies for our individual lives as consumers, businesspeople, and citizens. What it tells us is that we no longer have to play the zero-sum game. Instead of finding better ways to slice up the same small pie, in the alchemic world we can find a way to bake a new and bigger pie.

DEMAND SIDE ALCHEMY

According to conventional economic theories, if we have the technological ability to produce unlimited physical resources, which would mean that we also have the technological ability to produce unlimited quantities of finished products and services, our economy should grind to a halt. For once everyone received everything they wanted, they would no longer have a need to achieve anything. This is what probably concerned Keynes as he looked to the future from the depths of the Great Depression; perhaps he worried that even worse than the world of want he saw all around him in the 1930s might be the coming world of plenty—a world in which all wants were met and thus a world in which there was nothing more for people to do.

Like the great classical economists that came before him, Keynes underestimated the power of advancing technology. But while the nineteenth-century economists underestimated the capacity of technology to increase the *supply* of resources, Keynes underestimated the capacity of advancing technology to increase the *demand* for resources.

In the world we live in today, where advancing technology has been able to meet the basic primary needs for most Americans, advancing technology is constantly offering new products and services that before too long become considered basic primary needs by the majority of the population.

For example, before the invention of the first electric washing machine, around World War One, few Americans cared how many times they wore a shirt before they washed it, and clothing was constructed to require a minimum number of washings—shirts, for example, came with detachable collars and cuffs, the parts that got dirty most quickly.[13] Once the washing machine became available on a widespread basis, every American *had* to wear a clean shirt every day, and detachable collars and cuffs went the way of the horse and buggy.

When Henry Ford first invented a mass-produced automobile that was affordable by the common man, people scoffed at the thought of who would buy it—there were few paved roads available to go anywhere, and most people lived within walking distance of where they worked. Thanks to the automobile, within a very short period of time most people actually moved to a place—suburbia—where they needed it, and soon two cars, let alone one, became a necessity just to get to work or shop for daily necessities.

Back when the telephone first became available to businesses, most businessmen communicated through hand-delivered written messages that they originated by dictating to their secretaries. Many of them were convinced that using the telephone was a waste of time. After all, who wanted to dictate a message to a secretary, have it transcribed, then read by the secretary over the telephone to the recipient's secretary, and then transcribed by the recipient's secretary into a written message for the recipient? Of course, before long the telephone changed the way in which businesspeople communicated —causing them to speak directly to one another rather than through notes transcribed by their secretaries—and the telephone became an absolute necessity for every business.[14] (This story contains an important lesson for us today, since most people still use computers and other new inventions to merely modify existing obsolete ways of doing things—rather than reengineer the work itself to fit the ability of newly available tools.)

Today virtually 95 percent of the things we spend our money on— which most of us think of as *necessities*—were not even dreamed of when many of us were born. Electronic mail, fax machines, television sets, airline travel, Disneyland vacations, high-fashion clothing, stereos, VCRs, air conditioners, personal computers, day care, movies, fast-food restaurants, dry cleaning—the list goes on and on. Even the so-called traditional necessities like food, clothing, and housing are no longer necessities, in the sense that we consume quantities of them far in excess of our basic needs.

Fourth Law of Economic Alchemy

We state this ability of advancing technology to define new products and services, which soon become basic needs, as the fourth law:

By providing us with new products and processes that change the way in which we live, technology determines what constitutes a need, and hence the nature of consumer demand.

This fourth law regarding technology's ability to define the nature of demand is entirely analogous to the first law regarding technology's ability to define the nature of supply.

Fifth Law of Economic Alchemy

And just as we have a Second Law of Economic Alchemy to explain the supply of already defined resources, we have a fifth law to explain the demand for already-defined products. The fifth law states:

Technology determines the level of consumer demand by determining the price at which goods can be sold.

This may seem obvious, but it is amazing how few businesspeople understand the nature of demand in an economy where tomorrow's luxuries aren't yet invented and today's luxuries are fast becoming tomorrow's necessities.

In the world in which we live, where the technology explained by the first two Laws of Economic Alchemy is always expanding the supply—and lowering the price—of available resources, there is no absolute level of demand for any already defined product. From automobiles in the time of Henry Ford to personal computers today, the demand for a product is almost entirely determined by its price. For no matter how excessive the newly defined product may appear when it is first introduced, at some price the same consumer finds that he or she *must* have it, and probably have even more than one.

As the great U.S. economist, Nobel Prize–winner John Kenneth Galbraith, noted in 1958, "In the affluent society, no sharp distinction can be made between luxuries and necessaries."[15] The landscape of business failures is littered with companies that didn't realize that advancing technology would rapidly turn their so-called luxury products into necessities—by lowering the price. Dumont (televisions), IBM (personal computers), AT&T (telephones), Ampex (VCRs), and thousands of lesser-known companies failed to realize that their having the first product on the market meant only that they had a slight head start on becoming the first to make their product affordable by the average American consumer.

QUANTITY DEMAND AND QUALITY DEMAND

As we have seen, virtually 95 percent of the items demanded today by consumers are in excess of their most basic physiological needs. We call this type of demand *alchemic demand* in reference to the fact that it is created almost entirely by advancing technology. There are two fundamental types of alchemic demand: *quantity demand* and *quality demand*.

Quantity demand, the more rudimentary of the two, is the consumer's basic desire for more of what he or she already has: more food, a bigger house, an extra suit of clothing. This kind of demand may seem limited, but in fact it is typically much larger than the demand for the initial product. For example, from 1960 to 1988 the number of homes containing a television set rose from 90 to 98 percent—but the number of homes containing two or more television sets rose from 11 to 60 percent.[16] A men's clothing store might sell one hundred first-time suits a year to young men entering the workforce but two thousand suits a year to consumers who already own at least one or more. And for every first-time home buyer in the United States each year, there are at least five homes sold to existing home owners moving on to (usually) larger ones.[17]

If quantity demand can be thought of as the consumer's demand for a larger supply of an existing alchemic product, *quality demand* reflects the appetite for a different *kind* of product. In the case of television sets, quantity demand manifests itself in terms of a consumer's relatively simple desire to own more than one TV. Quality demand, by contrast, reflects his or her more sophisticated yearning for a *better* TV (say, a big-screen color receiver with remote-control capability and stereo sound) as well as for related but otherwise entirely new products (such as a videocassette recorder or a laser-disc player).

When Keynes and his successors worried about the likelihood that increasingly prosperous consumers would feel decreasingly motivated to spend, they were thinking mainly in terms of quantity demand. People might well want more food, a bigger house, an extra suit, standard economic logic told them, but there was a limit, wasn't there?

Well, no. What Keynes didn't realize was that when quantity demand is satiated—as it is these days among the vast majority of Americans—quality demand kicks in. When you have all the food, clothing, and TVs you need—as most Americans do today—you start wanting better food, better clothing, and better TVs. To put it another way, the typical middle-class American couple would probably have little if any interest in buying a third Chevrolet to add to the two they already own.[18] But they might jump at the chance to get rid of one of the Chevrolets and upgrade to a BMW. A young executive whose closet was filled with eight $400 suits would probably have little interest in purchasing a ninth one. But he might jump at the chance to purchase a new $800 designer suit.

Moreover, this flip in the nature of demand is not one-way. For as the consumer begins to satisfy his or her desire for higher quality, quantity demand once again begins to work its magic. Now the American couple wants *two* BMWs so they don't argue over who has to drive the Chevrolet. Now the young executive wants *seven* $800 designer suits because he no longer feels right wearing his older, $400 ones. Theoretically, of course, the demand for more and better goods will be satiated when the consumer finally owns a sufficiently large number of the best cars or best suits on the market. But as long as technology continues to advance, there never will be a best car or a best suit—at least not for very long. Each year a better one will be developed, and the process will start all over again.

Ironically, when it comes to understanding American consumers, no one seems to understand us better than the Japanese.

In the 1960s, the Japanese overwhelmed many of the world's markets with inexpensive products—in effect, satiating quantity demand. But in the early 1970s they turned their attention to increasing the quality of their goods, riding the alchemic shift from quantity demand to quality demand (leaving the now unprofitable market for cheaper goods to their imitators). In less than twenty years, they went from being known as the lowest-cost producer of almost everything U.S. consumers could want to being known as the highest-quality (and usually the highest-priced) producer of almost everything. In the 1990s they even began going after the U.S. consumer who already owned two Japanese cars and who wanted to trade up to a BMW. They introduced two new top-of-the-line automobiles—the Infiniti and the Lexus—which were highly successful in the midst of the worst car-buying years in decades. And they left General Motors in the dust wondering why their satisfied Chevrolet customers weren't buying any more of them.

The consumer's continual desire for higher-quality items is so incorporated into our marketplace that it is often transparent. Each year, as advancing technology lowers the cost of manufactured products, smart manufacturers, recognizing that they already have a relationship that they want to keep with an existing customer, automatically improve the quality of their products rather than lower the price.

Suppose you spent $300 on a thirteen-inch Sony color television in 1971 and went out in 1990 to buy its replacement. You would have been pleased to find that virtually the same television—a thirteen-inch model without remote control—cost only $150 (actually $47 in 1971 dollars after adjusting for inflation). But rather than purchase the same television, you would have probably elected to spend $400 ($124 in 1971 dollars) to purchase a twenty-seven-inch model with built-in stereo sound and remote control—or perhaps elected to spend $966 ($300 in 1971 dollars) on a Sony super-deluxe model with built-in VCR and Picture-in-Picture channel displays. Moreover, you would have found that Sony, aware that their satisfied customers wanted increasing quality rather than lower prices, no longer made a model equivalent to the one you purchased in 1971, having abandoned this (now) low-end market to its imitators.

Suppose in 1991 you entered medical school hoping to purchase a new $15,000 convertible automobile upon graduation in 1995. When you went to the dealer in 1995, you would have found that the car with all the features you wanted in 1991, say the equivalent of a 1991 General Motors convertible Geo, now cost only $10,000. But rather than purchase this car and pocket the $5000 savings, you would most likely have traded up to a now-$15,000 car that had all of the features of a $20,000 car in 1991.

This consumer-driven phenomenon of choosing increasing quality over lower price is so prevalent today that most people don't realize how much the material quality of their lives—from the improved quality and lower prices of their products—is steadily increasing. Whether you are talking about TVs or toys, automobiles or air conditioners, blue jeans or bedding, cameras or convertible sofas, refrigerators or recorded music, Americans today invariably enjoy better quality goods at a lower real cost than they did twenty years ago—or more than any other consumers at any other time in history.[19]

It wasn't too long ago that, when a person was late, the most common reasons were either a flat tire or a flooded carburetor— something that advancing technology (radial tires and electronic fuel injection) have almost completely eliminated from our daily concerns.

Paradoxically, lower prices and increased-quality products are usually reported in our media as a decrease rather than an increase in our material wealth. This is because our most common economic indicators such as gross national product (GNP) or retail sales are not currently indexed for either increasing quality or for price deflation caused by technology's ability to lower prices. For example, when the medical student in our example purchased his $20,000 car for $15,000, he experienced a $5,000 unreported increase in his material lifestyle —or if he had purchased his $15,000 original dream car for $10,000, it would have shown up as a $5,000 decrease in GNP or retail sales. Similarly, when the average cost of a new home is reported by our government, this figure is not indexed for the fact that it is more than twice the size of the average new home in the 1960s or that it contains features and appliances that alone make it worth twice as much to the consumer.

In the so-called recession of 1991 the retailers of America recorded their worse Christmas season in years—total retail sales for the holiday season were down 1.3 percent. But this figure is grossly misleading. Severe competition caused preholiday prices to drop on many items as much as 20 percent—or to put it in real terms, the children of America received as much as 18.7 percent more toys for Christmas in 1991. And this analysis doesn't include the fact that the hottest item of Christmas 1991—a $139 Nintendo video game—was functionally equivalent to a $1,000 rich man's computer toy just five years earlier.

The fact that the level of demand is determined by price, as explained by the Fifth Law of Economic Alchemy, may strike most readers as simple common sense. A student of economics might ask why something so obvious is even stated as a law of economic alchemy. This fifth law is part of the theory of economic alchemy because, *in a rapidly advancing technological environment,* there almost is no price too low for a product to be produced—or put another way, there is almost no level of demand too high.

The reason is what's commonly known as the learning curve. As explained by the First and Second Laws of Economic Alchemy, the expense of the actual physical materials and labor that go into each unit of most manufactured items is almost insignificant. Far greater are the fixed expenses—fixed in the sense that they remain the same whether you produce one item or one thousand—of research and development, retooling, marketing, and the like. Because these fixed expenses far exceed the marginal material expense that is attached to each item, the more items you produce, the lower the unit cost of each will be—and the lower the price you can sensibly charge consumers. Of course, the lower the price you can charge, the more demand there will be for your product—and the greater the likelihood that you will be able to sell the huge volume you needed to produce in order to achieve the economies you needed.

This may sound circular, but it works. Such is the magic of the alchemic power of technology.

These days this sort of learning-curve pricing is standard practice among smart manufacturers—in particular, the Japanese, who used it to take the VCR market away from the U.S. companies that invented the device. Conventional thinkers resent the technique even as they are steamrolled by it. They call it "dumping" and label those who practice it as unfair traders. In fact, there is nothing at all unfair about learning-curve pricing—except perhaps that in order to see its advantages, you need to recognize a few alchemic facts of life: namely that the level of demand is simply a function of price, and that what determines price is the level of our technology. Also, ironically for the Japanese, every VCR now sold in the U.S. and in Japan creates a demand for U.S.-produced prerecorded videotapes whose total cost is several times more than the cost of the VCR.

Many of the new products created by technology are by definition incapable of satiating the demand they create, for they are themselves alchemic demand machines that generate endless loops of continuing consumer need. For example, when a merchant sells a consumer a new VCR for $250, he is in fact creating far more demand than he is satisfying—in this case a continuing and potentially unlimited need for prerecorded movies, whose cost will far exceed the original cost of the machine. U.S. 1994 VCR sales were approximately $2 billion, while sales and rentals of prerecorded VCR tapes were approximately $18 billion. This same dynamic applies to a huge range of new products: cars, computers, cameras—the list is virtually endless. In purchasing them, consumers in effect are boarding an alchemic train of virtually unlimited demand.

This fact of alchemic life has enormous implications for every businessperson. Manufacturers and retailers who don't appreciate the extent to which their primary product may actually generate more demand than it satisfies run the risk of defining their businesses much too narrowly, just like the railroad barons of the turn of the century, who were left behind because they failed to realize that their business was transportation, not trains and tracks.

Why Retailing in the 1990s May Resemble Retailing in the 1950s
Amway's and Home Depot's Rising Stars May Represent a Return to Traditional Retailing

At the beginning of the twentieth century, it was apparent that rapidly advancing technology would make the necessities of life affordable for every American family. By the 1930s many economists were predicting that if government didn't institute higher and higher income tax rates, this rising affluence would lead to economic stagnation because people would become complacent when they obtained everything that they needed.

Today, we know that these economists were wrong because they failed to foresee that the same rapidly advancing technology would keep inventing new products that would keep expanding the average family's list of *necessities.*

From Frederick Maytag's aluminum-tub washing machine in 1922 to David Sarnoff's RCA black-and-white television set in 1939, the only thing growing faster than the affordability of existing products has been the continual array of new products that kept adding to the American lifestyle. This spawned the unlimited consumer demand for goods and services that caused the United States to grow from an agrarian nation into the world's greatest economic power in less than a few decades.

Some of the unsung heroes of this great economic boom were the department stores, developed in the United States by such innovative retailers as Marshall Field's in Chicago (1865) and Filene's in Boston (1881). By using better technology to centralize consumer credit, buying, and other functions of retailing, department stores quickly replaced the individual Main Street merchants from whom they themselves had sprung.

These department stores did a lot more than merely use technology to lower the cost of selling merchandise. The most important function they performed was educating their customers about new products that would improve their lifestyles. This fueled the never-ending cycle of consumer demand that defied then-conventional economic logic. Instead of going to the department store to purchase something you wanted, you went to the department store to find out about something you didn't know existed but that you couldn't live without once you learned about it.

Looking back on those days before the advent of television and mass media, we see that the department store alone served the two distinct functions of modern retailing—*education* and *distribution*. First, the department store *educated* its customers about new products that would greatly improve their lifestyles. Once it had taught customers what was available and assisted them in choosing the right product for their needs, it *distributed* the product from the factory to the consumers.

The traditional department stores fell into decline as advancing technology, such as universal credit cards and shopping malls, made most of their original innovations obsolete. Perhaps nothing took as great a toll on them as the development of television and mass media—developments that allowed large manufacturers to bypass the traditional department stores entirely in communicating directly with their ultimate customers.

Today most manufacturers "handshake" with their customers through the mass media, and the surviving retailers for most products are the lowest-cost, most efficient physical distributors of merchandise—like Wal-Mart, Target, and Toys "R" Us. These mass merchandisers almost exclusively distribute brand-name products to already educated consumers who know what they want. Customer loyalty has shifted from individual retailers like Sears, Macy's, and Safeway, to individual manufacturers or their products, like Sony, Levi's, and Proctor and Gamble.

Only twenty years ago, a commonly heard complaint about shopping in a retail store was that you, the customer, knew more than the clerks about what they were selling. Today this isn't even newsworthy, since most retail store shoppers assume that they are more educated about the products they want than the people who work there. Most surviving retailers have even abandoned the pretense of educating their sales clerks about the products they sell.

With the abandonment by most retailers of their traditional educational function, we have lost for many items the ability to educate consumers about new products and services that will improve their lives. A thirty-second television commercial can do a great job persuading millions of already knowledgeable consumers to buy more Pepsi or Ivory Soap, but it is not going to educate consumers about some completely new product or service that they haven't heard about.

Certain products and services require one-on-one customer education that only a trained user of the product itself can provide. The list of these items include VCRs in the 1970s, telephone answering machines and services in the 1980s, and better vitamins and nutritional foods in the 1990s. Moreover, because of the lack of customer-education vehicles today, there are many new products and services that, although they would greatly improve the lifestyles of their customers, have been around for several years but haven't yet made it to the mass marketplace.

For example, while interactive educational devices based on CD-ROM technology would greatly improve the education of virtually every child in America, until very recently they have languished in libraries and research laboratories primarily because there has not yet emerged an efficient way to educate parents about them. Packaged-food manufacturers have had the ability for years to improve the healthfulness of their products with synthetic fats and oils but similarly have not yet found a cost-efficient way to educate consumers about them.

One company that has retooled itself to serve the all-important educational function of traditional retailing is the Amway Corporation, which started in the 1960s as a direct marketing organization for proprietary soap products. Today's Amway distributors have virtually abandoned the physical distribution of their products and concentrate almost exclusively on educating themselves and their customers about new and innovative things that will improve their lifestyles. This has made Amway the retailer of choice for many of America's most innovative companies—particularly leading service organizations like MCI, whose intangible products require one-on-one customer education.

Another company that has capitalized very profitably on the need for customer education is Home Depot, Inc., which started in 1980 and quickly became the largest home-improvement retailer in the nation. Home Depot prides itself most on having product specialists in virtually every category of home improvement—teaching customers not only what they need but also how to install it themselves.

In the future, technological developments like interactive television for ordering merchandise and overnight or same-day shipping services for delivering it may let many manufacturers bypass retailers entirely in physically distributing existing products to their ultimate consumers. This may one day eliminate the majority of retailers that concentrate on physical distribution, like Wal-Mart, in favor of retailers that concentrate on customer education, like Amway and Home Depot.

This was evident right through the recession of 1991, when Amway's sales grew an incredible $1.5 billion, from about $3 billion to $4.5 billion, or in Home Depot's similar $1.3 billion rise in 1991, from $3.8 billion to $5.1 billion in annual sales.

However, the retailers specializing in customer education have a long way to grow before they seriously challenge the ones specializing in physical distribution. Traditional U.S. shopping center sales in 1994, mostly by the mass merchandisers like Wal-Mart and Sears, exceeded $900 billion.

TECHNOLOGY FEEDS ON ITSELF

When early humans first figured out how to control and use fire, they did more than discover a way to keep themselves warm on cold nights. They also laid the basis for a variety of other new technologies—such as cooking, lighting, and the forging of metals—whose development would wind up transforming the nature of human existence. Similarly, when William Shockley, Walter Brattain, and John Bardeen invented the transistor at Bell Laboratories in 1948, they not only gave the world a new and better kind of switching device; they also made possible the whole of modern electronics—telecommunications, computers, sensing devices, automated systems, and all the other new products and processes that are responsible for what we have come to think of as our twentieth-century way of life.

This is a fundamental characteristic of technological progress: New inventions are less ends in themselves than they are links in a continuing chain of innovation. That is, every major breakthrough spurs the development of not just one new device or service but an entire array of fresh products and processes; an advance in one area inevitably provokes advances in other areas. Technology, in short, feeds on itself.

Thus it is that we speak of the multiplier effect of technology. The higher the level of our technology to begin with, the faster that level will rise. As the level rises, the rate of progress escalates—leaping ahead more and more swiftly in an accelerating spiral until it reaches a critical state, at which point our technological capabilities can seem to be infinite.

Technology today has advanced to the point where, from an economic standpoint, there appears to be very little that it cannot do. Today even the long-derided goal of the ancient alchemists—to learn how to transmute base metals into gold—is an elementary exercise for nuclear physicists. Indeed, to the nonscientist at least, our technological capabilities seem so limitless that most people tend to assume that all they have to do is ask and technology will deliver. As a result, the process of innovation has been turned on its head. It used to be that an inventor would come up with some new invention and then consumers would figure out whether or not they could use it. Nowadays we decide in advance what we could use and then we tell the scientists and engineers to invent it.

The first great example of this sort of demand-driven innovation was the Manhattan Project, the United States' four-year, $2 billion effort to develop the atomic bomb during World War Two. In giving the go-ahead to the project, President Roosevelt was in effect ordering the nation's scientific establishment to invent a device—namely, a nuclear explosive—that not only was beyond the technological capabilities of the day but that many experts doubted would ever be feasible. The fact was, however, that the nation needed the bomb, and like the prototypical alchemic manager he was, Roosevelt believed in technology's ability to rise to the challenge.

A similar example of expecting technology to adapt to external considerations rather than the other way around was the Apollo Project. When President Kennedy announced in May 1961 that by the end of the decade the United States would land a man on the moon and bring him back safely, the technology necessary to perform such a feat simply did not exist. That, of course, was beside the point. As long as the consumer—in this case, the government—was willing to pay the price, it was assumed that technology could and would deliver. And, in the end, it did.

This is the essence of alchemic management. The new economic alchemists have such faith in technology that they design products without limiting themselves to the current level of technology. The only consideration they take into account is their reading of the marketplace.

Today, technology is advancing so rapidly that businesspeople cannot afford to allow their plans to be limited by what is currently possible. Those who do will not remain in business very long. The key to survival in the fast-changing alchemic world is to keep looking down the road, to anticipate what is likely to come next week, next month, next year—to base your plans on what you think will be, not what already exists.

The problem is, in a fast-changing technological environment, how can we determine what's likely to come tomorrow, let alone next week, next month, or next year?

We have seen in the First and Second Laws of Economic Alchemy how technology determines the definition and supply of physical resources; in the Fourth and Fifth Laws of Economic Alchemy, how technology determines the nature and level of consumer demand; and in the Third Law of Economic Alchemy, how information technology controls the advance of the overall level of technology. Having thus explained how technology is the major determinant of economic activity, we have arrived at our final law of economic alchemy.

The Sixth Law of Economic Alchemy

The sixth law, which explains how we can determine what's likely to come tomorrow, is stated as follows:

The immediate economic potential for an individual, an industry, or a society can be explained by examining the technology gap—the best practices possible with current knowledge versus the practices in actual use.

How many of us, after all, drive a car outfitted with the latest computerized fuel injection system, or live in a house built with the latest ceramic fiber insulation, or watch Jay Leno on a television set with the latest high-definition digital picture tube? How many manufacturers use nothing but the latest state-of-the-art CAD/CAM techniques to fabricate their products? How many distributors have fully outfitted all their warehouses with the latest automated materials-handling equipment? How many retailers track their inventory and monitor customer preferences with the latest point-of-sale laser scanning devices?

The answer, of course, is not many.

This is the essence of the technology gap. Since the beginning of recorded history, there has never been a society that was as efficient, effective, or productive as it was capable of being—capable not in some theoretical or idealistic sense, but capable in terms of the technology it possessed but for one reason or another did not use. In short, no society has ever—in economic terms, at least—lived completely up to its potential. The degree to which a given society or individual falls short of that potential at any given time—that is, the degree to which the advance of technology outstrips a particular society's or individual's ability or willingness to make use of the latest developments and breakthroughs—is the measure of its or his technology gap.

We can call each individual component of the technology gap a *ready-to-be-implemented technological advance,* or an *R-I-T.* An R-I-T isn't a pipe dream or an item on a wish list. It is a new product or process that is available to us today. It's just that, out of ignorance or indolence, we haven't yet gotten around to making use of it. A list of current R-I-Ts would include the computerized fuel injectors that haven't yet replaced mechanical carburetors, the radial tires that haven't yet replaced standard bias ply models, the electronic calculators that haven't yet replaced manual ones, the electric typewriters that haven't yet replaced standard ones, and the push-button phones that haven't yet replaced rotary models. It might also include the word processors that haven't yet replaced electric typewriters—though not necessarily all of them, since word processors are not yet cost effective for all users, especially when one considers the cost of training or replacing personnel who cannot or will not learn to use them.

Newness alone does not necessarily indicate the existence of an

R-I-T. Before we jump to any conclusions about a particular new product or process, we must first examine all of its interrelated attributes, such as its efficiency, cost, and reliability. A product has to be more than just new; it has to be both new *and* better—and it's not likely to be better unless it happens to be cost effective. Moreover, even if it is cheaper and easier to use, it might not be reliable enough. And the sum total of all of its various advantages and disadvantages might not be the same for each user.

Above all, what makes an R-I-T literally ready to be implemented is that it is *user transparent*—that is, from the standpoint of the skills required for its use, it is virtually the same as the product it is meant to replace. As far as the user is concerned, the only thing that has changed is that a job that used to be more difficult now seems easier. For example, from the driver's point of view, there's no difference between getting behind the wheel of a car with a computerized fuel injection system and one with a mechanical carburetor—except that the fuel-injected car has a lot more power and gets twice the gas mileage. Similarly, if you know how to use a rotary phone, you can use a push-button model without learning any new skills—yet you will be able to dial faster and more accurately. So too with an electric versus a manual typewriter.

Some new products never become user transparent; that is, however much their design is refined, they continue to require new operating skills different than the devices they are meant to replace. They can still achieve the status of an R-I-T, however, if their cost effectiveness is great enough to justify the time and trouble it takes to learn new operating skills. This was the case with the word processor, which, as it happens, seems to be becoming user transparent to a whole new generation of typists who have never even used an electric typewriter.

Overall, we can look at a specific office as a factory for processing information and say that its technology gap is the sum of the R-I-Ts it could sensibly employ but for one reason or another hasn't gotten around to installing—that is, the word processors, push-button telephones, and electronic calculators it hasn't yet bought to replace its typewriters, rotary phones, and mechanical adding machines. Similarly, we can look at a specific oil-drilling operation and say that its technology gap is the sum of the better but so far unimplemented drill-rig components, power supplies, and transportation systems that it could utilize on a cost-effective basis. (It should be noted, by the way, that R-I-Ts don't necessarily manifest themselves in the form of equipment of one sort or another. An R-I-T could just as easily reflect itself in terms of a better organizational structure, a better training procedure, or even just one better manager.)

Though they probably wouldn't put it in these terms, today's smart entrepreneurs almost universally look for the existence of R-I-Ts when deciding what new businesses to enter. That is, they recognize instinctively that in the modern alchemic world there is no point in trying to get into some particular business unless they have some *better way* of doing it—in other words, unless there is an R-I-T that they can implement or develop.

The logic is quite simple. The more R-I-Ts in a particular business, the wider its technology gap; the wider its technology gap, the greater its potential for growth.

How does the economic alchemist tell whether or not there are R-I-Ts out there waiting to be exploited? He or she studies each and every component of the business, from the efficiency of its equipment to the way it trains its people to its system of handling correspondence, to see whether or not each particular operation utilizes the most advanced technology available. In other words, he or she looks for the existence of individual technology gaps. The sum of these individual gaps is the business's overall technology gap.

Though we may take it for granted as basic common sense, this approach represents a profound departure from traditional business practice. Before the turn of the twentieth century, when technology advanced far more slowly than it does now, you could make it in business simply by being competitive. All you had to do was be as good as your rivals and you would attract your share of the market. Growth was mainly driven by population increase and classic economic demand for existing goods and services.

These days, by contrast, it is the prospect of providing new and better products and services—that is, the implementation of R-I-Ts— that drives most start-ups. After seven or eight decades of rapid and continuously accelerating change, consumers have no patience anymore with the status quo. Therefore, when it comes to starting a new business today, it is simply not enough to say that you are going to be just as good as the competition. You have got to be able to promise that you are going to provide your particular product or service better, cheaper, or faster—and preferably all three.

There is, of course, a difference between the way we experience technology gaps today and the way our ancestors did centuries ago. The difference is a matter of self-consciousness. Back in what we now call the Stone Age or the Iron Age, people didn't think of themselves as living in a Stone or Iron Age. Indeed, they didn't think of themselves as living in any particular age at all. Making that sort of distinction would have seemed pointless to them, as it would have to most of humankind for most of its history, because until relatively recently the vast majority of people thought of themselves as living pretty much the way people had always lived and always would live. Back then, the idea of change just wasn't in most people's vocabularies. Still less was the concept of progress. The notion that a different—not to mention a better—age was coming was simply inconceivable to the mass of humankind.

Today, of course, what's inconceivable is the notion of a static world. Unlike our ancestors, we expect things to change. Indeed, notions of change and progress are an integral part of modern people's worldview. Moreover, we recognize the agent of that change: technology. That's hardly surprising, for we have watched technology remake the world before our very eyes.

As a result, we are self-conscious about change in ways that our ancestors never were. We may not be able to anticipate what particular shape it will take, but we know that change of some sort is coming. It always has and it always will. Indeed, we pride ourselves on our ability to cope with change—to go with the flow, so to speak, to roll with the punches.

The new economic alchemists, of course, don't just roll with the punches. As we will see, they stay on top of change, managing it, orchestrating it, manipulating it to their advantage. In the context of business, they do this by studying their industry (or the industry they are thinking of entering) to see if there exists a technology gap to exploit. In other words, they look to see if the current practice in their industry represents the best available way of doing things. If it doesn't, that means there must be some R-I-T out there that they can adopt. This is precisely what virtually all successful modern businesspeople do. (Actually, they have no choice; the capital markets are no longer willing to finance companies that don't.)

When an economic alchemist finds and implements a better way of doing something, he or she keeps in mind the fact of its impending obsolescence. This is just what today's personal computer hardware and software manufacturers do. Hardware makers put extra expansion slots into their machines for circuit boards that haven't yet been designed or even envisioned, while software designers routinely build upgrade capabilities into their programs. But the personal computer business is hardly typical; few businesspeople think more than one product generation ahead.

5

WHAT'S HAPPENING

TO OUR JOBS

> Such a violent storm arose that the ship threatened to break up. They
> threw the cargo into the sea to lighten the ship. Then the sailors said to
> each other, "Come, let us cast lots to find out who is responsible for
> this calamity." Then they took Jonah and threw him overboard, and
> the raging sea grew calm.
>
> —JONAH 1:1-15[1]

We live in a time of unprecedented world peace and prosperity—an age dreamed about by the ancient alchemists, who sought peace and prosperity by trying to discover how to turn ordinary metals into gold.

For today, advancing technology has given us the ability to make much more than mere gold. We raise our fish in desert fish farms, we have conquered most of our major diseases, and we have at hand, for all practical purposes, an unlimited supply of what we once thought were scarce resources worth fighting wars over. Perhaps most telling, our greatest wealth is derived from our ability to electronically collect and process information with silicon chips, *which we derive from sand*. For as the mathematician Mitchell Feigenbaum once put it, "we make computers from dirt."

In our twentieth century, humankind's economic output over less than one hundred years has already exceeded the economic output of the previous one hundred centuries. And yet, as we approach the final years of this great century, fewer and fewer of us *feel* rich. And even among those of us who do feel rich, fewer and fewer of us seem secure in our newfound wealth.

For some of us, or for someone we love, it seems as if the alchemic age has passed us by. And all of us feel at times that we are trapped in the Red Queen's race in *Alice in Wonderland*—having to run faster and faster merely to stay in the same place.

The 1967 movie *The Graduate* offered with confidence a one-word answer for success to an aspiring college graduate—*plastics*. How many of us today with similar confidence could engage in such a discussion with our children when and if they turned to us for the wisdom of our experiences?

It seemed so simple in the past. The recipe for success was to go to school, choose an occupation or a company, and work in that field or for that company for the rest of your life. Looking back on just the past ten years, it seems as if this former recipe for success has become a recipe for disaster!

In 1985, there were approximately one hundred thousand people employed in a $2 billion industry manufacturing vinyl records—virtually all of whom were displaced as the digital CD swept the music business by 1990. Who could have foreseen in 1985 that an almost one hundred-year-old industry that survived through two world wars would dissolve itself in less than 5 percent of the one hundred years it took to develop?

In 1979, approximately three hundred thousand people were employed designing, manufacturing, and repairing mechanical carburetors—almost all of whom were similarly displaced in the 1980s by the electronic fuel injector, a device that performed the same function so much better that just one of its by-products was a doubling of the fuel economy of virtually every automobile on the road.

These and other technological changes caused the displacement of 20 million blue-collar workers in the 1980s, when it became socially acceptable in the United States to fire workers in obsolete occupations rather than to keep and retrain them. Moreover, the displacement of these blue-collar workers in the 1980s already pales by comparison to the displacement of white-collar workers that we have just begun to experience in the 1990s.

Those Americans who chose the other recipe for success, avowing loyalty to a company rather than to a specific occupation, have fared even worse. Thousands of companies have found that in a rapidly changing world they can no longer afford to honor their *unwritten contract* to take care of the employees who helped build their corporations. There were a few upright management teams that did try to honor this unwritten contract of postwar America. These upright teams either found their companies go out of business because of competition or found their management positions transferred by stockholders to new management teams—teams sometimes so young that they were often unaware that such a postwar unwritten contract might have even existed.

And yet, despite the ever-present complaints in the media and the demagoguery from our politicians, the cold hard economic fact is that we are richer than ever before. Far richer. But why is the fact that we are far richer cold and hard?

The reason is that, unlike previous waves of economic prosperity, our current wave of prosperity is not a wave at all, sweeping along in its wake all with whom it comes in contact. Our current period of prosperity looks like a wave only when measured in total terms, like rising gross national product, reduced inflation, or escalating retail sales. In reality, our current period of prosperity is more like an emerging range of mountains—large and strong, but with ever-increasing peaks and craters. While the entire range of mountains may be rising higher and higher above sea level, your perception of how high or low it is depends almost entirely on the internal vantage point from which you view it.

For the employees of the record companies headquartered in Los Angeles, the switch to digital CDs was a godsend because their firms now sell many times the amount of audio compact discs that they used to sell of vinyl records. But to the former employees of these same companies, who manufactured the vinyl records in Ohio and Pennsylvania, the recession of 1991 came as early as 1985 and still shows no sign of retreating.

For the high-technology manufacturers of electronic fuel injectors, and for society at large, the switch from mechanical carburetors created a whole new industry with tremendous social benefits—less reliance on foreign oil, a halving of automobile air pollution, and less frequent automobile breakdowns. But to the former carburetor mechanics and engineers who didn't have the skills (or the will) to switch to electronic fuel injection, America's just not the same kind of place anymore.

Yet the more closely we examine the components behind our emerging mountain range of economic prosperity, the more clearly we begin to see our current reality in a different light. As incredible as it may seem, the massive displacement occurring in our workplaces is actually the reason for, rather than a by-product of, our macroeconomic success.

Equally significant, once we understand *how* and *why* displacement in the workplace causes economic growth, we can apply the macro-economic alchemic principles underlying our total economy to our lives as individuals. This will insure, on a microeconomic basis, that we will thrive as individuals in scaling the next range of mountains ahead—the workplace of the twenty-first century.

Should You Quit Before You're Fired?
Why the Large Corporation May Be Obsolete

In 1931 an idealistic twenty-one-year-old British college student won a traveling scholarship to the United States. He was excited to be coming to the land of the entrepreneur—the land he had read so much about in works by authors like Alexis de Tocqueville and Horatio Alger.

When he arrived in the United States, the student was disappointed. He was surprised to find that in a land of so much opportunity, most Americans wanted to work for large corporations, rather than to strike out for themselves. He wrote a paper that attempted to answer the following question:

> Why, in a free-enterprise economy, would a worker voluntarily submit to direction by a corporation instead of selling his own output or service directly to customers in the market?[2]

The student was Ronald H. Coase, the 1991 winner of the Nobel Prize for economics.[3] The paper he wrote in 1931, which

he later published as "The Nature of the Firm," explained why
large corporations exist. Although the paper he wrote over sixty
years ago is today one of the most frequently cited works in the
field of economics, if Coase were to write this same paper today,
he might come to exactly the opposite conclusion.

Today, for exactly the same reasons that Coase cited in his
landmark work, many large corporations should not exist. Much
of the unemployment we are experiencing today is actually the
permanent dismantling of many of our large corporations—for
reasons precisely described by Coase more than half a century
ago. Today, employees of a large company might rightly ask
whether they should quit the corporation now, before it inevitably quits them by going out of business.

In "The Nature of the Firm," Coase explained that the corporation exists because of its ability to reduce the *transaction costs*
between individuals.[4]

For example, suppose a manager wants to dictate a letter and
have it typed. The manager could hire someone merely to type
the letter, but the transaction costs of doing so—finding the
typist, testing his or her skills, negotiating the price, and so forth
—would far exceed the cost of the work itself. To reduce these
transaction costs, the manager trades away hiring only the exact
amount of labor when and where he or she needs it. The typist
trades away his or her independence and higher per diem compensation for a guaranteed time and place to work.

Coase also examined why businesses produced goods and services themselves that were available at less cost from outside
firms—and he came to a similar conclusion. Considering the cost
of dealing with outside suppliers, businesses are often better off
internally producing many of the things they need.

Thus, according to Coase in the 1930s, large corporations exist
as an efficient form of business organization because they reduce
the transaction costs of doing business between different individuals and smaller firms.

However, as the large corporation continues to expand in size,
different costs increase—the costs of managing workers, the
costs of making erroneous decisions, and the costs associated
with hiring personnel who are not directly compensated for their
performance.

Coase wrote that the optimum size for the firm is that size at which these costs, the *inefficiency costs* inherent to being a large organization, equal the *transaction costs,* the costs that the individuals would have to incur among themselves if they were free and independent agents.[5]

According to Coase, a corporation will continue to grow in number of employees as long as the reduced *transaction costs* of having more people working for the single entity exceed the increased *inefficiency costs* of having a larger organization.

Today, however, for exactly this reason most large corporations should have far fewer employees, and many large corporations should not exist at all. This is because over the past sixty years the transaction costs of doing business between different entities have fallen dramatically, while the inefficiency costs of a large corporation have risen dramatically.

The transaction costs of working with outside suppliers and workers — communicating, delivering, accounting — are now so low relative to the value of the services or the materials being acquired that they are often no longer part of the decision-making process. Moreover, these transaction costs — telephone calls, overnight services, computerized invoices — should continue to decline.

Meanwhile, inefficiency costs have become a major component of doing business for large corporations. Since the inflationary 1960s, employees have gotten accustomed to receiving an annual raise independently of their annual performance. It is now commonplace in many firms for two employees performing the exact same job — one newly hired and one with seven to ten years experience — to have a 50 percent or greater difference in their salaries.[6] Moreover, large organizations have become obligated to provide employees services such as health care and retirement benefits — costs that increase each year independently of the efficiency of their employees.

The greatest reason that inefficiency costs have risen dramatically is the relative ineffectiveness of the large corporation — compared to the individual entrepreneur — in implementing technological change.

Traditionally, the very term "large corporation" connoted

being on the cutting edge of technology. Computers were once mainframes that were used only by large corporations, and only large corporations could afford to develop this technologically advanced equipment.

Today, however, many of the largest firms in America—IBM, Xerox, Texas Instruments, Hewlett-Packard, and so forth—are themselves simply providers of technology to third parties. The cutting edge of technology in most industries no longer belongs only to large firms that can develop it themselves. Instead, it belongs to the entity or individual that learns to use the newest third-party technology first.

The employees of large corporations, typically paid over time more for their duration rather than for their innovation, are sometimes the last to learn how to use the newest technology.

One way an employee can learn about where his or her employer may be heading is to look back on the raises received. He or she will clearly see how, directly from increased efficiency or performance, the employer made at least as much money as the employee received on each raise. If he or she cannot, it may be time to quit before being fired—either he or she may soon be terminated or a new competitor might put the employer out of business.

*P*rior to the twentieth century, most industries were organized around the apprentice-craft system, in which the worker learned his own trade and supplied his own tools. Management's job was merely to divide the work among the workers and see that they did it, rather than provide guidance or training to improve their labors.

The term "worker," or "laborer," as we know the term today, did not exist prior to the middle of the nineteenth century. Most of the important jobs in the Industrial Revolution were performed by skilled hands.

Back then, having a skill was more than the ability to earn a living —it was a way of life. In addition to current income, it provided social status through trade union membership and, most important, a legacy to pass on to one's children. Many family names (for example, Smith, Miller, and Brewer) were derived from such skilled professions.

Frederick W. Taylor (1856–1914), a great American inventor and engineer, developed a new system, where management took an active role in training and developing the skills of its workers, rather than merely coordinating their activities. Taylor called this new system "scientific management." Under Taylor's theory, managers had to do more than merely hire the best already skilled workers they could find and schedule their work; it was incumbent upon managers to develop job techniques and teach them, thereby enabling the workers to better perform their jobs.

This philosophy fit well with what was happening to the American labor supply at the turn of the century.

Why Immigrants Are Often the Best Employees
Newcomers Are Often the Fastest to Learn New Methods

Before the Civil War, most of the immigrants coming to America were either skilled laborers or professionals—self-motivated to come to the New World to try their fortunes. This changed after Abraham Lincoln became president of the United States.

In 1863 President Lincoln asked Congress to pass the *Act to Encourage Immigration,* which the president signed into law on July 4, 1864. This act allowed private companies to pay an immigrant's transportation expenses to the United States in return for a legally binding pledge of the worker's wages (as repayment for the cost of his or her passage) for up to twelve months.

Under this new law, which became known as the *Contract Labor Act,* private recruiters were paid fees for inducing foreign workers to come to the United States. Recruiting and transporting new immigrants quickly became the largest business in the United States. By 1880 the largest company in America was the American Emigrant Company, whose sole business was to recruit immigrants in Europe on behalf of American corporations and towns desirous of skilled laborers.

The efforts of these recruiting businesses were the scourge of European nationalists, who feared the economic loss of their skilled professionals.[7] In England, the press disparaged the U.S. recruiters, with one manufacturer protesting in 1865 that "the emigration of one spinner involves the stoppage of probably ten additional hands."[8] In France the same year, the government denied the U.S. consul at Marseilles permission to circulate copies of the Act to Encourage Immigration. And in Germany, the press accused the U.S. government of "swindling" in passing the Act to Encourage Immigration.[9]

However, ironically, while the emphasis of most of these programs was on skilled labor, the majority of people recruited were unskilled workers. Eager potential immigrants often lied to the recruiters about their skills, and in some cases may have even been encouraged to do so by their mercenary recruiters. Recruiting immigrants was a very lucrative business, with the recruiter paid on arrival for bringing over "skilled" workers —even if their skills didn't turn out to be what they were purported to be.

And yet, also ironic, in many cases these unskilled workers turned out to be more productive than truly skilled workers because the new arrivals were much more receptive to using the newest methods and tools in their work. For example, in the steel industry, at every step of production involving technological change after 1880, managers discovered that it was easier to teach new methods to completely unskilled workers than to retrain skilled workers from related crafts and industries.[10] By using almost exclusively immigrant unskilled labor and training them in the newest methods, the U.S. steel industry became the world's largest almost overnight—total U.S. steel production rose from twenty-two thousand tons in 1867 to 11 million tons in 1900.

The great steelmaker and industrialist Andrew Carnegie (1835–1919) was fanatical about continually training unskilled immigrants in the newest production methods. He became famous for his "scrap and build" policies, which consisted of utterly destroying his own steel plants and then starting over with new workers utilizing the latest technology. Complacent British steelmakers once criticized Carnegie's scrap-and-build policies, boasting that they (the British) were using the same methods and equipment for twenty years. "That," Carnegie replied, "is what is the matter with the British steel trade." [11]

Looking back today, we can easily see what was happening. Innovative American entrepreneurs were turning some of the world's least skilled people into the world's most productive, setting the nation on a course to becoming the greatest economic power in the world. But unfortunately, this is not how things were perceived by many existing Americans, who saw the continued waves of new immigrants as a threat to their economic security.

Each newly arriving group of immigrants became the scapegoat for the problems of those already in the United States who were unable or unwilling to make their own American dreams come true. Racist labor and political organizations were formed throughout America to disparage immigration. Italians, the largest group of new immigrants, were forced to attend all-black schools in twelve states. In 1875 *The New York Times* said of Italian-Americans that it was "perhaps hopeless to think of civilizing them." In a New Jersey mill town, several days of rioting erupted after a local firm hired fourteen Jewish-Americans. [12]

When the xenophobic native-born Americans were unable to stop immigration through intimidation of the new arrivals, they took their case straight to the consumer. The (white) union label was introduced for the first time in San Francisco in 1872 by white, unionized cigar makers to signal to consumers that their products were manufactured only by white, Caucasian hands.

We see a similar phenomenon today when certain American managers fail to maintain the design of their products or their plants at competitive levels. Rather than learn new methods of doing things that would allow the quality of their American-made products to speak for themselves in the marketplace, these managers attempt to use (or abuse) American patriotism —inducing consumers to purchase their inferior or overpriced products just because they are "Made in America."

But no group, organized or disorganized, did more harm to the immigrants, and ultimately to America itself, than the Dillingham Commission, which was chartered by Congress in 1907 to report

on the question of the new immigrants and the resultant mechanization of U.S. industry.

The commission, chaired by Senator William Dillingham from
Vermont, blamed the new immigrants for depressing wages, causing unemployment, and hampering the development of trade
unionism in America. The commission's biased report against
mechanization and immigration created a "Dictionary of Races,"
which concluded that "the new immigrants [mostly southern
and eastern European] were racially inferior to immigrants from
Western and Northern Europe." [13]

The fifty-two-volume report of the commission took more than
three hundred staff members over three years to complete and
became the basis for a body of legislation that severely restricted
the immigration of certain races, mainly those residing in southern and eastern Europe. Immigration from Asia and Africa was
basically prohibited.[14]

No less a great statesman than President Woodrow Wilson
fought the racist protectionists from 1912 until 1920; finally the
protectionists won when President Harding succeeded Wilson in
1921.

Supported by President Harding, the body of anti-immigration
legislation against southern and eastern Europeans culminated in
the Immigration Act of 1924.[15] The 1924 act was also known as
the Japanese Exclusion Act because it banned immigration entirely for persons of Japanese ancestry. The day the act took effect
was declared a national day of mourning in Japan in 1924, and
the anti-Japanese provisions were, shamefully, not repealed by
the U.S Congress until 1952.[16]

Immigration fell from over 1 million per year at the turn of the
century to less than fifty thousand per year during the 1930s—
coincidentally, this decline began the greatest depression the
country has ever known.

At the turn of the century, America was at the beginning of an age
of mechanization. Yet no one realized at the time that the mechanized
methods employed by these new immigrants—and their managers
who believed that their function was to develop and train employees

rather than just schedule their work—would eventually lead directly to increased prosperity for everyone, including the displaced skilled workers.

From 1880 to 1945, America developed from a backwards agrarian nation into the greatest economic power on earth. This growth was mostly due to the implementation of new technological methods by a (mostly immigrant) workforce that was not afraid to learn new things, combined with a uniquely American management style that took on the responsibility for employee training and development.

And as America developed, a new type of prodigious business organization emerged unlike anything the world had ever seen before, an organization so prevalent today that we completely take its existence for granted. And it is the decline of this type of organization that lies at the core of most of our employment problems today.

This organization is the large corporation that takes the responsibility for training its employees—General Motors, IBM, Citibank, Exxon, General Electric, and literally thousands more. These large corporations employ slightly less than half of all American workers today.

From 1920 until the mid-1980s, getting a job with one of these large companies was the dream for most young Americans—for such employment at an early age meant social prestige in the community, a steady path to success for those willing to work for it, and most important of all, job stability. There was an *unwritten contract* between the large corporation and the new young employee: If you work hard for us throughout your working life, we will take care of you and your family by giving you continual training, job stability, health care, and retirement benefits.

Then, in the 1980s, the system cracked. Twenty million blue-collar workers were let go—many of whom had spent their entire lives working for single organizations and who were totally unprepared to fend for themselves. And these mass layoffs by supposedly troubled companies only foreshadowed what was to come in the 1990s—similar layoffs of both blue- *and* white-collar employees by viable profit-making companies.

Large companies today are experiencing the dilemma faced by the passengers on the ship to Tarshish in the biblical book of Jonah—having to throw someone overboard in order to save the entire ship.

The Jonah Dilemma
The Truth About Why Many Companies Change Locations

Most large corporations today reward employees for duration, rather than innovation. Employees receive annual pay raises whether or not their individual contribution to the organization has increased—until the ax falls on them the hardest when times get tough.

Few companies have the moral stamina to insist that all increases in compensation be tied to both increased individual productivity and long-term corporate profitability—dooming their entire organizations to obsolescence when a new competitor enters their field. And whole communities are sometimes devastated when major employers find that moving their operations is the only socially acceptable method of firing workers whose compensation exceeds the level of the competition.

Large companies often face a dilemma similar to the one faced by the passengers on the ship to Tarshish in the book of Jonah. When a storm threatened their ship, they first tried throwing more and more of their cargo overboard to lighten their load. When that failed, they drew lots to determine the individual who was causing their problem—Jonah, who was fleeing the Lord— and threw him overboard in order to save the entire ship.

Today, corporations in trouble typically go through similar nonpersonnel cost-cutting experiences until they too painfully realize that in order to survive they must permanently eliminate many of the people who helped them build their company.

However, few companies facing the Jonah dilemma have the leadership necessary to make the tough decisions—and those that do often find that they need a subterfuge to cover their true intentions.

In the early 1980s my job was to locate major firms around the United States that could move to Texas and occupy office buildings owned by my real estate company.

In 1983, after waiting in the reception area of a Midwestern employer, I was escorted into the CEO's office by his executive secretary. After discussing the usual benefits of moving to Texas —lower taxes, right-to-work laws, inexpensive housing, and so forth—I questioned my host about the young receptionist who had gotten me coffee while I was waiting for our meeting.

"She sure seems efficient," I remarked. "How long has she been using that new personal computer?"

"Almost ten months now," replied the CEO. "She's able to produce with it almost three times the output of our ordinary secretaries who use IBM Selectric typewriters."

"How much does she earn?"

"About $18,000 a year," he replied.

"What about her benefit package?"

"She gets only two weeks vacation because she's new, and since she hasn't any dependents and is in good health, I guess her total benefits don't cost us more than $1,000 a year."

"Tell me about *your* secretary, the one who brought me into your office. I didn't see a personal computer on *her* desk."

"I know," he replied sheepishly. "She's been with me almost twenty years. I didn't have the heart to force her to learn how to use the computer—she's frightened by machines."

"How much does she earn?"

"About $35,000 a year."

"What about her benefits?"

"I know she gets four weeks vacation, because my office doesn't function during those four weeks when she's away. With her extended medical benefits and our contribution to her retirement plan, her total benefit package probably costs us about $14,000 per annum."

"Guess what," I chimed in. "When you move your company to Texas, your secretary costing your company $49,000 is going to stay in Ohio with her family. Your more productive receptionist costing $19,000 is moving to Texas, and if you'd like, I bet she'd love to be your new secretary. Moreover, if you think now that your personal office could be run more efficiently by starting over in Dallas, you should see what it's like out there on the floor among your middle managers, some of whom haven't learned anything new in decades."

The truth about most out-of-town corporate relocations is that approximately half of the employees—usually the higher-paid, less-efficient ones—don't relocate. Moreover, the company typically doesn't replace most of the employees who don't relocate, and the replacements it does hire are often employed at far less cost than their predecessors. While this can insure the survival of the company, it often causes devastation to the social lives of their employees and the local communities that they abandon.

*T*his oversimplified explanation is somewhat one-sided—most employees feel that they are being displaced more to increase shareholder profits rather than save entire organizations. Employees who have given their loyalty feel betrayed when they or their coworkers are displaced for reasons seemingly beyond their control, while employers feel that their increasingly mobile work force is no longer loyal to the organization that trained them in the first place.

But only in the 1990s has it become socially acceptable for some corporations to begin addressing these concerns out in the open. In the past, few companies would even admit to themselves that some of their least productive employees might be the ones who had worked the longest and the hardest to help build the company.

Sears and J. C. Penney Face the Jonah Dilemma

At the end of the 1980s, Sears Roebuck & Co. and J. C. Penney each announced that they would relocate their corporate headquarters—*supposedly* to take unrealized profits on their headquarters' buildings. Sears owned the one-hundred-ten-story, 1.8-million-square-foot Sears Tower in downtown Chicago, and J.C. Penney had a large building in midtown Manhattan.

What they both didn't announce was that their selling and administrative expenses as a percentage of sales had risen to record-breaking levels, almost double that of certain competitors like the Limited, Home Depot, and Wal-Mart.[17]

Both Sears and J. C. Penney immediately came under pressure

from many cities and states that wanted to add these prestigious companies to their local tax base. But this outside pressure was almost nonexistent compared to the internal pressure to remain in the same area exerted by the companies' own employees, anxious to keep their coveted positions without having to uproot their homes and their families.

J. C. Penney made the tough decision first and announced, to the complete horror of its employees, that they would leave the New York area and move to Plano, Texas. They sold their headquarters building at auction in May 1988 for $353 million, recording a $139 million profit on the sale, which helped offset their $150 million cost of moving.[18]

One reason Penney's $150 million cost of moving was so high was the very generous severance payments made to New York area employees who chose not to move with the company in 1988. These payments, often several times an employee's annual salary, were ostensibly made to compensate those who could not make the move to Texas for personal reasons. However, they had the possibly intended effect of causing an incredible *80 percent* of Penney's home-office employees to permanently leave the company and stay behind in New York.

While J. C. Penney has not publicly admitted it, when it arrived in Dallas it never replaced more than half of the employees that left the company in 1988. The results of eliminating more than 80 percent of their home office staff, and then replacing only half of them with younger and less expensive personnel, speak for themselves.

In 1989, one of the worst years in recent history for many of the nation's retailers, sales at J. C. Penney rose $1.3 billion, or 8.6 percent. More significant, profits, not counting the one-time sale of their New York building, rose a spectacular 23.1 percent. And these initial increases were only beginning as J. C. Penney, which was rated in 1990 as the top department store in the nation by *National Retail Federation Store* magazine, continued to out-shine its rivals straight through the tough times that followed in the early 1990s.

In contrast to Penney's decision, Sears succumbed to internal pressures and announced in 1989 that it would move from down-town Chicago to the nearby Chicago suburb of Hoffman Estates.

Many of Sears' senior employees even preferred the new suburban location because it was closer to where they lived. Meanwhile, the real estate market crashed during the two years they had spent arguing over their decision. In October 1989 they took their soon-to-be-vacated Sears Tower off the market; from the world's tallest office tower it became what a leading magazine called "the world's tallest white elephant." [19]

Between 1989 and 1990 Sears' earnings declined over $600 million. This was only the beginning of their problems, for Sears' debt became downgraded in 1990 and their stock price fell to about half the liquidation value of the company—which caused *U.S. News and World Report* to note that "a takeover could be Sears' ultimate bargain sale." [20]

Sears continued to react slowly with a new stream of layoffs every few months, cutbacks to pensioners' health benefits, and reduced holidays and employee discounts—all of which caused poor morale and failed to deal with the core problem: that Sears had far too many managers and employees being paid too much for too little work.

Finally, in February 1991, Sears management bit the bullet and announced that it would lay off over thirty-three thousand employees in 1991 alone.

During the first quarter of 1992, Wal-Mart passed Sears in sales to become the largest retailer in America, and J. C. Penney recorded the highest earnings in its corporate history.

*B*ut underlying this estrangement between management and labor is something much more profound. For this schism is about more than strained relations over employee productivity. Underlying these problems of management and labor is the permanent decline of what has been the traditional building block of American economic power, the large vertically integrated corporation.

Large corporations are comprised of parties organized for a common purpose. Yet they are typically comprised of individuals and organizations with divergent individual interests.

Employees work full-time for the corporation, are paid regardless of whether or not the activities of the corporation are profitable, and expect to receive raises every year. Managers are similar to employees, *plus* they expect to receive extra remuneration (in raises and bonuses) when the activities that they direct the corporation to pursue are profitable. Stockholders provide the money required to initially set up or expand the corporation in return for receiving the corporation's profits in perpetuity. And bondholders have similar interests to stockholders, except they receive a fixed rate of return on their investment in return for a more secure position in the investment hierarchy.

Any of these individuals or organizations may voluntarily leave the corporation at any time. Thus, all of the players must feel secure in their respective roles in order for the corporation to prosper. Even the "owners" are not permanently attached to the corporation—they may sell their shares at any time in today's liquid securities markets.

The original corporations were the great English trading companies of the sixteenth and seventeenth centuries, which were chartered by acts of Parliament. In the early United States, corporations were similarly chartered by separate acts of state legislatures until firms began complaining of special privileges unfairly granted to their competitors. Beginning with New York in 1811, states passed laws allowing any group of persons to achieve corporate status by simply satisfying a predescribed set of legal requirements.

Corporations grew regionally in number and size throughout the nineteenth century, paralleling the growth in America itself. But with very few exceptions, such as railroads and other businesses whose operations naturally crossed state lines, large national corporations didn't exist until a wave of mergers occurred between 1897 and 1902, producing hundreds of large companies. These corporations grew larger until another wave of mergers occurred during the 1920s; and a subsequent wave of mergers occurred in the 1960s, producing the very large multinational firms we know today.

There are three general types of corporate mergers—*horizontal, vertical,* and *conglomerate,* the explanations of which also illustrate the three ways large corporations expand, even without merging.

In a horizontal merger or expansion, a company seeks to become larger in its main business by acquiring or merging with another firm in the same industry. General Motors, for example, was established in 1908 when the Buick Motor Car Company bought the Cadillac and

Oldsmobile companies (Chevrolet was purchased later in 1911). The objective of a horizontal merger or expansion is to be able to control a bigger market and to be able to allocate fixed costs—like manufacturing, research, and distribution facilities—over a larger number of total products.

In a vertical merger or expansion a company moves forward or backward in its production process—acquiring or developing a firm that provides the components that go into its products. Examples of vertical mergers in the automobile industry include the acquisition in 1926 of Durant Motors by one of its suppliers, the Fisher Body company—and the subsequent acquisition of Fisher Body by its largest customer, General Motors.[21] More generic examples include a steel company's purchase or development of a coal mine or a large retailer's purchase of a manufacturer of one of its retail products.

In a conglomerate merger, a company acquires or merges with another company in a substantially unrelated business. The objectives of a conglomerate merger are usually financial—the goal is to have Wall Street, which relies heavily on current earnings in valuing stock prices, value the stock of the merged entity at more than the price of the two (or more) individual companies. A successful conglomerate merger might be formed between a company having good long-term prospects but little current cash flow and a company having good cash flow but declining revenues—for example, a merger of a new medical research firm whose products are under development with an older manufacturing firm whose revenues are derived mostly from expiring copyrights or patents.

Although a corporation can and does grow through all three of these types of activities, it was the vertical expansion of existing companies—either through acquiring their suppliers or through developing their own sources of raw materials—that primarily accounted for the growth of the large U.S. corporation we know today.

Most large oil companies, for example, are now almost completely vertically integrated—they drill for oil with their own rigs, transport the oil to their refineries in their own tankers and pipelines, refine the oil into gasoline and other products at their own refineries, and even sell the gasoline to the retail customer from their own service stations.

And yet despite the fact that today many of our larger corporations are vertically integrated, for most companies the reasons for vertical expansion have become obsolete. In fact, we are now experiencing the permanent dismantling of some of the largest vertically integrated corporations in America into much more productive specialized individual entities.

In order to better understand how this is happening and its dramatic effect on the workplace of the 1990s, let's examine how and why most large corporations expanded vertically in the first place.

The first reason that some companies originally expanded vertically was to obtain continuous supplies of raw materials and subcomponents. In the late nineteenth and early twentieth centuries, many sophisticated products and even some raw materials still came from overseas. Even slight disruptions in supply could shut down entire plants. In order to maintain a steady supply of raw material, or subcomponents, large corporations often found it advantageous to acquire or develop their own sources of supply.

This first reason for expanding vertically was also applied to the employees of the corporation. Because it was difficult to manage and communicate with individuals not located on site, corporations almost always found it more efficient to permanently hire full-time personnel rather than contract out the labor required for their work. The exception to this rule was in the hiring of professionals—such as accountants, lawyers, and certain types of technicians—whose expertise was highly dependent on their ability to keep abreast of developments in their respective fields.

The second reason for vertical expansion was that some large corporations in the United States were prohibited from expanding horizontally. The Sherman Anti-Trust Act of 1890, the Clayton Anti-Trust Act of 1914, and the Robinson-Patman Act of 1936 sought to limit corporations from expanding in their main line of business across state lines. Because of a fear of big business, these and other laws severely limited the expansion of large corporations into markets controlled by their competitors. Thus, because of government regulation, for many large corporations the only way to expand was up.[22]

A third reason that many companies pursued a policy of vertical expansion seems obvious—lower prices. If you are going to be using a lot of a product or service produced by another company, it stands to reason that you should be able to produce that same product or service yourself for a lower price—since you'll be saving money on marketing expenses, on inventory carrying charges, and, of course, by not having to pay the profits of your supplier.

The first reason for expanding vertically declined during the twentieth century as the nation began manufacturing most of the products it used to purchase from abroad and as the United States developed an unprecedented system of communications and transportation. It became relatively easy to communicate—most businesses had acquired telephones by 1920. And once a corporation had located a supplier, even in another region of the country, it was relatively inexpensive to transport materials—thanks to an elaborate system of highways and railroads.

The second and perhaps the greatest reason for initially expanding vertically—government prohibitions against horizontal expansion— declined in the postwar economy with the shift to consumerism. Federal regulation of big business shifted from the application of some arbitrary antibigness standard by Washington bureaucrats to the application of a cohesive "what is best for the consumer" philosophy by an enlightened electorate.

For example, in the 1920s, large retailers like W. T. Grant's began expanding across America—offering lower prices to consumers, to the detriment of much less efficient mom-and-pop stores. The government sought to stop such competition and even passed "fair trade laws" in the 1930s prohibiting all retailers from cutting prices on certain name-brand items. In contrast, in the 1960s, Sam Walton expanded Wal-Mart's into rural American towns—and the subsequent failure of certain local merchants was viewed as an inevitable by-product of much more desirable lower consumer prices. Congress made all fair trade laws illegal in 1975.

The third reason for expanding vertically—better supplies at lower prices—also rapidly disappeared after the Second World War. In almost every category, as the nation progressed, outside suppliers increasingly had the ability to supply subcomponents and raw materials at far *less* cost than a corporation could obtain or make these products for themselves. The reason has to do with something the economist Joseph A. Schumpeter (1883–1950) called *creative destruction*.

According to Schumpeter, the economic strength of a capitalist society lies in its continual desire to "incessantly revolutionize" its methods of production because of the pressures of competition. As

Schumpeter saw it, advancing technology continually produces new tools and better methods for every step of the production process at an ever-increasing pace. Even if a company has just designed and implemented a new tool, or even a whole manufacturing plant, competition in the capitalist system forces "creative destruction" of the just-built plant when, because of advancing technology, there is a better method available to produce a superior product.

Implicit in Schumpeter's theory of creative destruction is the view that almost anytime people start out from scratch to make something, they are going to be able to do it cheaper and better than *existing* companies in the field, which utilize, by definition, yesterday's technology. And also implicit is that, because of the pressures of competition, people and organizations will always purchase their supplies from the most productive sources as they become available.

Schumpeter, who saw creative destruction as the grease that kept the wheels of prosperity in motion, lauded the positive economic effects of the large corporation for its ability to commit massive sums to researching new technological methods—during the 1970s fully 10 percent of all American industrial basic research was conducted by Bell Labs.[23] But despite Schumpeter's praising large corporations for their research expenditures, in many cases the large vertically expanded corporation was a major deterrent in allowing creative destruction and its resultant economic growth to take place. Here's why.

Suppose a large automobile manufacturer in 1975, say Corporate Motors, vertically expands by building (or purchasing) a $500 million carburetor plant. In 1976 a new technology emerges allowing automakers to use electronic fuel injectors instead of carburetors. But the corporation, which just spent $500 million on the carburetor plant and just signed a three-year labor agreement with the plant's employees, is not going to switch to fuel injectors until it has recouped the investment in the carburetor plant.

Conversely, had Corporate Motors not vertically expanded and developed (or purchased) the carburetor plant in the first place, it would have been free to readily adopt the emerging technology. Corporate Motors would simply have stopped purchasing carburetors from one supplier and started purchasing electronic fuel injectors from another.

And unfortunately, our hypothetical story is almost exactly what happened in the United States during the 1970s. The Big Three American automobile manufacturers clung to their outdated carburetor technology while the Japanese and the Europeans—who had more recently tooled up their automobile industries—began offering cars in the United States with electronic fuel injection and other technological advances. In just the 1970s alone the Japanese and European share of the United States automobile market more than doubled.[24]

And this reluctance of U.S. companies to adopt new technology, due to the fact that most of them were large vertically integrated corporations, wasn't limited to the automobile industry. In consumer electronics, high-quality textiles, cameras, and even the machine tool business, foreign companies who were just coming on the scene captured significant interests in U.S. domestic markets. This was accomplished primarily because of the early adaptation by the foreigners of the newest technological methods, many of which were actually developed in the United States. It is a sad commentary on how far some U.S. manufacturers must have fallen behind to have their home markets captured by foreign competitors thousands of miles away.

Fortunately for the United States, as we'll see in a moment, in the 1980s a combination of foreign competition and something called the LBO caused American manufacturing companies to regain much of the competitiveness that they had lost in the 1970s. But before we explain how this happened in the 1980s, let's examine one of the *positive* effects that large vertically integrated corporations, which were often reluctant to adopt new technological methods, had on the American workplace.

In *Capitalism, Socialism, and Democracy* (1942), Joseph Schumpeter focused on the social turmoil that occurs in a rapidly advancing capitalist society as individuals are displaced from their jobs because of the implementation of better technological methods. In this book, Schumpeter incorrectly predicted the decline of capitalism because of the majority of the people in capitalist countries becoming displaced by rapidly advancing technology. The reason he was wrong was that, despite massive technological advancement from the 1940s through the 1980s, the majority of the people in capitalist countries were not displaced by the advance of technology. And the reason they were not displaced was that the large vertically integrated corporation served as a buffer in keeping down the level of creative destruction and its resultant displacement of personnel.

This is not to say that IBM, General Motors, AT&T, and the rest of the *Fortune* 500 didn't adopt great amounts of new technology prior to 1980. They did. But, because in most cases their own plants supplied the individual components used in their finished products, the rate of innovation that did occur was not at the higher level it would have been under a competitive supplier system, where they would have more rapidly adopted new technology as it became available.

Thus, until the mid-1980s, large corporations scheduled the implementation of new technology subject to the *unwritten contract* that existed between the corporation and its "lifetime" employees. This unwritten contract was the corporation's agreement to provide their workers with lifetime employment, health care, and retirement benefits—something they certainly couldn't do if their customers purchased from a continually changing list of suppliers or if their plants had to implement new technology before their employees were ready to absorb it.

Then, in the 1980s, the impact of two separate events forced U.S. corporations to begin implementing new technology as it became available, rather than when the corporations decided that they were ready for it.

The first of these events was the true globalization of the worldwide economy. Traditionally, the bulk of the trade between nations consisted of raw materials—oil, wheat, minerals, and other basic unfinished products. During the decades prior to the 1980s, most major countries developed their own manufacturing capabilities for sophisticated goods—cars, electronics, and subcomponents for all types of finished products—and they began competing with one another on a global scale. By 1980 a U.S. manufacturer needing, for example, automotive electronic components, could take its pick of products from Brazil, Great Britain, West Germany, France, Mexico, Japan, and a dozen other countries. Wherever U.S. manufacturers did not move fast enough to implement new technologies, foreign manufacturers quickly moved in—selling both subcomponents and entire finished products such as automobiles, televisions, and machine tools.

The second of these two events, which caused U.S. companies to get much more competitive in the 1980s, was a change in the way large corporations were governed. This type of change began with the conglomerate merger activity of the 1960s but was greatly accelerated by the leveraged buyouts (LBOs) of the 1980s.

By the 1960s the stock of almost all of the large U.S. corporations had become so widely held that the true owners, the stockholders, were actually no longer in control. Legally, stockholders were supposed to elect members to a board of directors, which would oversee the actions of the managers. But many of these directors either were members of management themselves or served at the pleasure of existing management. For all practical purposes, by the 1960s most large U.S. corporations were effectively controlled by existing management. Stockholders dissatisfied with current management were more likely to simply sell their shares than to make protests to current management and demand changes.

There were some exceptions to this general rule, but they were few and far between. In the 1960s the conglomerate merger became commonplace; one large corporation would make a tender offer for all of the stock of another corporation—in effect, buying management control along with the physical assets. But, thanks to an old-boy network that existed between most large corporations and their bankers, few of these conglomerate mergers were ever attempted on a hostile basis.

This changed on a wholesale scale in the 1980s, when corporate raiders such as Boone Pickens appeared making hostile tender offers for companies whose stock was selling below the price that the companies' assets would fetch at a liquidation sale. For example, in 1984, Pickens—claiming that the management at Phillips Petroleum had fallen so far behind that the company's oil reserves alone were worth more than the stock market's valuation of the company—made an offer for all of Phillips' outstanding stock with the stated intention of liquidating the company. Phillips Petroleum, in other words, was worth more dead than alive.

As the decade progressed, the action shifted from asset-based companies, like the oil firms, to manufacturing and retailing firms, like RJR Nabisco and Macy's. The corporate raiders soon realized that the really undervalued assets in America weren't the minerals in the ground but the operating companies that hadn't yet implemented new technological advances in their businesses. And in many cases, "new technological advances" was a euphemism for "too many employees doing too little work."

Old-line management didn't know what to do. They felt a moral obligation to honor their unwritten contracts with their lifelong employees, even if they no longer really needed them for new technically advanced positions. But if they continued to honor these unwritten contracts—either by delaying the implementation of new technology or by taking the time necessary to retrain their existing employees— management itself was subject to losing its own jobs when a corporate raider took over their company.

Moreover, the corporate raiders had an invisible partner in their deals that seemed to make them invincible. As unbelievable as it may seem, this invisible partner was the federal government, which subsidized up to 48 percent of the cost of their transactions. Here's how.

One of the controversies surrounding corporate income taxes has always been the issue of double taxation. Corporations pay corporate federal income taxes on their earned corporate income, pay the remaining amounts to their stockholders as dividends, and then the stockholders pay personal federal personal income taxes again on their dividends.

For example, suppose a company whose stock was selling for a $1 billion total valuation in 1985 earned $100 million from operations before income taxes. The company would pay $48 million (48 percent) in corporate federal income taxes, pay the remaining $52 million as dividends to its stockholders; and then the stockholders would pay $26 million (50 percent) in personal federal income taxes on their $52 million in dividends—which left the stockholders only $26 million of their corporation's $100 million in pretax operating income.

When Boone Pickens and the other corporate raiders sought to take over a company, they raised their funds from investors in the form of high-yield or "junk," bonds, which were actually equity instruments structured as debt securities.[25] This had the effect of eliminating most or all of the corporate income taxes on the companies they acquired.

For example, assume that a corporate raider purchased all of the shares of the above-described company for $1 billion—raising the $1 billion from investors in the form of 10-percent-interest junk bonds. Now the company's entire $100 million in pretax earnings would go to service the 10 percent interest rate ($100 million) on the $1 billion in junk bonds. Since interest on corporate debt is fully tax deductible, there would be no corporate income left on which to pay corporate income taxes—all $100 million in corporate earnings would go to the investors as interest on their junk bonds. Even if the investors paid $50 million (50 percent) of their $100 million in interest earnings in personal federal income taxes, the investors would still be about twice as far ahead ($50 million) as were the original stockholders, who were receiving the earnings of the corporation as dividends ($26 million).

Moreover, for the most part, the original stockholders that sold the stock of these corporations to the corporate raiders were the same individuals and financial institutions that purchased back the junk bonds issued by the corporate raiders. No wonder there was an endless supply of money for leveraged buyouts, or LBOs, as these transactions were called—the same people and financial institutions ended up with roughly twice the amount of annual return because of the virtual elimination of federal corporate income taxes. And all you had to do to get one of these deals going was show that existing management was underutilizing the corporation's assets and that you could do a better job. This wasn't very difficult to show when you had a silent partner—the federal government—offering you an extra 48 percent of your income from operations after you took over.

While there were many variations of the LBO game played throughout the 1980s, they almost all began with the same thing in common —a corporation that was perceived to be underutilizing its assets. And while the long-term impact of the LBOs are still being debated, the age of the complacent manager or corporation that could afford to wait in implementing new technology was over. Either you implemented new technology today or someone else would come in and do it tomorrow without you. And this applied to both the real implementation of new technological methods as well as to "downsizing" —the 1990s euphemism for firing underutilized employees as if unwritten contracts didn't exist.

American corporations began getting lean in the 1980s and recaptured much of what they had lost to foreign competition—the United States regained its title as the world's largest export nation by 1988. Real inflation-adjusted gross national product rose 24 percent during the Reagan years, and that was before adjusting the GNP for the fact that similar-quality manufactured goods—televisions, automobiles, textiles—cost much less in 1988 than in 1980.

Then, at the beginning of the 1990s, American companies started getting really lean. The so-called recession of 1991 provided corporate

America the excuse it needed. The ranks of the unemployed grew more than 40 percent to their highest level since the Second World War.

THE "RECESSION OF 1991"					
Year	1988	1989	1990	1991	1992
Unemployed[26] (millions)	6,701	6,528	6,874	8,426	9,384
GDP[27] (billions)	$4,900	$5,250	$5,522	$5,678	$5,951
Dow Jones (industrials)	2,061	2,509	2,679	2,929	3,284

But the second line and third lines in the preceding table tell what was really happening in the economy. While millions of Americans were being thrown out of work, the nation's domestic economic output, gross domestic product (GDP), continued the meteoric rise it had begun in the early 1980s. (GDP more than doubled from 1980 to 1992.)[28] From 1988 to 1992 the ranks of the unemployed swelled more than 40 percent, while the remaining employed American workers increased total national output more than twenty percent!

And this so-called recession of 1991 certainly didn't fool anyone on Wall Street. The Dow Jones Industrial Average rose more than 50 percent—right through the greatest period of unemployment since the Great Depression. In fact, percentage increases in the Dow Jones were so closely correlated to percentage increases in unemployment that they seemed to be joined at the hip. Moreover, a more detailed analysis shows that the companies leading the Dow's meteoric rise were the companies doing the most layoffs—the ones using the most nets! (See, in Chapter 8, "The Greatest Challenge of Our Century.")

Here is the challenge we face in our last decade of our greatest century. Changes that once took fifty years are now taking place in as little as five or ten. And yet, as we shall see, some of the pillars of our society are built on a foundation that resists, even fights, change. What we will need to thrive—and survive—in the years ahead is a new economic foundation for our businesses, our government, and, most important, for ourselves.

The future American workplace lies within this new foundation. Because of numerous technological advances in communications and transportation, and, most important, because of creative destruction, the most efficient form of manufacturing or service organization today is the focused, non-vertically-expanded business that can continually implement new technological advances.

The sources for these new technological advances will themselves be even more focused non-vertically-expanded business entities. And the ultimate sources of new technological advances for these even more focused entities will be the leanest, most efficient, entity of all— the individual who manages his or her own destiny.

We have already seen glimpses of this workplace of the twenty-first century, a workplace dominated by individuals rather than by organizations. In the near future, few of us will work for an organization that we do not, at least partially, control. And in the not too distant future, few of us will work for anyone at all. The day will come when the majority of Americans will effectively work for themselves—taking responsibility for their own training, their own savings, their family's health care—in short, taking responsibility for their own destiny.

6

THE WORKPLACE OF

THE TWENTY-FIRST

CENTURY

"Daddy, Daddy, you're home!" exclaimed the boy, running from the front porch carrying a ball and baseball bat. "Watch this!"

The boy tossed the ball into the air and swung the bat, completely missing the ball by over two feet.

"Strike one," the boy shouted. "Now watch this one, Dad."

The boy tossed the ball into the air again, and this time swung so hard that he almost lost his balance as he completely missed the ball.

"Strike two," he shouted even louder, and more excited. "Now, for the final pitch."

The boy choked up on the bat, planted his heels firmly on the driveway, and threw the ball high into the air. As the ball returned to earth he swung so hard that he fell onto the hard pavement, scraping his knee and again missing the ball by over two feet.

"Strike three," shouted the boy, panting on the ground from his fall.

The father ran over to help the exhausted boy get up from the driveway, trying to hide the disappointment he felt at his son's failure.

"So, what do you think?" exclaimed his son, beaming with pride.

"Not bad for a pitcher, huh, Dad?" [1]

This story illustrates what this chapter, and actually a great deal of this book, is really about. The father falsely assumes that the boy is failing when he continually misses the ball with each pitch. Yet the boy is oblivious to his father's disappointment as he marches on toward success.

People often think that they are failing when their business or job falls short of their economic expectations. Yet while they may not realize it at the time, like our aspiring Little League pitcher they too may be marching toward success. In economics, as in so many other fields, it is our initial failure at the traditional paths that usually provide us the opportunity we seek.

The subject of individual economic success has occupied people's minds since the beginning of time. However, for most of this time, the definition of "individual" meant a chosen few who originally achieved their privileged positions by force, and thereafter almost entirely by birthright. As society progressed, these chosen few evolved into the sovereigns of larger and larger nations, until their economic interests developed in the fifteenth century into a system called mercantilism.

The fundamental economic focus of mercantilism was the accumulation of wealth by the state, in which everything was typically owned by the sovereign and his minions. Sovereigns sought to increase their wealth through foreign trade, conquest, and the accumulation of goods for sale to other nations. These same sovereigns also directly controlled the internal production, exchange, and consumption of goods and services, and forced ordinary people to multiply, work hard, and avoid the consumption of even the most minimal of basic consumer products. The larger and more ill paid the population, the more low-priced goods that could be produced for sale to foreigners. One mercantilist writer had the following plan for the children of the poor:

> When these children are four years old, they shall be sent to the county workhouse and there taught to read two hours a day and be kept fully employed the rest of the time in any of the manufactures of the house which best suits their age, strength, and capacity.[2]

Outside of mercantilism, the concept of capitalism as we know it today—basically a free market economy where the individual is relatively free to pursue his or her own economic destiny—was so prevalent that it was hardly noticed. Virtually every book of the Bible, from Genesis through Revelation, is filled with references to the pursuit of personal economic sustenance (production, trade, property acquisition) by individuals relatively unfettered by state interference. It is primarily in the times when this did not occur that we begin to see the emergence of capitalism and economics as a separate discipline for study—a discipline that, until challenged by something like a mercantilist state, most people took for granted.

The Wealth of Nations, written at the close of the mercantilist era, was the book that established economics as an autonomous subject and launched the doctrine of free enterprise on an unsuspecting world.[3] Written in 1776 by the Scottish philosopher Adam Smith, *The Wealth of Nations* described how the unfettered pursuit by individuals of their own selfish interests leads directly to the increased well-being of the total society. The deeper and deeper Smith delved into the workings of the economy, the more fascinated he became by what he called "the invisible hand" that guided the unintended actions of individuals toward increased societal wealth.[4]

Today, *The Wealth of Nations* is remembered mostly for lauding the free market economic system we call capitalism. Yet its true contribution was in introducing the mercantilist world to the real cause of the wealth of nations—*the division of labor.* Using deductive logic, Smith scientifically explained the unlimited God-given ability of human beings to increase their productive output through increased specialization. And although Smith, as a progressive scientist in an enlightened era, avoided using *his* name, it is clear upon reading the original work that Adam Smith knew whose *invisible hand* was at work.

When I first studied the work of Charles Darwin in grammar school —*evolution* and the *theory of natural selection*—I became disturbed because it challenged my religious beliefs. Like many children, I had been taught to interpret the Bible literally, including the story of creation. It wasn't until I studied evolution again in high school that I realized Charles Darwin's theories *proved* rather than refuted my belief in God. Only a loving God could even dream of creating life forms so perfect that they could physiologically evolve on their own for continuous survival.

Similarly, although religious doctrine is absent from most of the work of the great economists of the past two hundred years, with the benefit of the twenty/twenty hindsight we enjoy today, it is almost impossible to study the areas in which they were correct without seeing God's handiwork in their theories. As explained in Chapter 2, only a loving God could dream of creating a world where the only limit to our wealth is the number of people we love. The more we specialize in a particular task, the greater our individual economic output. And the greater and more specialized our individual economic output, the more people we desire to share and trade with for their specialized economic produce, and the greater our total societal wealth.

When students study the physical sciences, they often find God absent from their initial discoveries. Science seems so exact in explaining the mysteries of the galaxy through deductive logic that religious doctrine seems superfluous. It is only when they develop a much higher knowledge in a chosen field—when the basic rules that once seemed so complex become seemingly obvious—that they realize that only a *God* could have created a world of such magnificent order and laid it open for us to discover how it works. Many of our great scientists, like Albert Einstein, started out as atheists but then became deeply religious in later life.

When it comes to teaching economics, one of the reasons we sometimes fail is that we are attempting to teach concepts that could only have been created by the most loving of deities, without acknowledging that such a deity even exists. And another reason we often fail to teach economics is the term we still incorrectly use today to define our modern free enterprise economy.

The term that we use to describe the economy described in the eighteenth century by Adam Smith—"capitalism"—was actually coined almost one hundred years later, in the nineteenth century, by Smith's severest critic, Karl Marx. To Marx the free market economy was not really *free* at all—it was controlled by whoever controlled the productive land and/or the material wealth, the *capital*. Marx coined the term "capitalism" as a negative contrast to his view of utopia —Communism—where the productive land and/or material wealth would be owned by the state.

Marx focused on the evils and early abuses in the unfettered free market system, attributing most of the blame to the owners of the means of production—the capitalists. Yet in reality, most of these abuses were not the result of the free enterprise system but were vestiges of the mercantilist economy that free enterprise was rapidly replacing.

Incidentally, while Marx's theories were based on Smith's cause of the wealth of nations—the division of labor—Marx's theories failed because they removed the individual's incentive to *want* to improve his or her skills through increased specialization. Nevertheless, young people are still attracted today to Communism for its idealistic solutions to our economic problems. As my mother says (paraphrasing Winston Churchill):

> If you're not a communist at some time before the age of thirty, you have no soul; and if you are a communist at any time after the age of thirty, you have no mind.[5]

Now that we live in a time when the theories of Karl Marx have been refuted by almost one hundred years of experience, it is time to remove Marx's pejorative term for our free enterprise system. We need to replace the word "capitalism" with a term reflective of the economy we live in today *and* the economy we can already see emerging in the twenty-first century—an economy, as we'll see in a moment, that will be almost entirely focused on the interests, values, and dignity of the human individual.

The *Random House Unabridged Electronic Dictionary* defines "humanism" as "any system or mode of thought or action in which human interests, values, and dignity predominate.[6] Thus, the new term I propose to describe our existing free enterprise economic system is "capitalistic humanism," defined as follows:

> Capitalistic humanism—an economic system combining free enterprise, humanism, and religious doctrine, in which the major unit of value (i.e., the "capital") is the single individual.

It is important not to confuse capitalistic humanism with secular humanism,[7] which promotes humanism without allusion to religious doctrine. In capitalistic humanism, economic laws are derived from God-given principles rather than from secular ones.

We have examined some historical facts behind the origins of our modern economy, and we have reviewed the origins of the basic economic premise behind the concept of unlimited wealth—the division of labor. Now let's examine how the division of labor has evolved in the past and how it is evolving today into the workplace of the twenty-first century.

The division of labor probably began in primitive societies between the sexes: Men built dwellings, hunted, and fought; women raised children and tended crops. As civilization developed, increased specialization led to the development of better tools and productive techniques, which in turn led to even more increased specialization and productive output.

By biblical times there were already at least thirty specialized professions within just the construction industry. These included brick makers, bricklayers, carpenters, carvers, caulkers, coppersmiths, designers, embroiderers, engravers, forgers, glassworkers, ironsmiths, leather workers, masons, metalsmiths, plasterers, potters, refiners, sculptors, seamsters, silversmiths, stonecutters, stonemasons, stoneworkers, tanners, tapestry makers, tentmakers, weavers, well diggers, woodcutters, and woodworkers—all of which are mentioned by name in the New and Old Testament.

But most of this process of specialization was so widespread and obvious that it was taken for granted. While the Bible has stories covering almost every aspect of human life, there is little mentioned about how one joined one of the more than 180 specific professions described, or how an existing member of one of these professions might improve his or her skills.[8]

The real accelerated development in the division of labor, and the resultant dramatic increase in productive output, began around the twelfth century with the development of organizations known as the craft guilds in England.

Craft guilds—also known as *corporation de métier* in France, *arte* in Italy, and *Zunft* or *Innung* in Germany—arose when groups of artisans united for mutual benefit. The artisans agreed to all share the same manufacturing technology, fix wages for their employees, and monopolize the local trade in their particular product or service. While these craft guilds are historically recorded as the forerunners of modern unions, they were really the opposite: organized entrepreneurs or owners rather than organized laborers. The public benefited only because of the high standards the guilds set for their finished work.[9]

The members of a craft guild were divided into three classes: masters, journeymen, and apprentices. The master, who typically owned the tools and the raw materials, functioned as a small-scale proprietor. Apprentices worked for room and board and lived in the master's house until they became journeymen, at which time they were paid a fixed wage for each day's work. The name journeyman is derived from the French word *journée,* meaning "day." Journeymen eventually became masters.

Craft guilds provided their members many benefits: professional education, mutual support in times of sickness, and even burial rites. The concept of providing these benefits laid the foundation for the nineteenth-century friendly societies that became the forerunners of modern insurance and savings associations.[10]

In many European cities, by the fifteenth century craft guilds had become the dominant economic, and sometimes political, force. However, craft guilds declined rapidly in the sixteenth century because of negative reaction to their monopolistic practices and the emergence of large-scale, more competitive methods of manufacturing. Craft guilds were legally abolished throughout Europe at the beginning of the nineteenth century.[11]

Unions began to develop in the middle of the nineteenth century, separately along craft or industrial lines, important distinctions that remain to this day.[12]

Craft unions, organized along lines based on professional skills, flourished in the construction, printing, and railroad industries. These well-managed unions provided an emerging America with new technology and high-quality standards for their work, and held their members together through a system of unemployment, sickness, and death benefits that the workers themselves financed. In many fields like construction and printing, dominated by many small firms unable to keep up with the latest technology, craft union labor became a highly sought after commodity by employers. Thanks primarily to the continuing professional education and regulation self-imposed by the craft unions on their members, the term "union labor" came to mean the highest in quality and performance standards.

This was not the case with the industrial or trade unions, organized along lines based on the industries in which people worked. These unions were composed mostly of semiskilled or unskilled workers who came together because they happened to work for a particular large company or companies in a specific industry. Trade unions attracted a lower standard of member than craft unions and provided the breeding grounds for many of the world's socialist and communist organizations.

Trade unions reached their lowest point during the Great Depression, having less than 3 million members in 1933. They might have disappeared altogether were it not for President Roosevelt's New Deal, which increased their numbers to more than 8 million by 1938 and more than 14 million by 1945. New Deal legislation such as the National Labor Relations Act of 1935 (also known as the Wagner Act) federally mandated employer recognition and collective bargaining with union representatives. In contrast with the craft unions, which were concerned with maximizing the productive output of their work, trade unions, for the most part, were primarily concerned with maximizing their return for duration rather than innovation in the workplace.

I should digress here and point out that there is another, more positive view of the development of trade unionism during the Great Depression. As I explained in *Other People's Money,* it is difficult for most people alive today to comprehend how badly off our nation was in March 1933, when President Roosevelt took office. National income had plummeted by 52 percent, declining to $40 billion from $85 billion just three years earlier. Banks were failing by the hundreds each month, leaving millions of depositors destitute: fully thirty-four of the forty-eight states had virtually no or only partial banking services by 1933.[13] The economy was so bad in the 1930s that many feared that the American experiment, begun in 1776, might be over. And no one, Democrat or Republican, seemed to be offering any answers—except the socialists and the communists.

Today, some of the New Deal legislation is disparaged as the beginning of the welfare state that may one day bankrupt America. And yet, upon reviewing the social, literary, and political context in which it was passed, one can argue that New Deal legislation actually saved the entire American experiment from revolution by establishing a political and economic safety net against socialism and communism.[14]

Led by the growth of the trade unions, union membership escalated in the United States after World War Two. By 1955, almost a quarter of the U.S. labor force, 24.4 percent, were union members. This figure fell slightly, to 22.6 percent, by 1970, primarily because of dramatic growth in the size of the total labor force itself—actual union membership rose from 17.7 million in 1955 to 20.8 million in 1970.[15]

Then, in the 1970s and 1980s, union membership plummeted as tens of millions of workers, having received wage and benefit increases primarily for their duration rather than their innovation in the workplace, were thrown out of work. Union membership as a percentage of the labor force fell to 18.2 percent in 1980 and 15.8 percent by the end of 1992.[16]

As already explained in Chapter 5, "What's Happening to Our Jobs?", most of these workers lost their positions because of a combination of events—only one of which may have been their union representation. And almost everyone expects new white-collar and continuing blue-collar displacement in the 1990s to make the tens of millions already thrown out of work pale by comparison.

So where is the answer for the workplace of the 1990s? The key to surviving and thriving in the workplace of the 1990s and the twenty-first century is found in the origins of the workplace of the nineteenth century.

The workplace of the twenty-first century will contain some of the best elements of the workplace of the nineteenth century. There will be a decline in scientific management; individuals will take the responsibility and receive the rewards for their own continuing professional education. There will be a return to the entrepreneurial spirit of the craft unions; individuals will once again be compensated for their performance and innovation, rather than for their duration. And there will be the emergence of a new benefit structure; individuals, not organizations or governments, will begin to take responsibility for their own retirement, health care, and the security of their families.

The Rise and Fall of Scientific Management

In the nineteenth century, most industries were organized around the apprentice-craft system, in which the worker learned his own trade and supplied his own tools. Management's job was merely to divide the work among the workers and see that they did it, rather than provide guidance or training to improve their labors.

Frederick W. Taylor (1856–1914), a great American inventor and engineer, developed a new system called "scientific management," in which management took an active role in training and developing the skills of its workers. This particularly American style of management fit in well with what was happening in the United States at the time. Over 1 million new immigrants were arriving each year, and some of the greatest fortunes ever created were made by the innovative entrepreneurs, like Andrew Carnegie, who trained them.

Taylor's system of management evolved into an American institution—the large corporation that assumed lifetime training and employment responsibility for the people it hired. Today this institution has become so commonplace that we don't even think about it as something new. When asking the question "What do you do?" you are equally likely today to hear, "I work for GM," or, "I'm with Citibank," as you are likely to hear, "I'm a doctor," or, "I'm a financial analyst."

But changes have occurred that now threaten the continued viability of the large American corporation—and with it the continued economic viability of up to half the jobs in our nation.

Corporations can no longer afford to guarantee lifetime employment, let alone provide it. The marketplace today changes so quickly that skills required only yesterday may be obsolete tomorrow. And customers, in order to remain competitive themselves in an international marketplace, cannot continue to purchase a company's product or service unless it is the very best available at the most competitive price.

To survive today, the corporation must look frequently at every task as if it were about to embark on a journey to a new kind of planet on a new kind of spaceship. In picking its crew, the corporation must select only the best people for the journey ahead—some of whom may not be the ones who were the most productive on yesterday's journey—to a different kind of planet on a different kind of ship.

Ideally, of course, and this is the management challenge of the twenty-first century, the crew on the journey yesterday should be—thanks to the manager who trained them—the ones best qualified for the journey tomorrow.

But nowadays and increasingly more so in the future, fewer and fewer companies have the ability or the inclination to take this challenge in training today's workers for tomorrow's jobs. This is primarily because there is less likelihood in our mobile society that employers will reap the benefits of what they sow.

Instead, employers find it more profitable to fire yesterday's skilled employee and hire tomorrow's—complete with whatever may be the requisite skills the employer needs tomorrow to serve its customers. This is causing the organizational focus and the educational focus to shift from the corporation to the individual employee.

Today there are tens of thousands of employee affinity groups defined by the industry in which they work—real estate (National Association of Realtors), computers (Electronic Industry Association), dentistry (American Dental Association), manufacturing (National Council of Manufacturers), and so forth. Traditionally, membership in these organizations was paid for by employers interested in coordinating industry activities. Today, membership is increasingly paid for by individuals interested primarily in increasing their professional skills and keeping abreast of employment opportunities within their industry.

In the near future we will see more major companies with no employees other than top management, who hire or subcontract skilled labor in the same manner professionals like lawyers or consultants are employed today—on a job-by-job basis. These new per diem employees will come with their own tools and maintain their skills through membership in their trade associations. In reality, these, and eventually almost all, employees will *be* professionals—for in the next century, because of increasing automation, there may be little or no demand for what we today call "labor."

This type of workplace, in which each individual will be primarily responsible for his or her own economic future, will come with enormous social dislocations as well as potentially enormous social benefits.

It will require the retooling of our public educational system to allow for the continuing education and retraining of adults. It will require unions to return to the original noble purpose for which many of them were founded—training and improving the economic output of their members. And it will require redefining the very role of our government and private institutions with respect to providing health care, retirement benefits, and numerous other social services.

But it also promises the potential to return our society to a notion prevalent in America throughout the nineteenth century, when Horatio Alger first began writing about the American dream: the notion that each person *individually* is responsible for his or her own destiny and that the only role of government is to guarantee that each person be given the equal opportunity to manifest his or her individual destiny.

*I*n 1991 the Nobel Prize for economics was awarded primarily for a paper originally written in 1931 explaining why large organizations exist (see chapter 5, "Should You Quit Before You're Fired?"). Ironically, for many of the same reasons explained in this paper, by the end of 1991 many such organizations were ceasing to exist as "large" organizations. These "large" organizations were firing employees on a wholesale basis and replacing their functions with smaller, specialized outside subcontractors. By the middle of the 1990s it was clear that this technique, popularly known as "outsourcing," was the way in which many large companies were going to thrive into the twenty-first century.

Outsourcing—
The Reconstruction of a
Catsup Manufacturer

Part 1—The Company

In 1980 a midwestern catsup company had a large vertically integrated manufacturing plant, employing eight hundred persons, where they mixed their catsup, made bottles and bottle caps, printed labels, and even folded their own shipping cartons. In addition to the eight hundred people employed at the plant, the company also had a fifty-person national sales force, a thirty-five-person advertising department, and a seventy-five-person accounting department—about 960 people in all, generating approximately $100 million in sales.

In 1990 this same company was doing $300 million in sales, with a bunch of computers and a total staff of twenty-five persons. Here's what happened.

It began in 1981, when their largest customer requested that the company put a new form of bar coding on its labels, which the printing press in the plant could not produce. When the catsup company looked into purchasing a more advanced press and retraining its printing employees, it found out that it was much less expensive to have an outside specialized printer supply them. By connecting to the computers in the plant scheduling the catsup production, this outside printer was able to deliver the new labels several times a day just when they were needed. The catsup company let go the twenty printing employees at the plant.

In 1983 the company heard about a large, highly specialized bottle cap maker who had developed a new technology for making bottle caps with a silicone seal that extended the shelf life of a catsup bottle from fourteen to twenty-four months. However, this bottle cap maker wouldn't sell the catsup company the equipment to make them—it would only supply finished bottle caps, at much less cost than the catsup company was currently spending to make their own metal bottle caps. The catsup company let go the forty-five employees it employed making bottle caps and switched to this outside supplier.

In 1985 the outside bottle cap supplier ran late on deliveries, causing the catsup manufacturer to go into the market for a backup supplier. They found three similar bottle cap manufacturers and thereafter divided their business between all four, so as never again to become dependent on a single source. Then one of the new bottle cap suppliers began packaging finished bottle caps on a paper roll, which allowed the catsup manufacturer to purchase an automatic bottle-capping machine that eliminated the need to unpack the bottle caps and manually put them onto each bottle of catsup. Before long all four bottle cap suppliers had this innovation, which allowed the catsup manufacturer to simultaneously increase capacity and let go over two hundred employees at the plant.

In 1988 a new supplier offered the catsup company a crystal-clear unbreakable plastic bottle for less than half what it cost the plant to make its own breakable glass bottle. And this new plastic bottle came with its own cap, eliminating a full manufacturing step and the need for the four bottle cap suppliers. Moreover, when the company began exploring how to modify the manufacturing plant to use the plastic bottle, the bottle supplier recommended a fulfillment plant. This outside fulfillment plant offered to mix the company's catsup according to its secret formula, fill the plastic bottles, put on the preprinted labels, and package the finished cases of catsup for shipping—all for 30 percent less per bottle than the cost to run the entire catsup plant.

This new fulfillment plant utilized something called "flexible manufacturing," which allowed it to switch entire product lines several times each day. Moreover, this fulfillment plant manufactured items for seven different food product companies—all of which shipped their products to the same food wholesalers. Thus, not only could the fulfillment plant save the catsup company money on mixing and bottling catsup, but using the fulfillment plant could save substantial amounts in shipping charges by consolidating the finished cases of catsup with the items from the other seven food product companies.

Once the decision was made in 1989 to switch all of the catsup production to the fulfillment plant, the catsup company located two similar fulfillment plants in different parts of the country and decided to spread out their business, so as not to become too dependent on a single plant. Similarly, by 1989 the catsup company was purchasing preprinted catsup labels from four independent companies and plastic bottles (with built-in bottle caps) from five independent sources. These individual firms were each so specialized in their respective businesses, utilizing the latest in the technology for their particular specialty, that the catsup company's cost per bottle of catsup in 1990 was only about a third of what it was in 1980, when they produced almost everything themselves.

This two-thirds reduction in cost allowed them to reduce the price of a catsup bottle by 50 percent and caused a six-times increase in unit sales—from $100 million to $300 million per year. Moreover, thanks to the fact that they no longer had a single plant with a limited production capacity, they were able to increase their sales whenever they needed to with no additional capital investment.

This ongoing relationship with three fulfillment plants, four separate label printing companies, and five separate bottle makers also seemed to guarantee that the catsup company heard about new innovations in each of these areas before any of its competitors. But the company, which had learned how fast things change from firsthand experience, was not leaving anything to chance. In 1990 they had three full-time people in each of these areas—fulfillment, product design, and packaging—whose sole job was to keep up with new developments in their respective fields and insure that the outside suppliers kept the catsup company ahead of its competition. The sole responsibility of these three in-house experts was to evaluate new technologies and write affirmative memos stating why they should or should not be adopted.

Outsourcing — The Reconstruction of a Catsup Manufacturer

Part 2 — The Employees

In addition to eliminating the eight hundred people they used to employ at the plant, by 1990 the catsup company had also reduced its home office personnel by a factor of five. Here's how this occurred.

In 1985 their top salesperson convinced management to let her organize the entire fifty-person sales force into an independent sales representation company owned by the salespeople themselves. By carrying other, complimentary lines of products along with catsup, some of which were also made at the large fulfillment plant, the salespeople became much more productive when they called on the food wholesalers. The catsup company's selling expenses as a percent of sales remained constant, while the salespeople's earnings rose considerably.

In 1987, responding to competition, the catsup company fired their thirty-five-person advertising department and outsourced this function to an outside agency on an annual contract basis. This insured that the catsup company would always learn what was new in the advertising world when other agencies visited each year to make a pitch for their business.

In 1988 the seventy-five-person accounting department was eliminated by a contract with a leading accounting services firm called Automatic Data Processing (ADP) — and now there were three additional outside accounting services firms claiming that they could perform the same function as ADP for half the cost.

So much outsourcing went on that by 1990 all that was left at the catsup company were twenty-five very high level managers to administer the various contracts with the outside suppliers and coordinate their activities.

Let's go back over the previous ten years and examine what happened to some of the employees.

When the catsup company first switched to using an outside

label printer in 1981, twenty employees did lose their jobs. But actually a number of new jobs were created at the label printer that received the catsup company's printing business—although these jobs were located far from the Midwest and required a higher skill level. The former printing press employees spent the next two years looking for work based on experience of having operated the now-obsolete brand of printing press—work that could not be found, since other companies stopped using similar equipment almost just as the former printing press employees came applying for jobs.

The same fate awaited the forty-five employees who made bottle caps in 1983. They, too, spent six months and more looking for work that could not be found, operating obsolete equipment. Before they realized what was happening, their unemployment benefits ran out and they had to take menial day and night jobs that did not allow them any time for learning new skills.

The bottle cap maker with the new silicone seal thought it had hit a home run in 1983—over the next five years it hired four hundred new employees to make its improved metal bottle caps as it captured business from food product companies nationwide. Then it, too, fell to the same fate that it had caused others to suffer, when the food industry switched en masse to using plastic bottles with built-in caps. Its employees, who had an exciting ride from 1983 to 1988 as the bottle cap company expanded, never even knew what hit them when the bottle cap maker declared bankruptcy in 1989.

Similarly, the plastic bottle manufacturer is currently riding its wave of prosperity. But storm clouds are gathering on the horizon—environmentalists are calling for an economic boycott of products distributed in plastic packaging that does not decompose in the environment. And while the bottle manufacturer is researching how to develop a biodegradable product, there is no guarantee that it will be the first to do so, or that whoever does first will be willing to license such technology to potential competitors.

On the whole, the nation greatly benefited. The price of a bottle of catsup fell by 50 percent—which meant that the $300 million in catsup produced in 1990 had an equivalent 1980 economic value of $600 million! Although technically this price reduction shows up as a $300 million *decrease* in GNP, it represented a $300 million real increase in economic wealth to the American public, far more than the amount the nation lost by the displacement of about eight hundred jobs. Even if one pretends that none of these eight hundred people ever got a job producing anything, American consumers directly benefited by about $375,000 per year for each one of the 800 jobs lost.[17]

*T*his story of the catsup company is somewhat atypical—few companies can undergo this amount of change in so short a time period. However, the story illustrates the types of changes that have taken place in the companies that have survived the past two decades. Because of a combination of true global competition, advancing technology, and a change in the manner in which corporations were governed, beginning in 1980 the genie of rapid technological implementation was let out of the bottle. And regardless of the social ramifications that this type of rapid technological change is having on our workplaces, there seems little possibility that the genie will ever return.

While the press remains focused on only the displaced-worker side of this phenomenon, outsourcing in the 1990s and the next century creates one of the greatest entrepreneurial opportunities of all time. The greatest reward awaits the displaced worker who can turn his about-to-be former employer into his first and best customer.

How to Quit Before You're Fired

If you work for a large company, here's how you can make something happen *for* you and your coworkers before it happens to you. Here's how to literally *quit before you're fired*.

First, analyze the work you perform each day from the standpoint of its contribution to your employer. What is the actual function that you do, how does it fit into the total objective of your company, and, most important, how does the company profit from what you do?

Then figure out how you, and perhaps several of your coworkers, can approach your employer to leave the organization and be simultaneously hired as an independent outside contractor.

For example, suppose you manage a warehousing operation involving stocking finished products on shelves and packing them to fill orders. You could form your own business with your coworkers to perform exactly that function as an outside contractor for your employer—perhaps initially renting warehouse space from your company and hiring most of the existing warehouse employees.

You should approach your boss asking to be paid for piecework—an amount per item for initially stocking the merchandise, an amount per day or month for storing the merchandise, and an amount for picking and packing each item to fill orders. You should also consider offering a total fixed price for an initial time period in return for a guaranteed amount of business. (See "Making Your Employer Your First Customer," which follows.)

Your profits should increase as soon as you take control. Here are a few reasons why.

First, if we assume you're savvy enough to work out an incentive compensation plan for your employees and coworkers, their individual productivity will take off. What you have to do is identify the work performed by each employee and establish an open compensation system based on their individual performance.

Second, with the extra time you and your coworkers have from your increased productivity, you will be able to lay off some of your employees. But rather than do so, you will probably go out to your former employer and other companies needing the same function and request more work. Moreover, when you start to perform services for different companies, in addition to increasing your profits you will be protecting yourself and your employees in case your former employer's business declines.

Third, and perhaps the greatest reason to go into business for yourself, you will be able to choose your own tools and implement new technology as it becomes available—rather than getting what is about to be last year's technology into next year's budget request, as you seem to now.

For example, virtually every company today has some sort of warehouse and inventory operation for their products and supplies. Today, a simple $1000 personal computer—which leases for as little as $50 per month—can run an inventory picking program that maintains a database of all items and their locations in a warehouse. In addition to printing invoices and tracking inventory, such a device can print a picking list of the items in the order that they are located—typically doubling the efficiency of the employees who pick the items off the shelves. Today, owing to the way many organizations postpone implementing new technology until it's often too late, less than 10 percent of the warehouses that could use such a simple computer program now have it.[18]

Unfortunately, today the process of employees leaving and then being rehired for the same task is already happening—but in a much more combative manner.

Because of declining sales at the end of the 1980s, General Motors eliminated thousands of basic engineering positions absolutely critical to the corporation. Most of these people—after being paid generous early retirement packages as incentives to leave the company—ended up working at outside engineering firms doing the exact same function on the exact same products. By 1990, GM was spending over $750 million a year on outside engineering and design firms.

While GM acknowledged that their cost cutting program didn't save them any dollars, top management boasted that these employees were now not on their payroll and could be eliminated at any time.[19] In commenting on what happened, GM's top management missed the main point. Individual entrepreneurs operate much more efficiently, even when these entrepreneurs are asked to perform the same task that they used to accomplish working for a large organization.

Convincing your employer to let you quit and go into business, with your employer as your first customer, could be a difficult task.

Some managers may be too jealous of their individual subordinates to even consider such a concept. You might need a hypothetical story to get a fair hearing when you first present the idea to your superiors.

Here's an example of how someone once accomplished such a diffi-cult task.

Making Your Employer Your First Customer

Approximately 1000 B.C., King David fell in love with another man's wife and had the man killed so he could take her for his own. The task of chastising the king for his misdeeds fell upon the prophet Nathan, a relative newcomer who succeeded to his position after the death of the prophet Samuel.

However, the prophet Nathan wisely did not go straight to the headstrong king and curse him for his transgression. Instead, playing on the king's upbringing as a shepherd, Nathan came to ask King David's advice about a rich man with many sheep who had callously slaughtered a poor man's beloved pet lamb. Upon hearing Nathan's story, David orders fourfold restitution, stating, "As surely as the Lord lives, the man who did this deserves to die."

Nathan then cries out, "You are the man," as David, realizing the terrible crime that he has committed, falls to the floor to beg forgiveness.[20]

Similarly, when approaching your boss with the concept of becoming an outside contractor, you might be prudent to first discuss the concept in generalities, implying that a third party has approached you at an attractive price to outsource the func-tion that you now perform for your employer. Then, once your superior is already considering the potential benefits to the com-pany, disclose that you, and perhaps some of your coworkers, are desirous of becoming that third party on the same terms that you have just discussed.

Getting your company to let you go into business for yourself might be easier if the work you perform for them now involves the use of company-owned capital assets like warehouse build-ings or sophisticated equipment.

The reason is that, given accelerated depreciation accounting policies, many large companies carry capital assets on their books at far less than their true value.[21] This means that if you can propose purchasing such equipment or buildings from your employer, the employer may be able to recognize significant book profits from the sale of such assets to you at highly advantageous prices. Moreover, if they're a public company, more interested in book profits than in cash, they'll probably finance the purchase of the assets themselves with low-interest and/or no-liability financing.

In the past it has been traditionally accepted that people leaving organizations go into business for themselves in competition with their former employer. Most of our successful entrepreneurial role models—e.g., Sam Walton of Wal-Mart or Ross Perot of EDS—all went into business as competitors of the firms they left.

However, in the future, as the building block unit of American business becomes much smaller and more specialized, it will become far more common to simultaneously leave your company and be rehired as an outside contractor or supplier—actually assisting in the survival of your former employer rather than in his destruction.

*I*n the manufacturing-based economy of yesterday, the building blocks of corporate technology included the large manufacturing plant and the mainframe computer. Companies that could afford such expensive plants and computers dominated their industries by achieving operating economies of scale—providing large numbers of employees with lifetime occupations.

In the service-based economy of the 1990s and the next century, the building blocks of corporate technology are the small entrepreneurial workplace and the desktop personal computer. Successful companies today dominate their industries "virtually," by utilizing an ever-changing list of efficient outside suppliers.

As the size of the building blocks of business has shrunk, so has the optimum size for individual organizations. This has created innumerable opportunities for entrepreneurs seeking to start their own business.

However, this stampede toward an entrepreneurial workplace is being impeded by outmoded government policies that subsidize large organizations at the expense of other American taxpayers. Indeed, if one didn't know that these policies originated when the majority of Americans used to actually work for large organizations, one might suspect that such policies were developed maliciously to keep workers from leaving their corporate employers and striking out on their own.

These insidious government policies affect the three things that employed individuals require most for long-term economic success—savings for retirement, continuing education, and health care.

Employees working for corporations are allowed to save for their retirement through company-sponsored pension plans. Employers deduct the full amount of their contributions from federal and state income taxes, and employees do not recognize these benefits as income until they are spent—typically when the employee retires, is in a much lower income tax bracket, and may even live in a different state without personal income taxes.

For example, assume an employee of a corporation contributes approximately $10,000 of his or her annual compensation to a company-sponsored pension plan, compounding tax free at, say, 10 percent per annum. In twenty-five years such contributions will compound to a retirement nest egg of $1,081,818.

Now assume that the same worker is employed by a company without a private pension plan and living in a state like New York or California, where the combined federal and state income tax rate exceeds 50 percent. If this worker wanted to save $10,000 toward retirement (outside of a retirement plan), he or she would have only $5,000 after paying personal income taxes on this amount, and thereafter interest on the compounding principal would also be taxed at 50 percent—lowering the 10 percent annual interest rate to 5 percent after taxes. In twenty-five years this employee making the same $10,000 pretax contribution will have a retirement nest egg of only $250,567–$831,251, less than if the self-employed individual were entitled to the same tax advantages as the employee of the large corporation.[22]

Put another way, an employee of a corporation saving $10,000 a year toward retirement for 25 years receives a $831,251 retirement bonus paid for mostly by the majority of U.S. citizens, who are not covered by a pension plan. No wonder so many people fear leaving their large employer—the government confiscates more than 75 percent of their retirement money just for going out on their own!

Over the past few years the federal government has made significant progress toward leveling the playing field between corporate employees and self-employed businesspeople—allowing in some cases a self-employed individual to save even more toward retirement than he or she could by participating in some company-sponsored retirement plans. But for the most part, this progress has been limited to assisting wealthy professionals and savvy entrepreneurs who have the wherewithal to implement fairly complex tax and retirement planning strategies.

The solution to this unfair situation is not to begin taxing employees of large companies for amounts contributed to their retirement plans. The solution is to allow every individual the same right—to level the playing field—and allow every U.S. citizen the right to save tax-free as much as they want toward their own retirement. This could be simply accomplished by allowing everyone, whether or not they work for a company with a pension plan, to put almost any amount of their pretax earnings into a tax-deferred savings account, or IRA.

One advantage of such a program might be the eventual elimination of defined benefit pension plans (popular in large organizations) in favor of individual retirement plans. It once made sense, when you worked for the same company all of your life, to have your employer manage your nest egg for retirement. It now makes no sense, when the average employee works in a single industry for less than 6.5 years, and for a single company for less than 4.5 years, to have your employer control what happens to your funds for retirement.[23] Once companies no longer received unique tax advantages in helping employees save for retirement, many would simply close their pension plans and transfer the existing proceeds to new individual retirement accounts managed by the people who really own them, their employees.

This potential elimination of many corporate pension plans would also curb abuses that exist today in a system where retirement savings belonging to employees are managed by their current or former employers. Assume a company has a fully funded defined benefit pension plan with $10 billion in assets that is obligated to pay employees a fixed amount upon retirement, say, a present value (based on actuarial tables) of about $10 billion. Typically, this $10 billion is managed by executives of the company, not the current or former employees who actually *own* the $10 billion. If the management of the pension plan makes risky investments and gambles the $10 billion into $15 billion or more, the company—not the workers whose funds were put at risk—actually makes the $5 billion in profit. Government regulations covering defined benefit pension plans currently allow employers to take out, as profits to the employer, funds in excess of actuarial amounts required to meet outstanding obligations. No wonder some pension funds in the 1980s gambled and lost tens of billions on junk bonds and commercial real estate. Had the investments worked out, all of the profit would have accrued to the benefit of the company, not the employees whose dollars were put at risk.

The second insidious government policy keeping individuals from striking out on their own is continuing education. Large companies spend billions of dollars helping their employees keep up with the latest technologies, learning how to use computers and attending local college courses designed to compensate for their individual educational deficiencies. In fact, some companies even pay the cost for employees to attend complete degree-granting undergraduate or graduate university programs.

While most of us laud such behavior, the ironic truth is that most of the cost of such programs is indirectly borne by other Americans, many of whom don't have the requisite education and skill to even get a job interview with these benevolent employers. Employers receive a full deduction from corporate income taxes for amounts paid to educate their employees, and employees are typically not taxed on the cost of such education paid directly by their employers.

In effect, similar to the benefits of saving money through corporate pension plans, 50 percent or more of such educational costs are borne by third-party taxpayers. It is cruelly ironic that our government indirectly pays the majority of the cost of educating citizens who already have a job, and little or none of the cost of educating unemployed citizens who require training or education in order to get a job.

And again, here, as with corporate pension plans, the solution to this terribly unfair situation is not to begin taxing employees of large companies for the amount of their educational benefits. The solution is to allow everyone the same right—to level the playing field—and allow every U.S. citizen the right to deduct from their income amounts spent on education and training by them or their employer. While this policy alone is probably not enough to get millions of unemployed people back to school and eventually to work, it would at least stop the discrimination against the unemployed by the employed. And it would send the right message to individuals contemplating leaving the large organization and striking out on their own.

The third, and probably the most onerous, insidious government policy keeping individuals from striking out on their own, is health care. By allowing large companies an unlimited tax deduction for the amount spent on their employees' health care and not taxing the employees for the benefits they receive, the federal government unwittingly subsidizes health care for middle- and upper-class individuals. Moreover, this massive indirect $100 billion subsidy lies at the root cause of our ever-spiraling health care costs.

Health Care

Fixing an Unfair Tax Code Would Make Health Care More Affordable

In the 1950s the United States had a 91 percent personal federal marginal income tax rate for high-earning corporate executives. Because 91 percent of any raises to this group would have gone to the federal government, these executives lobbied for (and obtained) the right to receive health care benefits tax free from their employers. Soon afterward, almost all employees of large corporations began receiving full health care benefits paid for by their employer.

The effect of this today is that we now have federally subsidized health care in the United States, but mostly for the people who need it the least. People who work for large corporations get 50 percent or more of their health care subsidized by the federal government through (1) the employer's receiving tax deductions for providing employee benefits and (2) the individual's not being taxed (state and federal) for the value of the benefits they receive. Meanwhile, poor and unemployed people (say, a single mother working part-time) receive only part or no tax deductions for what they spend on health care and must first pay income taxes on the money that they earn to purchase health care products and services.

However, the answer to this terribly unfair situation is not to begin taxing individuals or limiting corporate tax deductions for employee health care benefits. The answer is simply to level the playing field—allow all individuals, whether or not they work for a major corporation, to receive a full personal income tax deduction for every dollar they spend on health care. And, oddly enough, this simple equitable adjustment might have the unintended benefit of bringing our overall escalating health care expenses into line. Here's why.

The underlying problem with our health care system today is that most of us have few incentives to make rational cost-benefit decisions because someone else is paying 100 percent of the extra cost of providing us with services.

For example, in 1994 U.S. consumers spent about $90 billion on prescription drugs, mostly for name-brand, nongeneric prescriptions. More than 90 percent of these same drugs are available in generic form for less than $9 billion—and the generic prescriptions are often better products because they have been formulated or prescribed more recently. (Prescription drug companies limit informing customers of updated formulas because they might lose a customer to a competitive brand when the patient visits a doctor for his or her revised prescription.)

The reason that U.S. consumers have not flocked to less expensive (and often better) generic drugs is that the overwhelming majority of these consumers have their prescriptions paid for by third parties. As evidenced by the growth of Toys "R" Us or Sam's Club, American consumers will flock to anything offering them a better deal when it involves saving their money; but they have little interest in being inconvenienced when it involves saving someone else's money.

When was the last time you asked the price of a physician visit before making an appointment, or asked a hospital to provide you with comparable statistics regarding its performance in a certain area, or walked out of a pharmacy because its prescription prices were too high? Sadly, in today's health care industry, few health care providers have positive financial incentives to develop lower-cost products or services, because few of their individual customers want them.

Furthermore, approximately 20 percent of our total health care budget goes toward a woefully inefficient payment mechanism —which the insurers have little incentive to improve because such improvement would force them to pay billions of dollars to hospitals and other providers. (The "float," the difference between already provided services by doctors and hospitals and "intentionally delayed" payments by insurers, surely exceeds $10 billion.)

Employers, who started out thinking that they could give their employees a real benefit, with Uncle Sam footing more than half the cost, are now choking on rising health care costs. As their employees have come to view employer-provided health care as a right and not a benefit, most employers would give almost anything to take themselves out of the system.

Now, here's how a large part of the problem of escalating health care costs might be solved by simply leveling the playing field and allowing all consumers, not just those employed by large corporations, to take full personal tax deductions on health care expenditures.

Once consumers are allowed income tax deductions for their own health care expenditures, there would no longer be an incentive for corporations to offer health care benefits. Most companies would simply raise employee compensation by the amount of current health care plan costs and terminate their corporate health care plans. While employees might initially band together in work groups to purchase health care from the same providers, they would soon begin purchasing health care insurance as individuals or as members of other groups (e.g., churches, clubs) from the lowest cost source.

For example, let's say a company currently has a health care plan at a cost of approximately $3600 per year, or $300 per month per employee. The company would terminate that plan, raise salaries the same $300 per month per employee, and get their current insurer to guarantee providing all of their employees the same benefits for at least one year for the same $300 per month. In some cases employers would agree to withhold $300 per month from employees' paychecks and remit directly on their behalf to the health care insurer.

Simultaneously, a newly competitive *personal* health insurance industry would launch competitive plans for employees' health care dollar, with a wide range of benefits and packages—each tailored to the needs of different types of individuals. Because of the enormous paperwork cost of administering reimbursement to health care providers, one type of insurance product would soon come to dominate the marketplace.

The health insurance product that would soon dominate the marketplace would be a product with a high (say, $1,000) per person annual deductible. The reason is that while most people want a health care plan that covers all of their health care costs, they would quickly find out that a product with a higher deductible would reduce their annual health care premium by more than the deductible amount.

A person with a $3,600 annual premium for full (no deductible) coverage would find that his or her premium could be reduced by up to $2,000 a year if he or she would agree to pay the first $1,000 of his or her health care costs. The reason is that it currently costs an insurer $1,000 or more in paperwork to pay the first $1,000 of employee health care costs—paperwork involved in reimbursing myriad doctors, pharmacies, and hospitals for relatively small amounts.

Once most individuals begin paying themselves for the first $1,000 of their annual health care costs, they would become value-conscious consumers. They would start asking the price of each doctor visit before making an appointment. They would put up with minor inconveniences in order to save money on prescriptions. And they would begin asking normal market-type questions about the performance of each recommended therapy before agreeing to purchase a product or service with their own hard-earned money.

Overnight, an industry of cost-competitive health care providers and manufacturers would emerge. Our best and brightest minds would focus on how to efficiently deliver health care to millions of more people. Doctors and hospitals would have positive incentives to invest in equipment, technology, and better methods to make their services more efficient. Pharmacies would begin discounting name-brand drugs and educating their customers about generic substitutes. And some companies would even emerge concentrating on old-fashioned service—perhaps offering free doctor visits if you're kept waiting more than thirty minutes for a scheduled appointment.

No one has any idea of how efficient we might become when we apply Yankee ingenuity to the economic side of our health care system—because we have never tried it. Yet when we look at the growth of so many other industries—like food service, transportation, and consumer electronics—we can begin to get some idea of what might be possible.

Through innovative technology the restaurant industry lowered its prices so much that the demand for its product increased 1000 percent—from 1960 to 1980, Americans went from eating 5 percent to 50 percent of their meals outside of the home. Only thirty years ago a child's "Can we go out to dinner?" was met with, "What do think you we are—millionaires!" Today, such a request is usually met by, "What kind of food do you want?" Similar examples abound for the transportation, electronics, and hundreds of other industries that people once thought could never be made affordable on a mass-market basis.

In the United States innovative methods to efficiently provide more consumer products and services are constantly being developed. Sadly, not enough of these innovations find their way into the health care field because there is not enough incentive on the part of health care providers to implement them. In fact, in many cases where providers and insurers are reimbursed on a cost-plus basis, providers and insurers actually have significant disincentives to reduce overall health care expenditures.

And yet this entire system might reform itself when consumers begin paying directly for the first $1,000 of their family's health care costs. This will happen when we (1) uniformly subsidize the health care costs of every American, whether or not they work for a large corporation; (2) allow individuals to select their health care provider without the involvement of their employer; and (3) harness the power of consumer choice and free competition to motivate health care providers to develop more efficient methods of providing health care.

Today the greatest wealth in America is being amassed made by innovative individuals finding better ways to distribute already existing products or services. In the future, once we level the playing field and get employers out of a business that they shouldn't have gotten into in the first place, some of the richest fortunes in America will start being made by innovative individuals who find better ways to deliver affordable, quality health care products and services to millions more of our nation's citizens.

7

MONEY

In the temple courts he [Jesus] found men selling cattle, sheep and
doves, and others sitting at tables exchanging money. So he made a
whip out of cords, and drove all from the temple area, both sheep and
cattle; he scattered the coins of the money changers and overturned
their tables. To those who sold doves he said, "Get these out of here!
How dare you turn my Father's house into a market!" [1]
—JOHN 2:14-16

The misunderstanding of money and its function in society lies at the
root of many of our economic and social problems. Economically,
advancing technology is rapidly making money and its traditional
function in our economy obsolete. Socially, simple modifications in
monetary policy could quickly cause great reductions in crime and
increases in public revenues, leading to increased safety and prosperity for all.

Money traditionally serves three basic functions in society: as a
medium of exchange, as a standard of value, and as a store of wealth.
Understanding why and how each of these functions evolved is instru-
mental in understanding the changing role of money in our lives
today.

Money as a medium of exchange is one of the most important inventions of humankind. The potential unlimited wealth we experience
today as a result of increasing specialization could never have been
possible without it. Think how difficult it might be just to board a city
bus, let alone purchase a capital asset like a house or an automobile,

170 GOD WANTS YOU TO BE RICH

if you had to bargain with the bus driver for your fare each time you tried to board. Oddly enough, exactly this happened during the Great Depression in the 1930s because of a shortage of currency in circulation—the transit system in Salt Lake City was forced to begin accepting silk hose and toothpaste in lieu of cash for trolley rides.[2]

The use of money as a medium of exchange is its primary and most important function. Let's go back for a moment to Chapter 2, "The Covenant," where our fifty students were shipwrecked on a desert island, to illustrate how money works as a medium of exchange.

While the students on the island at first wanted to democratically rotate performance of the various chores necessary for their collective survival, by actually performing the chores the students quickly learned the primary tenet of unlimited wealth. The more each of us specializes in one particular task, the greater and more specialized our individual economic output, because of our increasing knowledge and our development of tools to assist in our tasks. The greater and more specialized our individual economic output, the more people we desire to share and trade with for their specialized economic produce, and the greater our total societal wealth.

But if the students had spent more time role-playing on the desert island, they would have soon encountered a limit to their seemingly unlimited wealth—the time it would take to locate another person who both wanted their specialized produce and also had something that they needed to trade for it, and the time it would take for the two of them to then agree on the actual price for one product in the terms of another (e.g., five sticks of firewood for two oranges). Moreover, they would have to start this entire process all over again for almost every transaction, for theoretically, fifty students producing just one product each could lead to up to twenty-five hundred unique barter transactions.

Over time, a market would have been established fixing the value of each commodity relative to the other. For example, five sticks of firewood might be accepted as worth two oranges, and an orange might come to be worth two apples—which would also mean that four apples was worth five sticks of firewood. Soon students would start acquiring more than they needed of certain nonperishable commodities, like sticks of firewood, just because they could trade these nonperishable commodities for other commodities. These sticks of firewood, acquired for their value as a medium of exchange rather than for their value as kindling, would be called "money."

Throughout the centuries thousands of nonperishable commodities, from coffee beans to palm fronds to precious metals, have served as money. The Bible lists hundreds of items used in bartering, ranging from grain to olive oil to wine, although by the time of the Exodus metals had come to replace most goods as a medium of exchange.[3] Early Egyptians shaped gold and silver into rings, bars, or rounded nodules for easier trading.[4]

Metals used as a medium of exchange were originally weighed on a scale at the place of transaction until they were eventually stamped into coins marked with their weight—although they still then had to be weighed for security, since their edges might have been filed or trimmed. Today, the coins of most modern countries have patterns stamped onto their edges and intricate designs over their entire faces in order to limit such tampering.

As certain commodities became accepted as a medium of exchange, these commodities also acquired the second function of money: serving as an abstract standard of value. Returning to our desert island, once it became accepted that one orange was worth two and a half sticks of firewood, and also accepted that one apple was worth one and a quarter sticks of firewood, two students might be willing to trade one orange directly for two apples. Or a student feeling that his or her labor was worth ten sticks of firewood per day would be willing to work directly for two oranges and four apples per day—the commodity firewood having evolved into an abstract standard of value as well as a medium of exchange.

Typically, the abstract standard of value for a commodity used as a medium of exchange, its monetary value, rises above its commodity value. For example, as explained in *Unlimited Wealth,* the *fundamental productive value* of gold as an industrial material in, say, dentistry, might be $250 an ounce relative to other metals and synthetics that could perform the same function. But the value of gold as a medium of exchange and as an abstract standard of value for other goods and services, its monetary value, might be as high as $400 an ounce.[5]

The monetary value for a commodity used as money rarely falls below its *fundamental productive value* as a commodity—primarily because when it does it is typically taken out of circulation as money and reverted back to its use as a commodity. This was the case in biblical times with copper or bronze, which started out as being used for money but was typically much more in demand for weapons or farming tools.[6] Rising silver and copper prices in the 1960s resulted in both the hoarding and melting down of coins, which forced the United States Mint to eliminate silver and copper from U.S. coins—today U.S. coins are made mostly of copper, except for the penny, which is mostly zinc with a thin copper coating.

As metals stamped with their weight (i.e., coins) became accepted as both a medium of exchange and an abstract standard of value, and rose to valuations far above the *fundamental productive value* of the materials used to make them, they became *fiat money*—money issued by governments with a decree that they are to be accepted by all. All currency issued by the United States government is *fiat money* and carries the statement "This note is legal tender for all debts, public and private."

Once a form of money becomes accepted as a medium of exchange and as an abstract standard of value, it typically acquires a third function—as a store of value or wealth. This function is not unique to money; any accumulated commodity can serve as a store of wealth. But storing wealth by accumulating money typically has lower transaction costs than storing wealth in the form of other commodities, like land or gold, that must be sold when the stored wealth is harvested for consumption. Of course, storing wealth in any form is inherently risky because there is no way of knowing the value of the wealth in terms of the commodities that are needed when the stored wealth must be harvested for consumption.

As we approach the twenty-first century, the prices of most commodities used as money are falling to their *fundamental productive value* as physical (e.g., nonmonetary) commodities. This began with oil and land in the 1980s and continued with gold in the early 1990s. These commodities are falling to their *fundamental productive value* because advancing technology is making obsolete most physical forms of money—as a medium of exchange, as a standard of value, and, most important, as a store of wealth. In order to understand how and why this is happening, let's first examine how money used as a store of wealth—savings—originates.

• • •

Borrowers are people or institutions whose consumption of money exceeds their current supply. In contrast, savers are people or institutions whose supply of money exceeds their current consumption and who seek to store their excess monetary wealth for future consumption. Savers seek to ameliorate the risk inherent in storing monetary wealth by receiving interest, which is simply the price, or rent, paid for the use of money over time. Curiously, while most people think of rich people as savers and poor people as borrowers, exactly the opposite has been true for most of the past one hundred years.

God Loves Savers[7]

Saving money, wrote Charles Dickens in 1864, is a practice that encourages its own success. "If you begin [saving] and go on with it for a little time, you come to have a sort of passion for it."[8]

But saving money is more than a commendable habit. It is a personal act of faith, a form of self-denial that expresses confidence in the future. A person who denies current comfort and pleasure for future happiness is demonstrating his or her belief in a destiny that can be controlled and improved.

It is one thing to pray in church for God's favor. It is an altogether different proposition to deny your loved ones food, clothing, and shelter that they need now in order to have a better life tomorrow. And this is exactly what immigrants in the United States today and in the past have done for generations in order to take control of their destinies.

As a child growing up in New York in the 1950s, I used to swing holding on to my father's hand as we entered both our synagogue on the Sabbath and the Bowery Savings Bank in the Empire State Building on deposit day. To him, the two institutions were almost one and the same. My father evidenced devotion to his God by making weekly visits to the synagogue, and he evidenced devotion to his children by making weekly deposits to the custodian savings accounts he had established for our education.

It is no mere coincidence that the churches and the savings

banks built by immigrants throughout America are so much alike. The vaulted ceilings, the echo of your footsteps on the marble floors, the high skylights designed to lift your vision upward together served the all-important purpose of fostering one's faith: faith in your new nation, faith in your God, and faith in your ability to take control of your destiny.

While the savings of immigrants collectively grew to the largest financial hoard ever known, the immigrants themselves were almost always poor people. They were day laborers and domestic servants, teamsters and hod carriers, ship's carpenters, tailors, and cigar makers. Theirs was a dream of an America of golden streets and limitless opportunities. It was a dream sustained by scrimping on meager wages to put away money for a better future. And as they saved, they actually financed themselves the very economic expansion that eventually would make them prosperous.

A turn-of-the-century journalist observed of the tellers' lines in lower-Manhattan savings banks: "Whether you are watching the sad-faced Jew struggling to save the passage money which shall free his family from Russian persecution, or the Greek who has left his beloved Peloponnesus to push a peddler's cart in the city streets, you must be at least conscious that you are standing close to the process of a nation's growth."[9]

The savings of immigrants seeking to improve their lives were responsible not only for the growth of the U.S. savings and loan industry but for much of the growth of the United States itself. The money deposited in savings banks was invested in homes and municipal bonds used to finance the infrastructure of our emerging nation.

Looking back, the willingness of these immigrants to save may seem to have been only prudent. But consider what courage their act of saving required. The poor, shabby newcomer to nineteenth-century America, perhaps an Italian peddler from southern Europe or a peasant farmer from Armenia, had to deprive his family of often basic necessities in order to salt away a few dollars in the care of a nameless banker operating from a storefront along a crowded, noisy street in Manhattan or Boston or Philadelphia. That immigrant, usually a victim of religious or political or economic repression, justifiably had no faith in paper money or coins not in his possession. Yet the immigrant saver still had sufficient faith in the American dream, and in the durability of the American political and financial systems, to bet that those few pennies and rare dollars would not only be secure, but be available when he or she needed them for medicine or a child's education or perhaps even the down payment on a modest frame house.

The origins and rich heritage of the savings industry are anchored in noble purpose—to provide common men and women with a way of accumulating modest wealth to improve their lives and the futures of their children. Indeed, they bear an indelible religious imprint, rooted in the philanthropic funds accumulated and disbursed by the church in the Middle Ages and the friendly societies organized in Europe during the late 1700s. As explained in *Other People's Money,* the model for the first modern savings institution was developed in a church in 1810.

In 1810 at Ruthwell Village in Dumfriesshire, Scotland, the Reverend Henry Duncan established the Parish Bank Friendly Society of Ruthwell. The reason that this institution is recognized today as the first modern mutual savings bank is philosophical. Existing friendly societies operated on the principle of charity: people banding together to help a neighbor in distress. By contrast, Dr. Duncan's Ruthwell bank was created to provide a way for one person to accumulate funds for his or her own benefit. The Ruthwell institution was not so much a charity as it was a repository for personal savings. In simple charity, a needy person is given help for reasons of mercy. But individual pride and dignity often reject charity. Avoiding the charitable motivation behind other friendly societies, Dr. Duncan wanted to encourage independence, self-reliance, individual pride, and dignity.

Today, conventional wisdom holds that one of the things wrong with our *economy* is a shortage of capital because consumers don't save enough money. This is far from the truth. Our economy is awash in capital, as evidenced by the lowest interest rates—the price of capital—ever recorded in modern times.

However, if we reflect back on Dr. Duncan and his noble intentions with the Ruthwell bank, the conventional wisdom is partially correct. Restated more accurately, one of the things wrong with our *society* is a shortage of faith because consumers don't *voluntarily* save enough money for their own future. Today, most Americans rely on social security, increasing taxation, corporate pensions, and other involuntary savings vehicles to take care of their future.

As a minister first and a banker second, Dr. Duncan's real noble intention was in providing something beyond economic sustenance in one's old age, the real rewards of voluntary savings: pride, dignity, self-reliance, and independence.

As the concept of saving money in conveniently located banks evolved, banks themselves evolved into two primary types of financial institutions—commercial banks and savings banks. Commercial banks, which originally had the exclusive power to take demand deposits and issue checking accounts, dealt exclusively with businesspeople and corporations. Savings banks, which originally could take only deposits requiring thirty days' notice of withdrawal and make limited types of loans on single-family homes, dealt exclusively with consumers. Then, in the 1970s, advancing technology and competitive pressures blurred the distinctions between commercial and savings banks. After the savings and loan debacle of the 1980s, new regulations came into existence effectively acknowledging that there is now little difference between most commercial and savings banks.

Today, approximately 2 million people go to work every day in commercial and savings banks throughout the United States. Sadly, while these 2 million people individually work very hard to diligently perform their functions, and include some of the most educated and potentially productive people in our society, the real benefits they provide to our economy could be just as well performed by two hundred thousand people or less. Most of these 2 million employees work for institutional dinosaurs that would, and should, have become extinct in the 1970s, were it not for the continued government subsidies that their employers receive at our expense.

How Customers Abandoned
Banks in the 1970s

After the collapse of the banking system in the 1930s, new legislation gave commercial and savings banks the exclusive right to take monetary deposits guaranteed by the full faith and credit of the United States government. To limit competition amongst themselves, until 1980 a federal regulation (Regulation Q) mandated the *maximum* interest rate paid by this monopoly on deposits—whoever heard of a government mandating the maximum rather than the minimum amount paid to consumers? In 1974, when the prime interest rate on loans soared to 12 percent, banks were prohibited from paying consumers any interest at all on their checking account deposits, and could pay a maximum of 5 percent interest on their savings deposits, even when these consumers borrowed back their own money.[10]

During the fifty years following the granting to banks of this monopoly to take insured deposits, banks lent their deposits to two primary types of customers: businesses and consumers. Over time, as is eventually the case with most monopolies, the banks failed to keep up with new technology necessary to continually serve the needs of these customers at a fair price. In the 1970s, the majority of businesses and consumers rejected the banks and took their borrowing business elsewhere.

At the beginning of the 1970s businesses constituted the largest group of borrowers from commercial banks. Creditworthy businesses borrowed money at the prime interest rate—the rate of interest the banks charged their most creditworthy, or "prime," customers. Other borrowers paid a rate of interest that was typically 1 to 3 percent above the prime rate, based on the security of their collateral. The prime rate for the coming week was set every Friday morning by the First National City Bank of New York (now Citibank) and then followed within hours by virtually all other banks worldwide.

On one such Friday morning in 1975 everyone expected Citibank to drop the prime rate substantially—overall interest rates had been steadily declining for weeks. Moreover, the Federal Reserve had just dramatically lowered the discount rate, the rate the Fed charged the banks themselves for borrowing excess funds. However, on this Friday morning, Citibank shocked the financial world by keeping the prime rate the same—in effect, arrogantly announcing that it saw no reason to lower its prices just because its costs had dropped. Customers, particularly corporate treasurers whose budgets had been decimated by the unprecedented rise in interest rates a year earlier, were furious.

One of these customers was the treasurer of the General Electric company, a major borrower that then had approximately $100 million in short-term loans outstanding with Citibank. This treasurer, it is told, was so angry that he began calling the treasurers of other major corporations to see who had short-term deposits at Citibank and other commercial banks—deposits that were earning far less interest than the prime rate. Within hours, the GE treasurer had secured agreements from several large corporations to lend their excess cash directly to GE at much better interest rates for both parties, bypassing the commercial banks.

Almost overnight, the commercial paper business was born as major corporations began directly lending one another their short-term cash.[11] After years of putting up with the arrogance and poor service of most commercial banks, their largest business customers didn't take much prodding to abandon them.

But GE and other new commercial lenders didn't stop there. Once they realized how inexpensively they could raise money from other potential bank depositors by offering them higher interest rates, GE and others began issuing lots of commercial paper and lending the excess amount to other businesses—going directly into competition with the commercial banks. Today, General Electric Capital, a wholly owned subsidiary of GE, is one of the largest lenders to businesses in the world, with over $65 billion in outstanding commercial loans. Moreover, the prime rate —which averaged almost twice the rate on commercial paper in the early 1990s—is now referred to as the "sucker's" rate by savvy borrowers.[12]

Today, the majority of short-term lending to businesses is accomplished via the commercial paper market—many businesses who still borrow from commercial banks do so because they are either too small or not creditworthy enough to issue their own commercial paper.[13]

It's also easy to see why large savers prefer buying commercial paper to making bank deposits. GE and other large corporations are more creditworthy than Citibank, and far more stable than most of the lesser commercial banks. Since large commercial deposits at banks aren't insured by the federal government anyway, why should any major depositor deal with banks known for poor pricing and even worse service?

At the beginning of the 1970s, consumers constituted the largest group of customers borrowing from savings banks and the second largest group of customers borrowing from commercial banks. Consumers typically borrow money from banks to purchase automobiles, major appliances, and homes. Enjoying a virtual monopoly on making loans to consumers, these banks' reputation for discourteous service was legendary—consumer bank lending officers typified the uncaring, insensitive bureaucrat in books and films for half a century.

And also in the 1970s, when consumers were given an alternative offering better service at lower prices, they, too, abandoned the banks in droves.

In the 1970s it became possible to calculate a consumer's creditworthiness at retailers via specialized computer terminals. Thanks to this and other technological innovations, by the end of the 1970s the largest lender to consumers in the United States was the General Motors Acceptance Corporation (GMAC)—a private company that raises funds in the bond and commercial paper markets and makes automobile loans direct to consumers at GM car dealers. The second and third largest consumer lenders by 1980 were similar organizations for the Ford and Chrysler companies, followed close behind by a financial subsidiary of Sears Roebuck & Company. In fact, Sears and other retailers became so proficient (relative to the banks) at financing the purchases of their customers that some retailers began making more money in lending than in retailing.[14]

These new consumer lenders had significant cost advantages over the third-party banks. First, by making their loans at the consumer's point of purchase, they reduced the distribution cost on the origination of their loans. As explained in "Distribution— The Greatest Opportunity in the 1990s" (see Chapter 4), distribution costs were becoming the largest component of the cost of most consumer items. Second, when a bank made a bad loan on a consumer item, the costs of taking title and reselling it—the reverse distribution costs—could exceed the original cost of the item. The original distributor, say a car dealer or appliance retailer in the continual business of selling exactly that same model of automobile or appliance, could obviously accomplish this reverse distribution task at far less cost—passing on the savings to consumers in the form of lower interest rates.

When it came to making mortgage loans to purchase homes, by 1970 most banks had acquired a reputation for disservice matched only by their capriciousness when consumers ran into trouble. In the 1970s banks began securitizing their mortgages— that is, selling new mortgages in pools to investors on a monthly basis. The third-party liquidity provided by the development of the mortgage-backed security business allowed nonbanks without proprietary sources of funds to enter the mortgage origination business. In less than twenty years the banks went from having a near monopoly on the mortgage origination business to a situation in which the majority of home mortgages are now originated by private nonbank companies.

How Banks Invented Fictitious Customers in the 1980s

Many, if not most, commercial and savings banks should have gone out of business when they were abandoned by their customers in the 1970s. But they didn't because of the monopoly they were granted back in the 1930s to take insured deposits backed by the full faith and credit of the United States government—in effect, a veritable license to print money at societal expense.

In the early 1980s, banks lobbied Congress and received the right to take in consumer deposits at any rate of interest and the right to invest these deposits in almost anything, regardless of the risk.[15] Then, since there were no real (i.e., creditworthy) customers around to borrow money at these higher rates of interest, the banks created fictitious customers to whom they lent money at higher and higher rates of interest, and then lent these customers even more money at even higher rates so that they wouldn't go into default when they couldn't repay their loans.

While such behavior with effectively public funds seems reprehensible today in the wake of the S&L scandal, such behavior was actually sound business practice for the owners of the banks. In 1982 Congress lowered the minimum capital requirement for savings banks to 2 percent of deposits. With only 2 percent of their own (stockholders') money at risk, the correct business strategy for these banks was to go all out and gamble their deposits, hoping for a windfall profit. If they won, the stockholders got to keep all the profits. If they lost, the federal government paid for up to 98 percent of the losses by paying off the insured depositors. Moreover, in the zero-sum game of most securities investing, half of these gamblers were bound to win at the expense of the half who lost, and some clever S&L owners hedged their bets by purchasing two or more banks and betting their respective portfolios on opposite positions.

The first group of borrowers invented by the banks were Third World countries. Originally, in the 1960s and early 1970s, most lending to these countries was soundly underwritten, based on their ability to repay. Loans were typically granted to develop infrastructure facilitating export, often the export of basic commodities that were sorely needed by the United States and other Western nations. Then, when world commodity prices collapsed in the 1970s, the banks made more loans to these same countries until, they thought, commodity prices would return to their pre-1975 levels. (Which never has occurred and probably never will.)

By 1980, the situation was hopeless. In the 1980s, as if they knew their time was running out, banks just kept making new, larger and larger loans to Third World countries, at higher and higher rates of interest, just to keep their existing loans from going into default. Since U.S. banks are allowed to record profits from unpaid interest payments on accrued borrowings, this Ponzi scheme continued until the late 1980s while these banks booked billions of false profits and issued hundreds of millions of dollars in dividends to their stockholders. Eventually, the U.S. government, under the guise of the Federal Deposit Insurance Corporation, was forced to pick up the multibillion-dollar tab. However, rather than close these institutional dinosaurs, political pressure from stockholders and employees forced the FDIC to merge many of them into the even larger dinosaurs they are today.

The second group of borrowers invented by the banks in the 1980s was the real estate industry. The majority of the savings banks in the United States were financially bankrupt in 1982 when Congress granted them the power to pay any amount of interest and to invest in almost anything they wanted. Racing against the clock to gamble themselves back into solvency, the savings banks increased their liabilities from $588 billion in 1980 to more than $1,295 billion by 1988—of which $972 billion came from high-interest consumer deposits and the balance was borrowed mostly from the federal government.[16]

The savings banks invested these funds in almost every piece of real estate they could find, driving the real estate prices up in a spiral that at first seemed to validate their prior real estate investments. Finally, after the owners of the savings banks and the Wall Street investment bankers had looted billions of dollars for themselves, the government stepped in and acknowledged the crisis. But again, rather than close down thousands of financial institutions that are simply no longer needed in our modern electronic economy, the government bowed to political pressure and kept the majority of these institutions in existence.

The simple fact is that twenty or forty years ago, when most business was conducted with cash, the United States may have needed 14,500 commercial and 3,500 savings banks. Today, when most business is conducted with checks, credit cards, and electronic transfers—and even cash is dispensed from conveniently located automatic teller machines—we still have about the same number of financial institutions and branches, although operating at a far less productive level.

In 1984 there were 3,057 savings bank branches with 15.8 million mortgage borrowers and 111.9 million depositors—about

5,168 borrowers or 36,605 depositors per branch. In 1991 there were 3,777 branches with 9.4 million mortgage borrowers and 81.3 million depositors—about 2,489 borrowers or 24,887 depositors per branch. Over a similar period, the number of commercial bank branches went from 57,010 to 64,006, with a correspondingly similar 50 percent reduction in productivity.[17]

Today, many of these surviving commercial and savings banks make little contribution to the economy. When interest rates and the demand from their borrowers began falling in the early 1990s, some of these institutions closed their lending operations entirely —converting their entire business to simply taking insured deposits and investing the money in higher-yielding Treasury instruments. The economy would be much better served if the U.S. government would close down these parasitic operations and make such Treasury instruments more conveniently available to consumers.

Should the spread decline between the interest rates these institutions pay depositors and the amount they earn from passive investments in government securities, it is only a matter of time before they begin searching for more risky, higher yielding, investments—and start the S&L crisis all over again.

According to *The Economist* magazine on December 6, 1993, this may already be happening. One newly chartered savings association in Dallas collects insured deposits and invests exclusively in risky distressed loans purchased from other savings banks. If it is successful in working these loans—primarily through strong-arm tactics—then the owners reap substantial rewards with little of their own money at risk. If the savings association is unsuccessful, then the taxpayers, once again, pick up the tab.[18]

If this Dallas savings association and most banks today had to fairly compete for their supply of funds in the open market, they would close overnight. The only reason depositors keep their money in such risky institutions is that the federal government insures 100 percent of their deposits.

But the biggest loser in keeping open most banks is the American public, and especially the more than 2 million people who work at these institutions. The average GNP per employed individual in the United States is approximately $47,000 per person, including the ones performing jobs that add little to our economic wealth. Releasing bank employees to take *real* productive jobs could increase our GNP up to $96 billion each and every year that these 2 million people were producing real goods and services desired by American consumers.

*T*he rate of interest in the economy, the price paid for the use of money, is determined by two primary factors: the supply of money available from savers and the demand for money by borrowers. When there is a shortage of money available, such as in prosperous times, when businesses and consumers wish to invest and spend, competition among borrowers drives the price, or interest rate, up. When there is a surplus of money available, such as in a depression, when businesses and consumers fear to invest or spend, the price of money, or interest rate, falls.

In the United States in the early 1990s, the economy began a long-term rise that shows no signs of abating even well into the next century. Theoretically, according to conventional economic theory, the price of money—the interest rate—should be rapidly escalating during such a period of prosperity when businesses and consumers desire to invest and spend. One decade earlier a similar economic boom caused interest rates to rise to all-time highs. In 1982 the interest rate on three-month Treasury bills was 14.04 percent, and the prime rate in 1982 averaged 18.87 percent.[19]

Yet interest rates, in the early 1990s and today, remain at all-time historical lows. In 1992 the interest rate on three-month Treasury bills was 3.43 percent, and the prime rate in 1992 averaged 6.25 percent.[20] While interest rates have risen since 1992, they show no signs of breaking into the continuous double-digit rates that prevailed throughout the previous two decades. A very close examination reveals what is going on.

In a traditional model of the economy, the rate of interest is a major determinant for businesses making decisions on new investments. A new plant or new equipment might yield a return of between 5 percent and 15 percent over many years, and thus the cost of the money required to build it is typically a major factor in making the decision to invest. As John Maynard Keynes correctly discovered, a government could control much of the economy just by artificially raising or lowering interest rates. Today this activity, conducted in the United States by the Federal Reserve Board through its open market operations, is considered a main function of a government, or central, bank.[21]

For example, suppose a business is considering building a $100 million manufacturing plant employing thousands of people that is expected to yield a 10 percent return on cost. If the cost of money to the business is less than 10 percent over the expected life of the new plant, the business will probably build the plant. If the cost of money is greater than 10 percent, the business will not build the plant. Since the cost of money to businesses is directly related to the overall interest rate in the economy, government actions to raise or lower interest rates are traditionally a major economic factor in expanding or contracting the economy.

But this is no longer the case. Both in recent years and in the foreseeable future, the accelerating pace of technological change is making such Keynesian monetary policy—artificially manipulating interest rates to control economic activity—obsolete. The reason is that for many businesses seeking to invest in new plants and equipment, the annual return on their new investments is far from 5 to 20 percent. Today, our virtual economy is so robust, and technology changes so fast, that many new investments must forecast a complete return of their cost in one to three years to be viable—or, stated more traditionally, have an annual return of between 100 and $33\frac{1}{3}$ percent.

Such fantastically high rates of return not only make obsolete traditional macro- and microeconomic models of finance; they also have the incredible salubrious effect of turning some of the fastest growing businesses in our economy into *net generators* rather than *net users* of new capital. This phenomenon causes interest rates to fall by reducing the demand for money by businesses, and also turns these same businesses from net borrowers in our economy into net savers. The capital generated by these new savers further increases the supply of money competing for the few remaining borrowers, driving interest rates down even further.

How Some Businesses Generate Capital As They Expand

In 1970, my partner and friend, Alan M. May, became the chief financial officer of Steak & Ale Restaurants, the first national restaurant chain to offer high-quality, upscale dining at reasonable prices.

Back then, a typical Steak & Ale restaurant cost approximately $1 million to open and yielded a gross return of approximately $250,000 a year, or 25 percent on each new investment. The $1 million paid for the cost of the land, building, fixtures, computer systems, furniture, advertising, supplies, and initial training for employees.

Alan's primary function was to continuously raise debt and equity capital on Wall Street to finance the growth of the company—by 1976 Steak & Ale had opened 110 stand-alone units. If we look back over this six-year period, while the company was wildly successful on Main Street and on Wall Street, from an actual cash flow standpoint it was a disaster. It had spent over $100 million in cash to open restaurants and was only just beginning to receive an annual return on this investment of approximately $25 million a year. Like virtually all growing companies in our then-traditional economy, it was a net borrower of enormous amounts of cash required to finance its growth.

Today, a new Steak & Ale restaurant unit is typically opened, in terms of 1976 dollars, for less than $150,000. The reason is that in our virtual economy, it is much more operationally efficient to lease almost everything required from specialized suppliers rather than to purchase or develop these items yourself.

The cost of purchasing the land no longer exists, since the best locations are typically in shopping centers, which are generating retail traffic long before the restaurant opens. Similarly, the cost of the building and sometimes of even the fixtures inside doesn't exist—landlords typically provide money for fixtures in return for increased rent over the life of the lease.

The computer systems are no longer developed in house but

leased short-term from specialized suppliers who provide service and training on short notice. Since several computer hardware and software suppliers compete nationwide for Steak & Ale's business, the company is assured a steady supply of new technology in this important area.

Advertising costs as a function of sales are also less for two reasons. First, by opening in shopping centers with steady customer traffic, each restaurant no longer has to rely as much on local advertising to tell the community that it exists. Second, the opening of each new restaurant unit actually reduces the cost of advertising as a function of sales, since already existing national advertising can now be amortized over a greater number of stores.

All told, in 1976 financial terms, the costs of obtaining these and other required items from outside suppliers has caused the net annual return from each new restaurant to fall from approximately $250,000 to $150,000 per annum—but this reduced $150,000 return represents a more than 100 percent annual return on the less than $150,000 it costs Steak & Ale to open each new restaurant. Put another way, each time Steak & Ale opens a new restaurant, the company receives back *each and every year* the entire cost of its expansion. This has caused Steak & Ale to go from being a net borrower, or user of new capital, to a net generator of new capital—even while it undergoes significant growth.

*B*eing a net generator rather than a net user of new capital, while undergoing significant expansion, is not limited to successful companies in the restaurant business. Today, many of the fastest growing and most desirable sectors of our economy are characterized by rapid technological obsolescence, effectively zero marginal product cost, and an abundance of outside suppliers—three characteristics that lead to companies becoming net generators of capital as they expand. Here's why.

In fields characterized by rapid technological obsolescence, a company can expect only a six- to twenty-four-month or less productive life from a new product or service. This means that a company would invest in such a field only if the return on such a product or service exceeded 100 percent a year—otherwise there would be no way for the company to hope to recoup its investment, let alone make a profit. Incredibly, the majority of new investments in our economy may soon lie in fields characterized by such salubrious rates of return.

For example, most products produced today by the entertainment business, one of the largest and fastest growing sectors of our economy, have an economically useful life of twelve months or less. This is not to say that a new movie or video game isn't useful one year after being released; it is useful. But from a standpoint of financial productivity, if it doesn't make back its entire cost within the first year after its release, it most likely never will. There are so many new movies and video games coming out to take its position in the marketplace, using even better technology, that a new release often has just one initial chance for success.

Almost across the board, the most rapidly expanding entertainment companies in the world generate, rather than consume, enormous amounts of cash as they expand. No wonder the most sought-after business prize of the 1990s was Paramount Communications, which in 1994 precipitated the largest takeover battle in history.

The ability of successful computer software companies to generate cash while expanding can make even the entertainment business seem cash deficient. Microsoft, which Bill Gates dropped out of college to start in 1975, rose to being one of the largest companies in the world in the 1980s without ever having to look outside for capital to expand.

Both the entertainment and the software businesses are characterized by effectively zero marginal product cost. That is, once their product or service is developed, it costs the company relatively little, or effectively nothing from a managerial standpoint, to produce each additional unit of the product or service that they sell. It doesn't cost the movie theater anything extra when it sells an empty seat. The cost of packaging and floppy disks is relatively insignificant next to the retail price of a software product.

In fact, many businesses today have a less-than-zero, or negative, marginal product cost—they actually profit even when their product or service is given away for nothing. A movie theater giving away an otherwise empty seat may find that the new patron purchases popcorn and candy that otherwise wouldn't have been sold, or tells his or her friends to go see the same picture. Software companies regularly give away products in order to develop loyal customers who will eventually purchase upgraded versions of the same product. In these and other cases, companies acquire an asset exceeding the value of their marginal cost each time they give away one of their products.[22]

Of course, not everyone in our economy works in the entertainment or software business, characterized by having a zero, or even negative, marginal product cost. A significant portion of our economy still lies in the manufacturing of basic products—food, electronics, publishing, products often synonymous with the names of the large companies (with large manufacturing plants) that make them. What is happening to these traditional businesses in terms of their demand for new capital as they expand?

These traditional businesses, too, have a reduced demand for expansion capital. And in some cases they too have greater than a 100 percent return on new investment. The reason is that although their marginal manufacturing cost can be greater than 50 percent of their sales price, their industries are increasingly characterized by an abundance of outside suppliers, which effectively allow for unlimited growth without outside capital.

In "Reconstruction of a Catsup Manufacturer" (see Chapter 6), we examined how in the 1980s a traditional large manufacturer went from having a large centralized plant with eight hundred employees, producing $100 million in sales, to a much more efficient twenty-five-employee virtual operation, producing $300 million in sales. Looking back, it is easy to see not only how the company tripled its sales without any outside capital but how it also set itself up for virtually unlimited growth in the future with no foreseeable capital requirements.

Our catsup company, like most of the manufacturing firms of yesterday that made it into the 1990s, survived and thrived because it shifted from making almost everything itself to relying on an ever-changing cast of outside suppliers. While these companies did so primarily to remain competitive with new technological advances, such a paradigm shift in their business strategy also had the effect of reducing or eliminating their need for outside capital. As long as there was a supplier or distributor ready, willing, and able to perform the required function, there was virtually no need to internally create additional capacity for expansion.

But what about all of these outside specialized suppliers? Don't they need a continual supply of expansion capital in order to supply their customers? Probably not. The reason is that often the most cost-efficient outside supplier probably already has a plant producing the product or service for someone else, and the reason that they are so cost efficient is that they are merely adding another shift to their existing production process.[23]

Business capital requirements are also being reduced because of the increasing speed of economic activity. From the implementation of just-in-time manufacturing methods to overnight delivery services, we have compressed the time it takes to turn raw materials into finished products, and to then get those finished products into the hands of the consumer. While such increased speed is motivated primarily by the rapid technological obsolescence of many products, it is also reducing the amount of fixed assets and inventory that a business must carry in order to serve its customers.

For example, at the beginning of the 1980s, a typical eighty-thousand-square-foot Wal-Mart department store had sales averaging about $100 per square foot, or $8 million per store. Such a store might cost about $4 million to build and carry an inventory worth about $1 million, which it turned over about every six and a half weeks. In other words, in order for a community in 1980 to enjoy the benefits of approximately $8 million in retail sales per year, the retailers providing such service required approximately $5 million in capital—a capital investment of approximately sixty cents for each dollar in annual retail sales.

By the end of the decade, thanks to technology and sales innovation designed to increase inventory turnover, many of these same eighty-thousand-square-foot stores had annual sales of approximately $300 per square foot, or about $24 million per store. Now, in order for a community to enjoy the benefits of approximately $24 million in retail sales per year, the retailers providing such service required approximately $5 million in capital—a reduced capital investment of only twenty cents for each dollar in annual retail sales.

Moreover, this two-thirds reduction in the requirement for retail capital came with many other social benefits. Over the long run, as less efficient retail competitors went out of business, it released approximately 160,000 square feet of additional retail space—space that enterprising entrepreneurs have just begun to focus on in providing new products and services that most of us haven't even dreamed of yet.

But overall, the greatest impact of the reduced demand for capital by businesses has been on the value of money used as a store of wealth. As businesses reduce their demand for money, and many of these same businesses turn into savers—further expanding the supply of money—the value of monetary wealth declines. This reduction in the value of money as a store of wealth is evidenced by the extremely low rates of interest we enjoy today.

Time, Inventory, and Money

Most of us are economically fulfilled when we complete our work and receive payment for our services. Yet, from a macro-economic viewpoint, nothing productive has really occurred until the end user of our product or service consumes it. Until a hungry person gets to eat, it doesn't really matter how much new food a farmer has planted or a food processing plant has packaged. Until a grandmother actually gets to hug her grandchildren on a holiday, it doesn't really matter how many new planes were financed or how many new airports were opened. As John Maynard Keynes noted in his *General Theory* in 1936, "Consumption . . . is the sole end of all economic activity."[24]

In our specialized economy, virtually every product or service is wholly or partially produced some amount of time before it is actually consumed. Items produced before their time of consumption are called "inventory." While accountants record inventory on a company's balance sheet as a physical asset, inventory has no real economic value—inventory consists of products or services that someone worked hard to produce but that aren't needed yet. Distributors add so much value in our economy because they find the end users who turn inventory into consumption "the sole end of all economic activity."

In our highly specialized economy, few of us actually get to see the real end user enjoy the results of our efforts. The inventory most of us produce sits on a theoretical shelf until it is demanded by the next step of production—in a long chain of interim consumption on its way to the end user. The amount of time that our produce sits on this theoretical shelf is actually waste because technically no one is yet enjoying the fruits of our labor. I've often hypothesized that the jobs with the most psychological rewards are the ones with the most end user contact because they produce real consumption (e.g., personal happiness) rather than inventory or just monetary rewards.[25]

While we might not think of it in these terms, the most successful businesspeople among us—our economic alchemists—spend most of their efforts reducing the amount of time, or inventory, that is required for a given level of business activity. New computers, better management systems, just-in-time control systems— these and almost all business tools today focus primarily on reducing the amount of time it takes from conception or production to consumption.

And of course, the resultant reduction in business inventory causes a similar reduction in the amount of money needed to finance a given level of business activity—further reducing our demand and need for money as a medium of exchange, as a standard of value, and as a store of wealth.

Twenty-one years before Keynes's *General Theory,* a different general theory put the subject of time in a new light with respect to physics. In his *General Theory of Relativity* in 1915, Albert Einstein explained that time is the most important aspect of a more general four-dimensional space-time continuum.

In a similar vein, we are just beginning to put the subject of time in a new light with respect to economics. Time, or the reduction of time in the economic process, is the most important aspect for us in managing our path to individual economic success.

We have seen how rapidly advancing technology is causing the value of wealth stored as money to decline. Such advancing technology is reducing the demand for money by businesses and is also increasing the supply of money from some of these same businesses, causing reductions in interest rates. But this phenomenon is not just causing the value of wealth stored as money to decline. It is also making the second function of money in society—serving as a standard of value—obsolete.

The reason is that the same advancing technology is causing unprecedented increases in the lifestyle of consumers, and these increases are not being recorded by the traditional monetary methods of tracking economic progress.

Traditionally and today, economic progress is recorded by what economists call the gross national product. GNP consists of the value, measured by the price, of all goods and services produced by a country. Since 1991, the U.S. Department of Commerce has been trying to shift from using GNP to GDP, or gross domestic product. The GDP is the GNP excluding all income from abroad, and is thus considered to be more accurate in recording national economic activity.

But both GNP and GDP are woefully inaccurate in recording what truly matters economically to most citizens of a country—their *real* economic wealth. Real economic wealth consists of such items as the size of their homes, the quality of their children's education, the amount and quality of their material possessions, and the amount of time that they get to spend with their families.[26]

For example, housing is the largest single component used in compiling the gross national product of the United States. The political pundits in our society like to remind us of the good old days when housing was more affordable. This is simply untrue. Americans spent the same 15 percent of their disposable income on housing in 1990 as they did in 1970, and housing costs as a percent of GNP have also remained relatively constant.[27]

Some economists using these figures would say that when it comes to housing, Americans live the same today as they did approximately twenty years ago for approximately the same cost. However, this statement, too, is far from the truth.

The truth is that, when it comes to housing, America was much better off in 1990 (and is today) than it was in 1970, and at far less individual cost. In 1970, there were 68 million units of housing in the United States serving a population of 203 million people. By 1990, the number of homes had increased 51 percent to 102 million units, while the population had increased only 22 percent to 249 million people. In other words, the number of people that could and did afford housing in just this twenty-year period increased at over 230 percent of the rate of the general population—over 33.7 million new units of housing were constructed.

While Americans in 1990 may have spent the relatively same 15 percent of their total collective income on housing as they did in 1970, in 1990 this same relative amount of total spending afforded 35.5 million more homes enjoyed by approximately 86 million more Americans. If the increases in the number of homes versus population are taken into account, the cost per housing unit in America from 1970 to 1990 actually fell by one-fifth, from 15 percent to 12 percent of consumer disposable income.[28] However, this real price reduction was never realized overall, because as relative prices fell, Americans opted to purchase more housing units—decreasing the average number of people living in each unit from 2.99 in 1970 to 2.44 in 1990.

And these reductions in the cost per home, and increases in the number of homes, don't even begin to factor in how much better the average single-family home was in 1990 than in 1970. (Over 72 percent of all occupied housing units in 1990 were single-family homes.) During just this twenty-year period, the average square footage of a new single-family home increased 39 percent—from 1500 square feet to 2080 square feet.[29] The number of new homes with more than two and a half bathrooms increased from 16 to 45 percent; the number with central air conditioning increased from 34 to 77 percent; and the number with enclosed garages increased from 58 to 82 percent— let alone the literally hundreds of other innovations, from kitchen appliances to swimming pools, that made most homes in 1990 considerably more comfortable and valuable than in 1970.[30]

Real Estate, Elasticity, and Interest Rates

When people first enter the market for housing—say, recent graduates looking for their first apartment—they typically set an amount that they are willing to spend on rent, based on what

they believe they can afford. If they find that the amount they
have decided to spend is higher than the cost of the apartment
they had in mind, they typically rent a larger apartment or one in
a better location. As their income increases, better housing is one
of the first things they acquire. Unlike almost any other single
consumer product, the demand for bigger and better housing is
virtually insatiable.

This process continues when a person or family sets out to
purchase a home. First, they look at interest rates to determine
the amount of mortgage loan that they can afford. Then they go
out to find a property in their maximum price range. When mortgage interest rates fall, as they have since the 1980s, prospective
purchasers of new homes literally have, and spend, more than
they would have in prior years—although some of their newfound wealth ends up in the hands of sellers, who benefit from
the increased competition for properties. No wonder the rate of
interest is the largest single economic component governing real
property activity.

Economists use the term "elastic" to refer to such a dynamic
relationship between demand and price. The demand for housing
by individual consumers is one of the most elastic relationships
in our economy.

Oddly enough, almost the exact opposite relationship exists
for commercial (i.e., nonresidential) real estate—its demand is
virtually inelastic. When a business requires more operating
space, no amount of price increase seems to deter the business
from renting it—mainly because the typical business spends ten
to twenty times the cost of its rent on salaries and equipment. A
business occupying ten thousand square feet, spending up to $4
million per annum on salaries and office expenses, doesn't really
care if its rent is $10 per square foot ($100,000 per annum) or
$20 per square foot ($200,000 per annum), as long as the space
is functional for its use. This phenomenon causes commercial
rents to skyrocket in an expanding economy when different
businesses compete for immediate occupancy of the same space.

Unfortunately, real estate developers almost invariably misin-
terpret such rapid price escalation as skyrocketing demand for
more and more expensive space, and typically then build several

times the amount of new, higher-quality, space that the market really can absorb. Then this same inelasticity works in reverse. No amount of discounting or price concessions by the developers can get tenants to rent space that they don't need—the real operating expenses (salaries and equipment) of the business using such space makes such discounting of the rental price financially irrelevant.

Returning to residential real estate, the reduced interest rates we enjoy in the 1990s are causing a boom in home purchasing that is reverberating throughout our economy. As the major cost factor of owning a home—the interest rate paid on the mortgage —declines, consumers opt for purchasing larger and better homes. And when consumers acquire new homes, they typically purchase new furniture, appliances, and services to accompany it—causing these consumer product businesses to expand.

Moreover, the more these businesses expand their production, the lower their cost to the consumer because of increasing economies of scale. This makes the millionaire luxuries of yesterday —home theaters, swimming pools, convertible automobiles— affordable necessities to many American homeowners.

These increases in real wealth—larger homes, newer neighborhoods, consumer appliances—remain unnoticed by those using money as a standard of value to determine wealth. Economists, media pundits, and government officials often fail to realize what is happening, because the consumer is now purchasing an increased market basket of goods for effectively the same (monetary) price.

*T*hese unrecorded increases in economic prosperity aren't limited to housing or household furnishings. Automobiles, personal electronics, vacations, clothing, food—advancing technology causes the price of almost every one of these products to decline every year. Sometimes this is not readily apparent, for the following reason.

Most Americans associate lower prices with cheaper quality. So rather than lower the actual selling price when advancing technology lowers the cost of production, most businesses opt to give the consumer a higher-quality product for the same price. This phenomenon is so ubiquitous that in virtually every field consumers simply expect that next year's model will give them considerably more quality or value for about the same price.

A typical new American automobile selling in 1995 for $15,000 is the functional equivalent in terms of features of an automobile that sold in 1991 for $20,000 or more. If we use money as the standard of value to record automobile progress, such increased functionality could show up as a $5,000 reduction in gross national product rather than a $5,000 increase in consumer real wealth. Fortunately, yesterday's buyer of a $20,000 automobile is not pocketing the $5,000 savings and buying the same car for $15,000—he or she is opting to purchase for $20,000 or more an automobile with features that may not have existed four years ago at any price.

In attempting to keep the "standard" in money as a standard of value, economists use something called the consumer price index (CPI) to adjust over time for increases (inflation) or decreases (deflation) in general prices. The CPI, also referred to as the "cost-of-living index," is the monetary price of a market basket of goods and services purchased by urban consumers representative of the majority of the U.S. population. However, as we have seen in just these few examples, the CPI has become virtually obsolete by its inability to take into account a continual, ever-expanding market basket of goods and services. This was foreseen almost forty years ago by the great economist and Nobel laureate John Kenneth Galbraith, who said, "In the affluent society, no sharp distinction can be made between luxuries and necessaries."[31]

We have examined how money is declining in value as a store of wealth and how money is becoming obsolete as a standard of value. Now let's examine what is happening to the original and most important function of money in an economy—serving as a medium of exchange.

Money used as a medium of exchange is the lubricant for our entire economy. Without it, the unlimited wealth we experience today as a result of our specialization of labor simply could not exist. However, since money itself has no actual value—money is valued only for the things that one can buy with it—it is important not to have too much or too little of it around. Having too much money in circulation causes inflation—a decline in the value of existing money. Having too little money in circulation causes deflation and can bring commerce to a screeching halt—just like having too little lubricant in a machine.

Ever since money evolved from *commodity money* to *fiat money*—from gold, olive oil, firewood, and the like to government-issued paper currency—one of the greatest challenges facing the central bank of every nation has been controlling the amount of money in circulation. The history of the United States and almost every modern government is rife with the trials and tribulations of managing the money supply.[32]

Throughout its early existence, the United States was plagued by financial panics that occurred whenever large numbers of people attempted to turn their bank deposits into currency. After the severe panic of 1907, debate ensued on the question of establishing a central bank to regulate banking and the supply of money, and the Federal Reserve System was created in 1913.[33]

Although its role has been continually debated over the years, the primary goal of the Federal Reserve is to regulate the money supply to promote real economic growth. The major tools the Federal Reserve has to accomplish this goal are the ability to control the amount of currency in circulation and the ability to control the amount banks are free to lend (bank money), which ultimately shows up as money in the form of checking accounts.

Originally, the supply of money in the economy was simply the amount of currency in circulation. As technology made checking accounts possible—which allowed banks to lend out more money than they had on hand in currency—the definition of the money supply was expanded to what economists now refer to as M_1. M_1 consists of currency in circulation (outside of banks) plus balances in checking accounts (bank money). Later, as technology made certain savings accounts almost as accessible as checking accounts, the definition of the money supply was expanded to M_2. M_2 consists of M_1 plus near-money in savings accounts and money market funds.

Recently, as more technology has made additional types of money almost instantly accessible, the Federal Reserve has begun using the additional terms "M_3" and "L" to define the money supply. M_3 consists of M_2 plus large time deposits (over $100,000) not originally included in M_2. L consists of M_3 plus other investments that most people think of in monetary terms, like savings bonds, short-term Treasury instruments, and commercial paper. Below is a recent breakdown of the money supply as defined by the Federal Reserve.

MONEY STOCK AND LIQUID ASSETS (BILLIONS)[34]

Currency	$ 292
Travelers checks	8
Demand deposits	341
Other checkable deposits	385
M_1 (subtotal)	$1,027
M_2 (M_1 + near-money)	$3,504
M_3 (M_2 + large deposits)	$4,174
L (M_3 + money investments)	$5,059

But while the Federal Reserve has attempted to keep up with the changing definition of money by adding large deposits and effectively liquid monetary investments, the chart doesn't even list the three fastest growing forms of money today: credit cards, other forms of "private money," and electronic transfers. These types of money, the supply of which is almost completely in the hands of the free market, will soon constitute the majority of the money in our economy used as a medium of exchange.

In 1980 there were 86 million U.S. credit card holders spending $201 billion per annum; in 1991 there were 111 million U.S. credit card holders spending $481 billion per annum; and by 2000 there are projected to be 125 million cardholders spending $882 billion per annum.[35] And little if any of this amount is regulated, or even monitored, by the Federal Reserve, because the majority of credit cards are issued by private companies outside of Federal Reserve regulation.[36]

Assume for a moment that M_1 has a velocity of five—that is, the amount of M_1 turns over five times each year. This would mean that if the GNP was about $5,000 billion, the proper amount of M_1 necessary to sustain such a level of economic activity would be about $1,000 billion. Now assume that a new person graduates from college and gets a new job for $25,000 per annum producing new products or services. Now that GNP has increased by $25,000 per year, the economy would demand an increase in the money supply of $5,000.

In the past, increasing the money supply by $5,000 in such a case was the job of the Federal Reserve, or central bank. However, today, months before the new person graduates from college and starts working, American Express and other private credit card companies send the aspiring graduate multiple credit cards offering approximately $5,000 in combined purchasing power—$5,000 in more lubrication for the economy. If this amount is too large an increase in the money supply, experience (painfully) causes the private companies to cut back on the size of their credit lines. If it is too small, the amount is increased as soon as the new college graduate demands and demonstrates the capability to handle it.

The existing credit card business is just one of hundreds of forms of new money that are emerging from the private sector. In 1994, companies across the United States were scrambling to begin issuing electronic "smart cards" in prepaid monetary denominations for use in telephone and transit systems—cards that become almost identical to currency once more vendors and retailers begin to accept them.

Airlines in the 1980s invented a form of private money known as frequent flier miles, which could originally be redeemed only for more airline flights. But by the end of the decade frequent flier miles were being issued by thousands of nonairline companies and being accepted for hundreds of unrelated products and services. From hotels and rental cars to purchasing a bicycle or an evening with one's favorite movie star, frequent flier miles became enormously popular with consumers—in some cases even more popular than currency itself, since they allowed consumers to purchase certain items that money couldn't buy. In 1994, the front-page headline of the Sunday *New York Times* called frequent flier miles the new "Currency for the Earthbound."[37]

Private credit cards, electronic smart cards, frequent flier miles, and the electronic transfer of funds between nonbank financial institutions are collectively becoming the "new money" that most of us will use in the next century. The supply of this new money, which in many cases represents a return to the bartering days of yesterday, is controlled almost entirely by the free market. Underlying the new money explosion is the information explosion, which allows consumers and businesses to track their imaginary electronic wallets and keep abreast of the goods and services available for purchase.

Bartering itself, for many of the same reasons, is on the upswing— most major companies experimented with bartering their goods and services in the 1980s. According to the publisher of *Barter News,* "by 1990 in the U.S. alone there were over 500 privately owned trade exchanges issuing their own debits and credits between over 300,000 individual companies—effectively over 500 autonomous federal re-serve chairpersons controlling their own form of currency."[38]

In primitive times, as the specialization of labor increased before the development of money, wealth was limited by the time it took to locate another person who wanted your produce and who also had something that you needed to trade for it. Today, led by *Barter News* and other innovative organizations using the latest in information technologies, we are approaching the time when every producer will have the ability to instantaneously locate parties that want their pro-duce and parties that have what they need—eliminating money en-tirely as a medium of exchange.

Moreover, even producers of goods and services who do not want current consumption in return for their produce—savers—could par-ticipate in this type of barter. In cases where their customer is a creditworthy institution like General Electric, producers desiring sav-ings would be much better served getting GE commercial paper rather than currency—GE commercial paper has an AAA credit rating and pays a higher rate of interest than the best U.S. government securities. Additionally, for nonsavers, it is only a matter of time before organiza-tions like GE Capital figure out how to pay employees and suppliers with user-friendly commercial paper accounts that can be automati-cally debited with proprietary GE plastic credit cards.

The private sector, able to issue exactly the type and amount of money desired by consumers and businesses, is rapidly replacing one of the most original functions of government—issuance and control of the money supply. Moreover, reporting and audit trails already in place on these new types of private money actually eliminate much of the opportunity for thieves to prosper from criminal activity—what good is stealing money that you can't spend? From the placing of photographs and fingerprints on credit cards to elaborate telephone voice identification systems, the private sector is far ahead of the government in reducing most types of property crimes that involve private money.

Returning to the Federal Reserve chart showing the breakdown of the money supply, one might rightfully ask, Where *is* the $292 billion in U.S. currency currently in circulation—$1,143 for every man, woman, and child living in the United States? Certainly most people we know, especially our children and elderly, aren't each carrying around $1,143 in hard currency. A closer examination of the denomination of the bills comprising this $292 billion reveals where it might be located.

How to Hit Criminals Where It Hurts the Most

There are currently over six $100 bills in circulation for every man, woman, and child in the United States[39]—or over twelve $100 bills in circulation for every one of the 128 million people over sixteen years of age in the labor force.[40] The majority of these 1.57 billion $100 bills are held by drug dealers, vicious criminals, and millions of otherwise ordinary citizens who cheat the rest of us every day by not paying taxes on their incomes.

In our modern economy, where most law-abiding citizens prefer to use checks and credit cards for most of their financial transactions, the $292 billion of currency in circulation—which includes over $157 billion in $100 bills—represents in large part the savings and the working capital of the underworld and the underground economy.

Confiscating this hoard of savings and working capital would deal a crushing blow to drug dealers from which many would never recover. It would also serve as a powerful deterrent to those nontaxpayers among us who seek to have other citizens pay for the benefits they enjoy in American society.

Here's how this could be accomplished almost overnight. The president of the United States would appear on television and make the following announcement:

My fellow Americans. The Secret Service believes that many of the $100 bills in circulation might be counterfeit. But no legitimate owner of even a single $100 bill is at risk. The United States government will stand behind every $100 bill in circulation, counterfeit or not, and replace it with a new, different-looking $100 bill. All citizens need to do is to bring their existing $100 bills to any bank, where they will be exchanged for the new $100 bills. Old $100 bills will not be exchanged after twelve months, and banks will be paid a fair amount for each $100 bill they exchange. And finally, each person will be asked to fill out an identification form when they exchange their $100 bills—so the Secret Service can investigate in case any of the $100 bills they exchange turns out to be counterfeit.''

Of course, probably almost no one who has obtained $100 bills illicitly will show up to exchange them. After twelve months have passed, the Treasury could declare all unexchanged $100 bills void and record the total amount of voided bills as a gain in federal revenues. If we assume that there is one $100 bill legitimately in circulation for every person in the labor force, only 128 million of the 1,570 million outstanding $100 bills might be exchanged—which would yield the U.S. Treasury that year an immediate revenue bonus of approximately 1,290 million $100 bills, or $129 billion.

And the bonus to the U.S. Treasury wouldn't stop there. For many years to come, billions of more dollars in taxes would be paid by certain American taxpayers who currently take unrecorded income in the form of currency from their customers. Once a significant part of their savings had been wiped out, these otherwise ordinary citizens would think long and hard before taking unreported cash as their remuneration—always fearful that the government might do it again with the new $100 bills or even bills of lesser denominations. The size of the black market economy in the United States is currently estimated to exceed $500 billion per year—almost 10 percent of the entire gross national product.

But the real gain to American society would not be in catching the income tax cheaters. The real gain would be in permanently wiping out hundreds of thousands of career criminals who operate billion-dollar illicit operations—like drugs, prostitution, and gambling.

These "businesspeople" would not lose just their savings; they would lose their working capital and their medium of exchange. Almost overnight, their businesses would be crippled, because their suppliers would no longer accept their currency and their customers would no longer have available an untraceable means to pay for their illicit goods and services.

8

GOVERNMENT

When Samuel grew old, he appointed his sons as judges for Israel. But
his sons did not walk in his ways. They turned aside after dishonest
gain and accepted bribes and perverted justice. So all the elders of
Israel gathered together and came to Samuel at Ramah. They said to
him, ". . . now appoint a king to lead us, such as all the other nations
have." This displeased Samuel; so he prayed to the LORD.
And the LORD told him: "Listen to all that the people are saying to you;
it is not you they have rejected, but they have rejected me as their
king. . . . Now listen to them; but warn them solemnly and let them
know what the king who will reign over them will do."
Samuel told all the words of the LORD to the people who were asking
him for a king. He said,

*This is what the king who will reign over you will do: He will
take your sons and make them serve with his chariots and
horses. . . . Some he will assign to be commanders of thousands
and commanders of fifties, and others to plow his ground and
reap his harvest, and still others to make weapons of war and
equipment for his chariots.
And he will take your daughters to be perfumers, and to be
cooks, and to be bakers. And he will take your fields, and your
vineyards, and your oliveyards, even the best of them, and give
them to his servants. And he will take the tenth of your seed,
and of your vineyards, and give to his officers, and to his
servants. And he will take your men-servants, and your
maid-servants, and your goodliest young men, and your asses,
and put them to his work. He will take a tenth of your flocks,
and you yourselves will become his slaves.
When that day comes, you will cry out for relief from the*

king you have chosen, and the LORD *will not answer you in*
that day.

But the people refused to listen to Samuel. "No!" they said. "We want
a king over us. Then we will be like all the other nations, with a king to
lead us and to go out before us and fight our battles." When Samuel
heard all that the people said, he repeated it before the LORD.
The LORD answered, "Listen to them and give them a king."
—1 SAMUEL 8:1, 3-7, 9-22 (NIV)

The optimum form of government has been a subject for debate ever
since the people of Israel asked the prophet Samuel to anoint them a
king. Samuel, who believed that the laws of God were enough for all,
saw only the evil inherent in any form of government controlled by
human beings. In contrast, the Israelites who asked Samuel to anoint
them a king believed that an authoritative form of government would
give them improved justice and a stronger national defense.

Approximately seven hundred years later, Aristotle defined three
types of governments: *monarchy*—government by a single individual;
aristocracy—government by a select few; and *democracy*—government by many. Later Greek philosophers named these three types
degenerately: *tyranny*—rule by an individual in his or her own self-
interest; *oligarchy*—rule by a select few in their own self-interest; and
ochlocracy—mob rule.[1]

In addition to the best type of government, the purpose for even
having a government has also been debated over the ages. The best
definition for the purpose of having a government is contained in the
opening sentence of the Constitution of the United States:

We the people of the United States, in order to form a more perfect
union, establish justice, insure domestic tranquillity, provide for the
common defense, promote the general welfare, and secure the blessings of liberty to ourselves and our posterity, do ordain and establish
this Constitution for the United States of America. (Philadelphia,
Pennsylvania, September 17, 1787)

The Constitution of the United States, and the subsequently added
ten amendments known as the Bill of Rights (along with similar bills

establishing individual rights in England, France, and Canada) became the cornerstone of what is now mistakenly called "democracy" throughout the world.

It is a mistake to call these countries democracies because democracy, as was foreshadowed twenty-four hundred years ago by the critics of Aristotle, eventually means ochlocracy, or mob rule. If the majority of the people are given the right to vote on whatever they wish, it is only a matter of time before such a majority votes out the rights of a minority.

The United States, like many "democratic" countries in the world today, is a *democratic republic*—a democracy *subordinate,* or *subject to,* the rights guaranteed individuals by the U.S. Constitution, which includes the Bill of Rights.

But the United States Constitution is even more than the document that established the Bill of Rights and our form of government. Looking back over the past two hundred years, we see that the U.S. Constitution was and still is the most powerful business treatise ever written —leading directly to the emergence of the United States as the greatest economic power on the earth.

Among its many features, when it comes to economics, Section 8 of Article I of the U.S. Constitution gave Congress the right[2]

To establish post offices and post roads . . .

To promote the progress of science and useful arts, by securing for limited times to authors and inventors the exclusive right to their respective writings and discoveries . . .

To regulate commerce with foreign nations, and among the several states, and with the Indian tribes . . .

To establish a uniform rule of naturalization, and uniform laws on the subject of bankruptcies throughout the United States . . .

To coin money, regulate the value thereof, and of foreign coin, and fix the standard of weights and measures . . .

Equally important to what Article I, Section 8, of the Constitution allowed is what Article I, Sections 9 and 10, of the U.S. Constitution did not allow. They prohibited Congress and the individual states from restricting the free flow of commerce between themselves, and between themselves and other sovereign nations. Nowhere before had the principles of unlimited wealth and the laws of Abraham been so codified in a secular document. These sections state:[3]

> No state shall, without the consent of the Congress, lay any imposts or duties on imports or exports, except what may be absolutely necessary for executing its inspection laws . . .

> No preference shall be given by any regulation of commerce or revenue to the ports of one state over those of another: nor shall vessels bound to, or from, one state, be obliged to enter, clear, or pay duties in another.

> No tax or duty shall be laid on articles exported from any state.

From an economic standpoint, the genius of the U.S. Constitution was the model it established for the continual advance of technology and economic prosperity. Looking back with twenty/twenty hindsight, it seems as if Washington, Jefferson, and our other Founding Fathers knew that whatever wisdom they possessed was transient; that advancing technology and evolving politics would make today's heresy into tomorrow's dogma, and vice-versa; and that the most loving gift they could give their fledgling nation was the ability to continually evolve on its own.

Today's Heresy Is Tomorrow's Dogma[4]

In 1954, J. I. Rodale was convinced that he had made the most important discovery of his life. This was no small conviction for a man who was already the author of several best-selling books, the founder and publisher of *Prevention* magazine, and the chairman of Rodale Press — the largest health-oriented publishing company in the world.

Rodale had discovered that eating large quantities of red meat and dairy products dramatically increased the risk of heart disease, and that increased physical activity actually decreased rather than increased the risk of having a heart attack. Meanwhile, the government was spending millions encouraging Americans to eat more red meat and dairy products at every meal, and most doctors were telling patients with heart disease to reduce or eliminate physical activity. No wonder heart attacks were the leading cause of death in America!

Rodale wrote about his dramatic findings in two books: *How to Eat for a Healthy Heart* and *This Pace Is Not Killing Us*. Convinced that he could help change the diet and health of the nation, J. I. attempted to have them widely distributed. But like many prominent authors in the 1950s, he was under suspicion by Senator Joseph McCarthy's Subcommittee on Investigations, and the large New York publishers refused to have anything to do with his new books.

No problem, J. I. thought; his company would publish the books and distribute them through bookstores along with other Rodale Press publications. He was wrong. The bookstore distributors also refused to carry J. I.'s new books. Still undaunted and convinced that he could save millions of lives, J. I. had Rodale Press distribute his two new books along with a third book on family health, *The Health Finder*. Taking full-page advertisements in national publications, Rodale offered them via mail order for as little as $5.95 for all three.

The Federal Trade Commission ordered the advertising stopped, claiming that certain statements and testimonials used in the advertisements were unsubstantiated. Similar actions taken by the FTC earlier against other publishers, including Prentice Hall, had gone unchallenged.[5]

Rodale was furious. He felt that the FTC action was a blatant violation of the First Amendment guarantee of freedom of the press, and he fought back on constitutional grounds with Arnold Porter and Abe Fortas of the respected Washington law firm of Arnold, Fortas, and Porter. Fortas subsequently withdrew from the case when he was appointed a justice of the Supreme Court of the United States.

The FTC scheduled hearings before an FTC examiner, in which Rodale was ordered to present proof that people who purchased the books and followed their advice would, indeed, reduce their risk of heart disease. At these hearings, the nation's most respected medical professionals testified that there was no correlation between heart disease and eating large quantities of red meat and dairy products, and that following Rodale's advice on increasing physical activity could be fatal.

The FTC examiner ruled against Rodale. Rodale appealed the case to the full five-member commission, mainly on grounds that the First Amendment prohibited the FTC from regulating information-based products.

At the appeal to the full commission, fearing that the FTC might lose on the constitutional issue, the commission refused to rule on the First Amendment question. Instead, in closed-door session the commission re-examined the evidence presented at the original hearings and trumped up a new charge against Rodale — that the advertisements did not accurately describe the information presented in the publications. The commission then went on to convict Rodale of this new charge without notification, violating his right of due process, guaranteed by the Fifth Amendment. The full commission voted four to one that Rodale Press "cease and desist" from advertising, directly or indirectly, that readers of their publications will improve their health.[6]

During the 1960s the case dragged on through the U.S. Court of Appeals and seemed eventually headed for the Supreme Court.

In legal proceedings Thurman Arnold introduced new testimony from some of the same leading medical experts that the government originally used at the initial FTC hearings to discredit Rodale's publications. One by one these "experts" refuted their original testimony and admitted that over the years many of Rodale's original claims had become established medical facts. Arnold felt that there could never be a better example of what our Founding Fathers may have had in mind when they made freedom of the press the very first item in the Bill of Rights. The FTC attempted to back down, dropping the original complaint against the Rodales on December 4, 1968.

Then, in 1971, J. I. Rodale dropped dead on live national television while describing his legal problems with the federal government. Until he actually stopped breathing and turned blue, everyone watching the Dick Cavett show that evening thought that J. I. was facetiously faking a heart attack in order to make a point about his troubles with the FTC.

While the case never reached the Supreme Court, on July 2, 1971, the FTC promulgated a new policy stating that they would no longer require advertisers of information-based products to establish the efficacy of their claims. Perhaps more than any other single action by the U.S. government, this policy allowed the health and fitness industry to grow to the level it is at today.

Advancing technology causes the world to change so fast that today's heresy is often literally tomorrow's dogma.[7] Thanks to the Constitution and its guarantee of free speech, along with courageous men like J. I. Rodale who risked everything they had to keep the United States on the course set by our Founding Fathers, these changes are incorporated into the U.S. economy faster than in any other place on earth.

In Rodale versus the FTC, as in so many other cases that continue to establish our constitutional freedoms, it is hard not to see the invisible hand of our Father guiding the work of our Founding Fathers when they met in Philadelphia during the summer of 1787.

*I*n Chapter 6, "The Workplace of the Twenty-first Century," it was explained how Darwin's theory of natural selection proves rather than disproves the existence of God: Only a loving God could have created life forms so "perfect" that they would evolve on their own in response to changing environmental conditions. Similarly, when it came to establishing a new nation, only leaders guided by such a loving God could be instilled with enough humility to believe that they did not then possess all the answers. Recognizing this fact, our Founding Fathers established a system where neighboring states freely competed on economic matters and continually learned from one another's successes and mistakes.

In colonial times and, sadly, often today, when a neighboring country or state discovers a better way to produce something, the typical governmental response is protectionism—taxing or even prohibiting the higher-quality or lower-priced product from reaching the consumers of the less efficient state. Over the long run this not only injures consumers at the expense of inefficient domestic producers; it can even cause the collapse of whole domestic industries. Such collapses occur either because domestic producers lose access to higher-quality subcomponents for their products or because, absent competition showing them what they're missing, domestic producers fail to keep up with advancing technology.[8]

The Wealth of Nations, written in 1776 by the Scot Adam Smith, described how competition—fed by numerous individuals each pursuing their own selfish interests—creates wealth. Borrowing from established precedents in the United Kingdom, Article I, Section 8 of the U.S. Constitution seeded the advance of technology by federally protecting the rights of authors and inventors. But it was Article I, Section 10 of the Constitution that assured that the innovations of these authors and inventors would be put to widespread use faster in the new United States than anywhere else on earth.

Section 10 geometrically expanded the universe of freely competing entrepreneurs by eliminating protectionism between the states, accelerating the *creative destruction* process later described by economist Joseph Schumpeter.[9] And equally important, by leaving most of the regulation of commerce to the states, the Constitution subjected the evolving laws of each state to the same process—leading to the creation of a legal system that fostered wealth like none other. Thanks to the U.S. Constitution, *creative destruction* was applied not only to private businesses but also to the actual laws and regulations of each state.

For example, the Constitution is silent on one of the most important concepts inherent in establishing a government—laws regarding the ownership of real estate—and even goes out of its way to insure that authority to make such laws remain with the individual states.[10] Because of this, the laws relating to owning and borrowing on real estate developed differently in almost every state and are still evolving today to meet changing requirements.

When the law in a given state, say, Texas, was too favorable to borrowers of mortgage money, more settlers came to Texas until excess losses by lenders caused them to stop lending in Texas and seek more business in Oklahoma. When Oklahoma then began to grow at the expense of Texas, the Texas legislature was forced to make their mortgage financing laws more reasonable to lenders. Over hundreds of years, this process of economic "natural selection" developed a balance of state laws and regulations that are now the true most powerful economic asset of the United States.[11] Sales taxes, transportation regulations, highway construction, business legislation, consumer legislation—in each and every one of these important economic areas, it is the free competition between the states that keeps the United States from going the way of virtually every other formerly great empire.

Turning Swords into Plowshares (Almost)

In the first half of the 1980s, a nuclear confrontation between the Soviet Union and the United States seemed inevitable. In 1983, hundreds of people, including a U.S. congressman, were killed when Korean Air Lines flight 007 was shot down by Soviet fighters. In 1984, an important editor of *U.S. News & World Report* was arrested and accused of espionage in Moscow. And throughout the 1980s, the United States actively supplied Stinger missiles to the rebels fighting Soviet troops in USSR-occupied Afghanistan. The tension was best typified by President Ronald Reagan's history-making faux pas—unaware that he was on the air before a weekly radio broadcast, Reagan repeated, "The bombing begins in ten minutes," to set the audio levels on his microphone.

Although I grew up watching my neighbors build bomb shelters in the 1960s and I had learned in elementary school how to place my head between my legs and avoid the flash in case of a nuclear attack, I knew firsthand that the average Soviet citizen did not seek world domination or want nuclear war. My father had emigrated from Russia; I had friends throughout the USSR since 1965, when I became an amateur radio operator; and I first visited the USSR in 1969 at age fifteen to play chess for my high school.

In 1985, I was the managing partner of an international real estate development firm when reformer Mikhail Sergeyvich Gorbachev became the Soviet premier and announced a new policy called glasnost.[12] Within days of this announcement, I was in Moscow seeking to put together large real estate projects that would help the emerging Soviet economy. Although I worked diligently during the next five years, all of these projects failed and ended up costing my company millions of dollars.

The reason we failed had nothing to do with the strong economic need for these projects, the desire on the part of the Soviets to see them completed, or the way in which we conducted our business. The reason we failed has everything to do with the United States Constitution and tens of thousands of federal, state, and local laws and regulations that developed in the United States over the subsequent two hundred years.

Our major project in the USSR was a ten-thousand-hectare industrial park near Vladivostok, the largest Soviet warm water port, located just 350 kilometers from the Japanese coast. Vladivostok is a virtual duplicate of old San Francisco, down to the cable cars built at the turn of century by the same cable car company. Economically, it is the terminus of the Trans-Siberian railroad to Europe and the site of several airports, and was the center of Soviet military power in the Far East. When we signed the deal to build an industrial park with air, rail, and sea access, we were convinced that we couldn't fail, because of the extremely high demand for distribution and transportation facilities in nearby Japan.

For example, in the late 1980s there were over one hundred dedicated Boeing 747 air freight trips each week between Tokyo and Los Angeles at revenues exceeding $200,000 per flight. Once in Tokyo, air freight often waited at the crowded Tokyo airport for up to three days to clear Japanese customs before being put on a boat to its ultimate Japanese destination—the Japanese use water transportation for bulk goods similar to the way the United States and Europe use rail. In contrast, our company could fly freight containers from L.A. to Vladivostok via Anchorage, put the freight on a Japanese ship in Vladivostok for an eighteen-hour boat ride to, say, Yokohama, and still beat the normal L.A.-Japan delivery time by twenty-four to forty-eight hours at less than half the cost.

To serve this market, we set up an air freight company in partnership with ANT, a division of the largest Soviet airline consortium. ANT supplied us with sixty Ilysushin-72 freight planes and three hundred Soviet pilots. We supplied the freight customers, the fuel, the ships to go from Vladivostok to Japan, and American navigators for the L.A.-Anchorage leg of the flight. The nickname of our company was "Swords into Plowshares," based on the quotation of the prophet Isaiah: ". . . they shall beat their swords into plowshares, and their spears into pruning hooks; nation shall not lift up sword against nation, neither shall they learn war any more." [13] We even leased an airfield that the Soviets claimed was used by fighters that shot down KAL 007.

Four months before we were scheduled to begin flying, the director of ANT was arrested by Soviet authorities and held without bail for six months for allegedly selling tanks to the Baltic republics. Not only did our deal blow up; I personally came under suspicion when certain Soviet hard-liners began inquiring what we were planning to ship in the Ilysushin-72 freight planes. [14] The inquiry halted Swords into Plowshares and several of our other Soviet projects for months. As was later explained in an excellent book on doing business in Russia, the director of ANT was set up by anti-Gorbachev forces in order to make a political statement against perestroika during Gorbachev's 1990 campaign for president. [15]

When the deal continued months later, I learned one morning how naive we were in trying to develop a large-scale real estate project in the disintegrating Soviet Union.

We were negotiating that morning with a Japanese multinational that wanted to lease sixty hectares (about 148 acres) of land in our industrial park for a lumber processing facility. This company wanted to bring in raw lumber from Australia and process it on demand for their Japanese customers. They were willing (and preferred) to supply their own electricity, communications, labor, housing for their workers—in short, they simply wanted to pay land rent with hard currency and be left alone.

"Nyet, nyet, nyet, nyet, nyet," stammered our Soviet joint-

venture partner. "You cannot make your own electricity; there is a law against it; we will supply you whatever you need." After a pause the representative of the Japanese company asked what the price was for electricity supplied by the Soviet state.

"Ha," the Soviet smiled with pride, "in the Soviet Union, all electricity is free." The Japanese were silent. Like us, they anticipated the day when the Soviets would install electrical meters and begin charging for electricity.

"Good," replied the Japanese negotiator, "but we want a clause in the lease that if the USSR ever begins to charge for electricity, we will either be able to make our own electricity on-site or that the price charged will be no higher per kilowatt than the best international rate."

As the negotiations continued, the Soviets kept insisting they could not allow the Japanese to make their own electricity and that they would not agree to a cap on the price that they might charge for electricity. Meanwhile, the Japanese kept raising the price of such a cap until they were offering to pay the highest rate allowed in downtown Tokyo or any similar world capital.

At that point I realized what was happening. The Soviet Union had no law to allow charging for electricity, and therefore no one had any authority to bind the eventual makers of such a law to a cap on the price they could charge. A similar catch-22 situation existed for communications, labor laws, and most of the reasonable rights of quiet enjoyment that any tenant requires in a real estate title document. Worse still, the centralized government in Moscow, which prior to 1985 might have had the authority to grant such rights to a foreign investor, was on the verge of collapse. These and other legal quagmires put the Japanese multinational, and negotiations with all other prospective tenants, on permanent hold.

A similar experience awaited me the following month in Czechoslovakia, which had just gone "capitalist." Recognizing the need for established law as a foundation for economic growth, the Czechs had modeled their entire government on the U.S. Constitution. Unfortunately, it wasn't enough.

Our company was planning to renovate a building on Wenceslas Square in Prague to house a U.S. Department of Commerce commercial library and a large McDonald's restaurant. Just before we were to begin construction, the son of a pre-World War Two owner of the property challenged the validity of the Czech government's title to the property. While both the Czech government and the challenger to the title wanted our project to go ahead—since it would greatly increase the value of the property, regardless of who ended up as the owner—the legal system would not let us proceed. There was no precedent under Czech law to allow us to put the profits and/or title into escrow while we completed construction and the Czech courts determined the rightful owner of the property. Both tenants went elsewhere during the ensuing delay.

I returned to the United States and purchased a new house in Dallas, Texas. When I went to the title company to sign the papers, I was amazed at how efficient everything was—the legal description of the property, the title insurance policy, the easements granted to the utility companies and other necessary service providers—all of which contributed to my peace of mind in purchasing the property. For the first time, I realized the real foundation of our prosperity—the United States Constitution and the tens of thousands of federal, state, and local laws and regulations that have painfully evolved over the last two hundred years. While many people focus on what can be improved in our legal system, when it comes to guaranteeing the rewards for individual effort that cause unlimited wealth, no other system in the course of human history has ever come close.

*E*very action has an equal and opposite reaction.
—Newton's Third Law of Motion, 1684–1687

Although Isaac Newton wrote these words about physics, they have always been true about government. Virtually every action of government is *an equal and opposite reaction* to some apparent societal problem or injustice.

This is the major challenge facing government today. In reacting to events of the past, government action typically ends up focusing on alleviating the symptoms of problems rather than on fixing the underlying causes of problems. Moreover, with a seemingly endless series of contemporary crises to react to, there is no time for government to be *proactive*—to focus on what we can be, rather than just trying to fix past inequities.

Such was not the case when our country was founded back in the late 1700s. Washington, Jefferson, and others were reacting to the events of their time when they wrote the Constitution. But because of the sheer physical limitations of getting everyone together in one place, let alone disseminating information to the thirteen state legislatures that would have to ratify their actions, our Founding Fathers had lots of time to contemplate proactive action. Although the colonies originally declared their independence in 1776, they did not agree on the Constitution until 1787—and then it took three more years, until 1790, to obtain ratification from all of the original thirteen colonies.[16]

As was already demonstrated in the way the Constitution laid the foundation for our economic prosperity, this time taken is reflected in how focused the Constitution was on the future of building a great nation, rather than on a morass of current events, which seems to dominate our legislative process today. The framers of our Constitution either understood the concepts of unlimited wealth or were guided by an invisible hand that knew where they should be going. The Constitution promoted economic competition between individual businesspeople and individual state governments, and established the public sector as the supplier of last resort rather than the usurper of private sector opportunity. It is important to appreciate today how radical this devotion to private enterprise was back in the eighteenth century—the age of mercantilism—when the definition of government itself often meant the state control of economic activity.

But in promoting private enterprise and free competition, the Constitution was not blind to economic reality and technological economies of scale. The founders of the United States recognized that there were certain activities then best performed by a central organization or government—like national defense, regulation of bankruptcies, coining money, and establishing a post office. These and other services centrally provided by the federal government promoted the economic welfare of every state.

However, over time changes occurred in the underlying technology that originally made the government better at providing certain services than the private sector, and in most cases the government was not politically able to react to such changing technology.

It once made (and still does make) economic sense for the government to build and maintain roads, airports, and other key transportation facilities—to ensure every American the right to efficient and open transit throughout the United States. The U.S. interstate highway system, developed through a unique cooperative effort of federal, state, and local government, is the envy of the free world and was a major factor in making the United States the world's leading economic power. Its success lies in the way the federal government sets the uniform standards for safe and easy access but allows the individual states to design the routes, acquire the land, and let the (private sector) contracts for construction. (States claim reimbursement for a majority of the cost once projects are completed in accordance with federal specifications.) Without such federal intervention, it is unlikely that states would have gone out of their way to connect their cities with those of neighboring states, which would have limited the total size of our regional economies and the increasing specialization that spurs unlimited wealth.

It once made economic sense for the government to set up the U.S. Post Office for efficient communication between all Americans. But today, even with enormous federal subsidies, the U.S. Post Office is often the highest-priced, lowest-quality provider of each of the services it offers. This is because in a federal institution with guaranteed employment, the employees and managers of the U.S. Post Office have little incentive to implement new advances in technology.

It once made economic sense for the government to mandate a monopoly on long-distance telephone service so that every American could be connected to one another—if this hadn't occurred, who knows how long it might have taken to get service to more remote parts of the country? But in the 1970s, when technology had advanced to the point where multiple long-distance carriers could economically serve customers anywhere and connect to one another, the federal government terminated this monopoly. The resultant competition between different long-distance carriers caused the price of a long-distance call to fall to a fraction of what it was—greatly benefiting American consumers and the entire U.S. economy. Sadly, however, this example of government relinquishing unnecessary control is an exception rather than the rule.

It once made economic sense for the government to set up a single government-run school in each locality to insure that every American child would receive quality education. But today, advances in transportation, the shift to an urban economy, and advancing educational technology have made the entire concept of government-owned schools obsolete. Just think what shopping malls, airline service, motion pictures, and television programming might be like today if there was only one government-owned provider of each service in each location. Moreover, because of its inability to adapt to changing technology, the $330 billion virtual government monopoly on primary and secondary education has become a major impediment in keeping every American child from receiving quality education.

What's Wrong with Public Education

The 180-day U.S. school year was designed in 1860 for an agrarian economy in which children were needed at home to help with chores and harvesting. Today, when most other industrial nations have a 220- to 240-day school year, more than just our educational calendar remains in the nineteenth century— teaching methods themselves also haven't changed in over 130 years.

Schools today fail not only the less intelligent students, who need our help the most, but also our brightest students, who should need our help the least. Thousands of the most successful people in the postboomer generation, from Steven Jobs to Bill Gates, dropped out of or never attended college.

In the 1970s my colleagues and I at the University of Pennsylvania worked on interactive computer-based "teaching machines" that we saw would one day bring the best teacher of every subject to every student. Such interactive technology would allow educational institutions to break free of their communist mentality—all students could learn at their own pace and in their own manner. Moreover, this technology could also allow teachers to be uniformly judged on their performance in motivating students from similar groups to learn—which would allow school districts to begin paying educators more for innovation on the job rather than for duration.

Sadly, as this technology progressed in the 1980s, rather than be incorporated into the $330 billion educational system, it exploded into a new $20 billion video game business. And in the 1990s, as private sector companies began producing complete educational curriculums on CD-ROM for home use, it seems as if this technology will benefit middle- and upper-middle-class students, who, on a relative basis, need it the least.

The cost of providing educational CD-ROM technology to 50 million U.S. schoolchildren is minuscule compared to what is wasted every day by a system that currently pays teachers for how long they have been teaching rather than how well they teach. It would cost about $300 per student per year to provide every child with a CD-ROM personal computer, contrasted with the more than $7,500 that U.S. school systems currently spend per student per year on K-12 education.

In the middle of the nineteenth century, Abraham Lincoln and other farsighted Americans saw the economic wisdom in mandating publicly financed education for every American child. Citizens were forced to pay educational taxes based on the value of their personal wealth as determined by the appraised value of their real estate, rather than on the number of children that they sent to public school. Our leaders correctly hypothesized that the economic rewards from educating every American child would accrue uniformly to the entire economy, and thus should be borne by individuals in proportion to their wealth rather than in proportion to their number of children.

Unfortunately, the means rather than the intended end of this process became fixed—the value of a person's real estate in our nonagrarian urban economy bears little relation to his or her personal wealth. Today, the financing of public education through real property taxation rapes our inner cities, federally subsidizes "private" education for the upper middle class, and denies disadvantaged children access to the American dream by denying them the ability to meet the children and families of more fortunate Americans.

One of the first things an upwardly mobile family does as they prosper is move to a location where their children can receive a better education. Typically, this means moving to an area where the citizens voluntarily vote in high tax-deductible property taxes earmarked for education, and zoning requirements designed to

GOD WANTS YOU TO BE RICH

keep out the less fortunate. This wouldn't be so insidious if the

keep out the less fortunate. This wouldn't be so insidious if the federal government weren't the 50-percent-or-more silent partner in the process. By allowing individuals a federal tax deduction on their real property taxes, along with allowing communities to finance exclusive public education through tax-deductible real property taxes, the federal government massively accelerates this unnatural process of economic segregation.

In the Pulitzer Prize–winning 1960 novel, *To Kill A Mockingbird,* Scout Finch invites her less fortunate classmate home to dinner and then makes fun of him when the boy pours molasses over his meat. After being chastised by her father for embarrassing her guest, Scout begins to appreciate how fortunate she is relative to her poverty-stricken classmate. As the story develops, both children greatly benefit from getting to know someone from "the other side of the tracks."

This type of sharing and learning between the different social classes was an integral part of the American experience. But since World War Two, it has been happening less and less, partially because of misguided federal policies that subsidize the education of the upper middle class by allowing them to pay for technically public "private" schools through tax-deductible real estate taxes on their homes.

Thus, two apparent problems today with public education are the lack of technological innovation and the way government indirectly subsidizes better schools for middle- and upper-class students. Unfortunately, our state legislatures are beginning to focus only on the funding issue—passing "Robin Hood" laws that mandate the same amount of spending per pupil in each district.[17] Unless they find a way to deal with the first issue—the lack of technological innovation that results from paying teachers for duration—the states' good intentions to equalize public education will be for naught.

If states simply try to equalize spending per pupil without reforming the entire system, our public schools will "equalize" —insuring that every student receives an inferior education, not just the economically disadvantaged. The reason is that there is little or no correlation between the amount of money spent per pupil and the quality of public education.[18] This is because increasing funds for education typically means just paying more to those teachers who have been teaching the longest, rather than paying more to those teachers who are teaching the best and utilizing the latest technology.

*I*n education and in most other consumer services provided by government, the inability of the public sector to keep up with technology causes economic destruction. The accelerating migration from cities to suburbs, and more recently from developed states like California and New York to less developed ones like Texas and Arizona, is tied primarily to technological stagnation by existing government providers of services.

In New York and San Francisco, the average city employee in 1991 earned $34,812 and $44,736 respectively, contrasted with, say, Houston and Phoenix, where the average city employee in 1991 earned $26,568 and $36,708.[19] Surprisingly, despite significantly higher costs of living in certain cities, the average annual wage paid to municipal employees across the nation, approximately $31,800, is relatively constant. Yet belying these numbers are tremendous differences between what taxpayers receive from their municipal employees.

In New York and San Francisco, per ten thousand population, there are respectively 532 and 358 municipal employees, in contrast with Houston and Phoenix, which have 123 and 112 municipal employees per ten thousand population.[20] Assuming a relatively constant level of municipal services, the employees of Houston and Phoenix are approximately 400 and 300 percent more efficient than their counterparts in New York and San Francisco. Or put another way, after adjusting for differences in total population, for every municipal employee in Houston or Phoenix there are roughly four municipal employees in New York and three municipal employees in San Francisco.

Such massive differences in employee productivity translate directly into businesses and consumers paying three to five times the amount per capita in urban taxation. City taxes per inhabitant in New York and San Francisco were $2,190 and $1,302 respectively, in contrast with Houston and Phoenix, where city taxes per inhabitant were $440 and $335.[21]

But Houston, Phoenix, and other cities with relatively high municipal employee productivity are not far behind their less fortunate counterparts. Without competition to spur the implementation of newer and better methods to accomplish their tasks, it is only a matter of time before the productivity per municipal employee in these newer cities falls to the dismal level of their older competitors.

In the private sector over the past few decades, *creative destruction* spurred by competition has caused the displacement of tens of millions of American jobs. But the increases in productivity from such displacement have dramatically improved the economic lifestyle of almost every American—and even caused the formation of more jobs than were originally displaced. Total employment between 1980 and 1992 grew 20 percent, from approximately 100 to 120 million employed people, almost twice the rate of growth of the total population, which grew 12 percent from approximately 228 to 255 million people.[22]

However, little of this displacement and increased efficiency has taken place in the public sector. When it comes to purchasing computers and training their employees how to use them, or simply establishing a better route for sanitation workers to use in picking up refuse, the longer our municipal employees remain on the job, the more inefficient they seem to become at their tasks. Creative destruction simply does not exist without competition. In the absence of a competitor forcing individuals and organizations to implement new technology, no one seems to be able to put in the extra hours necessary to learn the better methods that drive our modern economy.

So what is the answer? How can municipalities and state and federal governments get off the one-way ride to economic collapse that seems to be their destiny?

The answer is privatization—the elimination of virtually all municipal employment for other than police, fire, and other social-type services. This answer is nothing new—it has been suggested by countless studies and commissions ever since Roosevelt's New Deal spawned the growth of government activity. However, it is now time to get serious about its implementation.

It is time to recognize that most of our efforts toward privatization have failed. Regardless of the potential benefits, democracy will simply not allow the termination of the jobs of a significant percentage of the voting members of a community. Instead, communities must be willing to bite the bullet and buy out the jobs of existing municipal employees.[23] Otherwise, rising inefficiencies in the municipal workplace, which are far more expensive than simply rising salaries, will cause the economic collapse of their communities.

> . . . eye for eye, tooth for tooth, hand for hand, foot for foot, burn for burn, wound for wound, bruise for bruise.
>   —EXODUS, 21:24–25 (NIV)

Crime is the area where our government has failed the most. Federal, state, and local governments currently spend approximately $78 billion each year on criminal justice—$39 billion for police, $29 billion for prisons, and $10 billion for courts.[24] Looking back over the number of crimes committed and how these costs have risen over the past twenty years, it would seem as if the amount of crime is directly proportional to the amount spent to prevent it, rather than the other way around. Each year approximately 23 million, or 25 percent of all U.S. households, are touched by crime—a household is considered touched by crime if during the year a member of the household experienced a burglary, theft, or assault.[25]

But surprisingly, despite the endless barrage of media attention paid to this epidemic, there is a relatively simple *economic* reason why crime is out of control. This reason is that the real costs of crime are not borne by government: The real costs of crime are borne by the private sector, and the agenda of the private sector in combating crime is often diametrically opposed to the agenda of the public sector.

While government spends $78 billion each year on criminal justice, the private sector spends an additional $596 billion on the failure of government to stop crime, broken down as in the chart below.[26]

PRIVATE SECTOR CRIME COSTS (billions)	
Private security	$ 64
Loss of life and work	$202
Crimes against businesses	$120
Stolen goods and fraud	$ 60
Drug abuse	$ 40
Drunk driving	$110
Total private sector cost	$596

The government agenda in combating crime is focused on the biblical concept of retribution—eye for eye, tooth for tooth. The private sector agenda is focused on dealing with the aftermath of the government's failure to stop crime—insurance claims, moving to safer neighborhoods, and so forth. If both parties were to work together to prevent crime—rather than deal with its aftermath—crime could be reduced considerably. This would have already occurred were it not for the economic schism in criminal justice economics between the public and private sectors.

When a person is incarcerated for a crime, the cost of incarceration is borne entirely by the public sector. Today, approximately $29 billion is spent by federal, state, and local governments to incarcerate approximately 750,000 criminals—an average of about $38,667 per criminal per year. Each year millions of criminals are released before serving the full term of their sentences because the public sector supposedly doesn't have enough money to keep them all incarcerated. While approximately 750,000 criminals are now behind bars, an additional 3.65 million criminals are under "correctional supervision," on probation or parole. Over 81 percent of criminals are recidivists—having been convicted at least twice for separate offenses.[27]

The public sector decision to release a criminal before serving his or her sentence is often driven by the $38,667 annual public sector cost of keeping them incarcerated. Yet, once released, the cost to the private sector per released criminal greatly exceeds $38,667 per annum. Dividing the $674 billion public *and* private sector annual cost of crime by the 4.4 million known criminals yields an annual cost to society per criminal of $153,182. Moreover, if one excludes for a moment the 2.67 million criminals on probation and only considers the 1.3 million more dangerous criminals in prison or on parole, then the annual cost to society per freed or incarcerated criminal rises to a staggering $518,000 per annum![28]

In other words, if the public sector had to bear the real costs of releasing criminals before serving their completed sentences, there would probably be far fewer released criminals and far less crime. Here's an economic way to accomplish this goal that would also give each state legislature the power to regulate a tolerable level of crime in their communities.

A statutory amount of victim compensation could be set by each state legislature for each type of crime—ranging from, say, $100,000 for a murder or rape down to $10,000 for an auto theft. When one of these crimes is committed by a person who is out on probation or parole—that is, a known, already convicted criminal whom the state has affirmatively decided to let go free—the state would be forced to pay 80 percent of the statutory amount to the victim (or insurer) and 20 percent to the police department responsible for the arrest and conviction. This way, the state would be held accountable to the private sector for their actions when they allow a convicted criminal the luxury of going free before serving their full sentence.

For example, assume a known recidivist is being considered for probation whose statistical profile says that he has an 80 percent chance of being arrested during the next two months for auto theft. The judicial authority considering the release would weigh the $8,000 expected state cost (80 percent of $10,000) in victim/police compensation against the $6,444 two-month incarceration cost (one-sixth of $38,667 per annum). In this case, the expected value of denying probation to the judicial authority would be a positive $1,556. By raising and lowering the amount of victim compensation paid for each crime, a state could economically regulate a tolerable amount for each type of crime against its humanitarian desire to grant early release for convicted offenders. Moreover, the economic argument of *having* to release convicted criminals just wouldn't hold true anymore.

Some people might argue that such a process would end one of the greatest things about the U.S. criminal justice system—the latitude granted our judicial authorities to show mercy in special cases. Unfortunately, while this is partially true, no one is showing mercy to the victims of violent or economic crimes. My immigrant father once explained to me how the U.S. system of justice is founded on the principle that it is better to let one hundred guilty criminals go free than have one innocent man convicted of a crime that he did not commit. It wasn't until years later that I realized the fallacy in this approach— one hundred guilty rapists, for example, cause the deaths and ruin the lives of thousands of innocent women per year.

Our criminal justice system seems to function on the concept that criminals are like Jean Valjean in Victor Hugo's *Les Misérables,* an otherwise honorable man who spent decades in jail after stealing a loaf of bread to feed his family. However, the truth is that the overwhelming majority of criminals today are professionals—vocationally committing hundreds or thousands of crimes day in and day out until they finally get caught. And once caught, after making bail they typically commit even more crimes in order to raise the money for lawyers and other expenses of journeying through the court system. To the professional criminals that commit most property crimes, getting arrested, making bail, going to court, and even serving time in jail are viewed as nothing more than one of their costs of doing business.

In 1985 the city of Baltimore experimented with a program in which persons arrested for auto theft were scheduled for speedy trial and bail was limited and set at very high levels. Within months the rate of automobile theft fell 95 per cent as Baltimore's auto thieves moved on to more hospitable environments. Unfortunately, the city was forced to abandon this experiment and focus it efforts on crimes that received more public attention—having an automobile stolen for most people is nothing more than an inconvenience, because of the proliferation of auto insurance.

One might think that automobile insurers or manufacturers would be willing to fund such extra efforts on behalf of municipalities to reduce auto theft. Sadly, while numerous ways exist to eliminate automobile theft almost overnight, there is little economic incentive to do so, since our society has unwittingly built a system that economically thrives on this and other types of property crime.

Automobile Theft

Every year approximately 1.3 million cars are stolen in the United States—which causes billions in economic losses to society. Poorer owners are especially hard hit by this crisis because they usually cannot afford comprehensive automobile insurance.

Most stolen automobiles are disassembled and sold for spare parts, particularly body parts, which are needed by collision repair shops. This was well illustrated by the T-top craze in the early 1980s. Few manufacturers back then made replacement T-top roof panels because a car is often beyond repair once collision damage has affected the roof. Meanwhile, owners seeking to purchase replacements for their stolen T-top roof panels created a spiraling demand for more (stolen) roof panels.

It is estimated that today the majority of the large parts used by collision repair shops may come from stolen vehicles.[29]

Yet, as incredible as it may seem, one of the major reasons we have not solved this problem lies in the fact that two of the largest beneficiaries of stolen cars are the automobile insurance companies and the new car manufacturers.

The automobile insurance companies benefit because in most states they are allowed to raise their premiums only by the amount by which their losses increased during the previous year, plus a percentage markup for profit and overhead. Thus, ever-increasing automobile theft rates lead directly to ever-increasing profits for the automobile insurance companies. Many of them might even go out of business if fewer cars were stolen, since their initial gains in reduced claims would be more than eaten up in lower premiums the following year.

Automobile manufacturers and dealers benefit even more from motor vehicle theft. The 1.3 million annual victims of motor vehicle theft represent a significant portion of the approximately 10 million annual purchasers of new motor vehicles. Indeed, an auto dealer's best customer is typically a victim who has just received a check from his or her insurance company and needs an immediate replacement for a stolen vehicle.

No wonder the automobile insurance companies and manufacturers haven't yet gotten together to solve the problem of auto theft!

And yet solving the problem of automobile theft can easily be accomplished.

Insurance companies should simply not pay for any collision repairs unless the invoice from the body shop contains a certificate of origin for all parts costing more than $100. This would force the body shops to ensure the legitimacy of their purchases and ultimately eliminate most of the market for stolen vehicles.

The insurance companies should be given time to develop their own system for accomplishing this goal, with the state or federal government ready to mandate a system if they fail to voluntarily comply. To insure compliance of the insurance companies, the states should allow them to share part of the savings in reduced claims, rather than have to apply 100 percent or more of these savings toward reducing premiums.

Since the 1970s, the federal government has taxed automakers for the cost to society of their vehicles that have below-average fuel economy. It is time to similarly begin charging automakers for the cost to society of their vehicles that have above-average theft rates—a stolen vehicle costs society a lot more than a vehicle with below-average fuel economy. This would encourage the automobile manufacturers to develop better antitheft devices and parts-registration systems.[30] Additionally, each automobile manufacturer should be required to pay $100 or more to the local police department wherever a vehicle is reported stolen.

A similar private sector solution to a public sector problem was accomplished earlier in this century when every state, working with the automobile manufacturers, implemented a system of government automobile registration using vehicle identification numbers (VIN). The VIN has virtually eliminated the domestic market for whole (that is, nondisassembled) stolen vehicles by eliminating the demand for them; no one wants to purchase a motor vehicle that cannot be registered. (The few stolen vehicles that are not disassembled are shipped overseas intact.) VIN numbers could also be used today to recover most stolen vehicles within minutes of being taken.

Most progressive cities today have instituted "toll tags" on their toll roads and bridges—electronically readable window stickers that allow drivers to pass through toll booths without stopping and receive a monthly bill showing the exact time and place of each toll use. If an electronic copy of each vehicle's VIN were built into the windshield of every car, a stolen vehicle could be located in minutes when it passed through a toll booth or by a highway access point. What would be the point of stealing a car that you couldn't drive on a major road?

In the alchemic world we live in, virtually everything, including property crime, is driven by demand. Once we understand this, we can solve the problem of automobile theft by concentrating on reducing the demand for stealing cars in the first place rather than by trying in vain to reduce the seemingly endless supply of car thieves.

The main reason we still have automobile theft, and many other socioeconomic problems, is that we have been trying to apply outmoded economic supply-driven concepts to problems that require innovative alchemic demand-driven solutions.

*U*nemployment is another area in which the well-meaning intentions of government have had the opposite effect.

The overwhelming majority of unemployment today is caused by technological change. Such unemployment is actually the first sign of economic growth—provided that technologically displaced workers obtain jobs producing new products or services that add to our overall wealth.

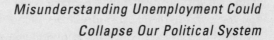

The Greatest Challenge
of Our Century

Misunderstanding Unemployment Could
Collapse Our Political System

Imagine a self-sufficient island with ten men, all of whom make their living by fishing with poles from a communal boat. Along comes a missionary who shows the men a new, technologically better way of fishing—using a large net instead of ten individual lines. Now two fisherman, one to pilot the boat and one to throw the net, can catch the same number of fish as ten fishermen could with lines.

On the surface, unemployment on the island has risen from zero to 80 percent, since eight of the ten fishermen are now out of a job. Yet although eight of the men are no longer working, the island society as a whole is still as wealthy, because two fishermen using the net catch as many fish as ten did with lines.

Now the island society must decide how to feed and clothe the eight unemployed fishermen. The options are simple: They can tax the two working fishermen 80 percent of their earnings and redistribute this 80 percent to the unemployed, or they can help the eight unemployed fishermen develop new jobs that will add to the wealth of the community.

The former option sounds ludicrous. What society would increase the marginal tax rate to 80 percent (or more) on the producers of society (in our example, the men with the nets)? Yet, during the first half of this century, this was the world's primary response to short-term unemployment as the implementation of technological advances made certain people far richer than their neighbors. Between 1913 and 1960, the United States and western Europe instituted highly progressive income taxes, increasing the personal marginal income tax rate to 91 percent and more on the producers of society. Over roughly the same time period, eastern Europe became Communist (effectively 100 percent taxation), removing the individual's incentive to implement new technological methods and putting their economies into a long-term economic spiral.

For all their good, the massive productivity increases made possible by advancing technology (in our example, two men performing the work of ten) have not occurred without problems. On the positive side, society has become much richer as the temporarily displaced individuals found new, more productive jobs that added to our total economic wealth. Today virtually 95 percent of our economy involves producing new and innovative products and services that didn't even exist fifty years ago. On the negative side, however, the increased speed with which this is occurring today is causing massive social displacement. Indeed, we may even be approaching a time—perhaps in this decade—when the majority of the workers in our society at a given moment may be technologically displaced.

The economist Joseph Schumpeter's last great book, *Capitalism, Socialism, and Democracy* (1942), focused on the social turmoil that occurs in a rapidly advancing capitalist society as individuals are displaced from their jobs by the implementation of better technological methods. While Schumpeter praised such technological advancement for increasing the size of the total economic pie, he predicted that capitalism would eventually self-destruct, because the people displaced by advancing technology would democratically vote in a socialist form of government. He further predicted that after many years of socialism and the resultant economic decay that socialism would cause, the same people (or their children) would turn vehemently capitalist and start the cycle all over again.

As evidenced by recent events in eastern Europe and the former Soviet Union, Schumpeter correctly predicted that socialist countries would democratically turn capitalist. But his dire prediction for capitalist countries has not yet occurred. This is because, despite massive technological advancement in capitalist countries from the 1940s through the 1980s, the majority of people were not permanently displaced by the advance of technology. They were not permanently displaced because society developed a need for new employees who could produce new goods and new services, and the ability to train these new workers, at a pace exceeding the rate of displacement from their old jobs.

However, in the early 1990s, the rate of technological advancement greatly accelerated, displacing millions of Americans from their jobs. It now remains to be seen

(1) whether the same advancing technology can again develop jobs fast enough for these displaced Americans;

(2) whether our government will be able to modify existing educational and vocational programs to assist displaced workers in adapting to new opportunities; or

(3) whether, if neither of these events occurs, our government will begin implementing socialist and other antigrowth policies designed to limit technological displacement—in effect killing the goose that has been laying our golden eggs since the beginning of this century.

It is all-important that every citizen of every country understand how technological displacement has caused society to grow in the past and how it will allow society to grow in the future. If we fail to understand this, Schumpeter's dire prediction for our capitalist nations may still prove true.

We have the economic power to employ all technologically displaced workers. This is because, by definition, the wages of the technologically displaced workers are being earned by the employers who laid them off and by the (often higher paid) remaining employees who operate the machinery or equipment that displaced them.

And as explained in Chapter 4, "Economic Alchemy," by the Fourth and Fifth Laws of Economic Alchemy, the stockholders of these employers and the remaining higher paid employees have an unlimited demand for new goods and services that hopefully will be ultimately produced by the displaced employees.

However, because our society is built on an economic and educational model that assumes that workers will learn a profession or trade and perform that function for the rest of their lives, too many of our displaced workers do not find any job within a reasonable time period, let alone a new or better one that adds to their and our overall wealth. The reason is that we do not currently have a system that reaches out to the displaced worker offering education for tomorrow's jobs as well as the opportunity to find one.

Today, the median length of time that an average employee stays within a single industry, let alone with a single employer, has fallen to 6.5 years—ranging from twenty-five years for barbers to less than 1.5 years for food service personnel. No wonder unemployment is skyrocketing!

Over one hundred years ago our leaders realized the economic wisdom of using public funds to educate every American child— correctly surmising that the financial rewards of educating children would accrue to the entire economy. Similarly, this same wisdom should apply today to using public funds to re-educating every displaced American worker. And fortunately, such efforts could be initially accomplished without new expenditures merely by productively redirecting funds from existing programs.

Unemployment Compensation

At the beginning of the 1992 presidential election campaign, the Democratic and Republican Parties squared off on the issue of unemployment compensation.

The Democrats wanted to extend unemployment benefits from roughly six to twelve months—arguing that because the economy was recovering more slowly from the "Reagan Recession," laid-off employees needed more time until their employers called them back to work. The Republicans counterargued that the economy was recovering faster and that benefits should be extended from six to only eight months. The two parties finally compromised, and Congress extended unemployment benefits to nine to ten months (depending on individual state contributions).

The real losers in this debate were the unemployed—the overwhelming majority of whom were thrown out of work by technological change, not the 1991 recession. What these displaced employees needed was education on how to repair electronic fuel injectors instead of carburetors, or how to make digital CDs instead of vinyl records—not longer unemployment compensation periods and meaningless political promises.

What our government should have done to help these people was to give them what they really needed—six months in cash benefits to feed their families *plus* six months in education benefits—and make using their education benefits mandatory in order to receive their cash benefits.

For example, suppose an unemployed person in a certain state received a six-month cash unemployment benefit of $150 per week. Now, he or she would receive the same cash benefit to support a family plus a six-month education benefit worth $150 per week, both redeemable at any licensed education or training center. The center would dispense the $150 cash benefit only when and if the displaced employee showed up for $150 in mandatory education courses.

The government wouldn't have to worry about the quality or the content of the privately provided education courses—the free market would determine the best curriculum. Newly unemployed people would flock to the best courses (résumé writing, improving job skills, typing, and so forth) to help them get a job before their six months of benefits ran out. Unemployment benefits are given only to formerly employed people, virtually all of whom desperately want to get back to work.

There is nothing new about the unemployment we are experiencing today, except for the increased speed with which it is occurring. Changes that used to take fifty years now occur in five or ten years, causing us to deal with the problems of retraining existing employees within single lifetimes, as opposed to passively waiting for their descendants to choose other, more productive occupations.

Fortunately, the answers to unemployment and most of the social problems in this decade lie in learning from experiences that occurred in the past five decades. However, it is necessary to condense time when studying them, so we can develop innovative solutions that can be implemented in much shorter periods of time.

9

LEADERSHIP

The hunting dog marched proudly in front of the hunters, keeping a watchful eye behind to make sure that he was being followed. When the hunters turned to go in the opposite direction, the dog sprinted to a new place in front of them, again proudly proclaiming his place as their "leader."

Politicians today are like hunting dogs—carefully watching the latest poll to see which direction the public wants to go, and then adopting this position as our "leaders." This is fortunate because today we no longer need so-called wise leaders who "know better than we do" to make laws controlling our lives. Today, thanks to the revolution in information technology, we debate every issue—in newspapers, on radio and television talk shows, with our friends and family—until we, as a people, reach a consensus on where we want to go. Then there never seems to be any shortage of "leaders" waiting to claim the credit for taking us there.

In the past, when most jobs were menial, managing typically often meant ordering subordinates to work a certain way. Today, when most jobs require more brains than brawn, ordering subordinates to work a certain way is a sure-fire recipe for disaster. Managers must now educate their subordinates *why* they should work in a certain manner, until everyone reaches a consensus on how to proceed.

Similarly, in the past, when only a small minority of the public was capable of understanding the issues and there was no effective way to communicate with them, political leadership typically meant our legislators doing what they thought was best and then communicating afterwards with their constituents. Today, political leaders must help educate their constituents to develop a consensus in order to succeed. This process also has the added benefit of insuring the successful implementation of legislated changes in public policy, since the majority of the public should already be supporting these changes before they are passed by the legislature.

For example, as a nation in the 1970s we developed a consensus that we were willing to be inconvenienced as consumers in order to leave this land a better environmental place for our children. Since then, our legislatures have passed hundreds of laws and regulations that have made a real difference in cleaning up and protecting our environment. Moreover, while developing this consensus our society automatically obtained the voluntary compliance of the people that count the most—the schoolchildren and adults who practice conservation and recycling every day in their communities.

Science fiction writers and theologians have dreamed of the utopian day when our spiritual senses will be united into a collective consciousness. Today, for at least most economic issues, the end goal of such a dream is almost at hand. Thanks to instantaneous and ubiquitous electronic communication, most people wanting to contribute to the decision-making process are involved, and our political leaders rarely take a position without first finding out where the collective consciousness or consensus is on each issue.

Protecting the environment, eliminating smoking in public places, reducing the size of government, replacing welfare with workfare, maintaining private health care, eliminating trade barriers with our neighbors—these are but a few of the hundreds of areas in which our legislators have recently responded to the general consensus—often a consensus that emerged only once the issue was thrown open to national debate.

And this recent responsiveness of federal, state, and local government to their constituents is just the beginning. By the end of this decade, thanks to numerous forms of interactive electronic technology, our legislators will literally be polling every one of their constituents on virtually every issue. This will complete the shift of political power that began this century with the start of the information age— the shift of political power from those skilled in politics to those skilled in educating the public, particularly about economic issues.

In Chapter 3 (see "John Maynard Keynes") we saw how one can

often learn more from studying the mistakes of our greatest minds rather than from studying where they were correct. Joseph A. Schumpeter was clearly one of the greatest minds ever when it comes to understanding the true value of the entrepreneur and how an economy functions in a rapidly advancing technological age. But so far, Joseph Schumpeter has not been correct in what he regarded as his greatest work—his prediction of the self-destruction of our capitalist societies.

The word "economics" comes from the Greek word *oikonomia,* meaning the "management of a household:"[1] While today "economics" has come to mean the study of business and government issues by professional academics, the real economists in our society are the ones who practice economics—the hundreds of millions of people seeking to economically manage their own households or lives every day.

And when it comes to *continually* proving Schumpeter wrong in what he regarded as his greatest triumph, there is nothing more important than the role that now befalls you, the real economist, the reader of this book—the role to continually teach every member of our society *how* and *why* we live in a world of abundance, and *how* and *why* God wants every one of us to be rich. God bless you.

APPENDIX

The Principles and Six Laws of Economic Alchemy

The theory of economic alchemy explains how technology determines the nature and supply of our physical resources, what controls the speed with which technology advances, how technology determines the nature and level of consumer demand, and how we can use the technology gap to see what's ahead around the corner. The following is a brief summary of the three principles and six laws of economic alchemy.

PRINCIPLES OF ECONOMIC ALCHEMY

1. Technology is the major determinant of wealth because it determines the nature and supply of physical resources.
2. The advance of technology is determined mainly by our ability to process information.
3. The backlog of unimplemented technological advances (the "technology gap") is the true predictor of economic growth for both the individual and society.

THE FIRST LAW OF ECONOMIC ALCHEMY

By enabling us to make productive use of particular raw materials, technology determines what constitutes a physical resource.

Definitional Technology—technology that gives us the ability to define valuable physical resources.

THE SECOND LAW OF ECONOMIC ALCHEMY

Technology determines our supply of existing physical resources by determining both the efficiency with which we use resources and our ability to find, obtain, distribute, and store them.

Quantity Technology—technology that determines the available quantity of already-defined physical resources.

Use Technology—technology that determines the efficiency by which we use physical resources.

Supply Technology—technology that determines our ability to *find, obtain, distribute,* and *store* physical resources.

$W = PT^n$

W stands for wealth, P for physical resources (that is, the traditional measures of wealth, such as land, labor, minerals, and water), T for technology, and n for the exponential effect of technological advances on themselves.

THE THIRD LAW OF ECONOMIC ALCHEMY

The rate at which a society's technology advances is determined by the relative level of its ability to process information.

Information-Processing Technology—technology that gives us the ability to distribute information.

THE FOURTH LAW OF ECONOMIC ALCHEMY

By providing us with new products and processes that change the way in which we live, technology determines what constitutes a need, and hence the nature of consumer demand.

THE FIFTH LAW OF ECONOMIC ALCHEMY

Technology determines the level of consumer demand by determining the price at which goods can be sold.

Alchemic Demand—demand for goods and services in excess of basic physiological needs.

Quantity Demand—demand for more quantity of an existing already-owned product.

Quality Demand—demand for a different quality version of an existing already-owned product.

THE SIXTH LAW OF ECONOMIC ALCHEMY

The immediate economic potential for an individual, an industry, or a society can be explained by examining the technology gap—the best practices possible with current knowledge versus the practices in actual use.

R-I-T (Ready-to-Be-Implemented Technological Advance)—a fully developed better product or method that is ready to be put to use.

User Transparent—from the standpoint of the user, requiring no additional skills or training than the product, method, or practice it is meant to replace (applies to R-I-Ts).

NOTES

Chapter 1: God Wants You to Be Rich

1. Paul Samuelson and William D. Nordhaus, *Economics,* 12th ed. (New York: McGraw-Hill, 1985), 4.

2. This exact statement appears also in Mark 10:25 and Luke 18:25 in the same context.

3. In Matthew 19:17 Jesus states that one must follow the Ten Commandments in order to get to heaven. The rich young man then asks: "All these things I have kept from my youth up: what lack I yet?" Jesus then explains the obligation of the rich to help the poor (Matthew 19:21).

4. After the idle laborers go into the fields and work, they are paid the same for one hour of work as was promised earlier to a group of laborers who worked for an entire day. When the earlier group protests that they were cheated, they are admonished because they were paid exactly what they had originally bargained for; they were not injured in any way by the generosity shown by the foreman to the second group, who had shown the initiative to begin working without a contract (Matthew 20:1–16).

5. At New York University, we try to accomplish this by using the "case method" of instruction—students are asked to write papers and make presentations in first-person form, setting themselves up as the protagonist in each situation.

Chapter 2: The Covenant

1. The word "seed" in this chapter is translated from the Aramaic word *zera,* meaning "posterity" (Genesis 22:1–18).

2. "Neither shall thy name any more be called Abram, but thy name

shall be Abraham; for a father of many nations have I made thee" (Genesis 17:5).

3. Genesis 23:1–20.

4. At this point I also ask the schoolchildren to vote on whether we should invite a passing ship of fifty destitute foreign schoolchildren to come live on our island and share our newly developed wealth. If the lesson has been successful, during the ensuing debate the students realize themselves that they and the new immigrants will both become even richer when the newcomers are welcomed with open arms into our island society.

5. Richard Rodgers and Oscar Hammerstein, "Happy Talk," *South Pacific,* 1958.

Chapter 3: The Search for Camelot

1. Paul Zane Pilzer, *Unlimited Wealth* (New York: Crown Publishers, 1994), xiii.

2. The world's most popular textbook on economics defines the science it aims to teach as follows: "Economics is the study of how people and society choose to employ *scarce* resources that could have alternative uses in order to produce various commodities and to distribute them for consumption" (emphasis added). Paul Samuelson and William D. Nordhaus, *Economics,* 12th ed. (New York: McGraw-Hill, 1985), 4.

3. Nobel Prizes were established by philanthropist Alfred Bernard Nobel (1833–1896), a Swedish chemist and inventor who invented dynamite as a safer form of volatile nitroglycerine. The first Nobel Prizes were awarded in 1901 in the fields of physics, chemistry, medicine, literature, and world peace.

4. This processing of the whale products at sea (mostly boiling down the blubber into whale oil) had the additional benefits of reducing pollution in the home ports and returning the unused products to the ecological chain.

5. While commercial production of oil from shallow reservoirs began in 1857 in Romania, Drake's well, which produced twenty-five barrels of crude oil per day, is generally credited to have begun the modern petroleum industry. "Petroleum Industry," *The Grolier Encyclopedia,* 2/47.

6. R. D. Collison Black, "William Stanley Jevons," *The New Palgrave: A Dictionary of Economics* (London: Macmillan Press Limited, 1987), 1013.

7. John Tierney, "Betting the Planet," *The New York Times Magazine,* 2 December 1990, 76.

8. Black, "William Stanley Jevons," 1012.

9. Tierney, "Betting the Planet," 76.

10. The eleven-year solar sunspot cycle was first identified (as a ten-year cycle) in 1843 by the German astronomer Samuel Heinrich Schwabe. Jevons, using statistics of fluctuations in grain prices, identified an 11.11-year cycle, which he attempted to tie to new astronomical data that the sunspot cycle might be eleven (rather than ten) years. This work is significant in the context that, at the time, the entire study of business cycles was in its infancy.

11. "Population," *The Grolier Encyclopedia,* 6/34.

12. Ronald Bailey and Bruce N. Ames, "Raining in their Hearts," *National Review,* 3 Dec 1990, 32.

13. "Squeezing in the Next Five Billion," *The Economist,* 20 January 1990, 19.

14. John Lukacs, "Alexis de Tocqueville," *Scribner's Writer Series on CD-ROM—European Writers,* 1985, vol. 6, 893–912.

15. The median-size new home in the U.S. was approximately one thousand square feet in 1960 and rose linearly to approximately two thousand square feet in 1990.

16. The general U.S. population increased from approximately 180 million to 280 million persons (55 percent increase) during this period, while the number of owner-occupied housing units increased from 33 million to 59 million (81 percent increase). U.S. Department of Commerce, Bureau of the Census, *Statistical Abstract of the United States: 1989* (Washington: Government Printing Office, 1989), 706.

17. A labor department study of 5.1 million workers displaced between 1979 and 1984 showed that nearly one-third had earnings gains of 20 percent or more, although one-fifth had taken pay cuts of 20 percent or more. Robert J. Samuelson, "The American Job Machine," *Newsweek,* 23 February 1987, 57.

18. Pilzer, *Unlimited Wealth,* 179–181.

19. Janet Bodnar, "How TV Sees the Economy," *Changing Times,* December 1989, 89.

20. The reason is that in a rapidly changing technological environment there are no economic "cycles"—the marketplace for a particular good or service becomes technologically obsolete long before patterns have a chance to repeat themselves.

21. Nancy J. Perry, "The Bright Man's Burden," *Fortune,* 9 November 1987, 160.

22. John Weber, "There's No Depression in Ravi Batra's Royalties," *Business Week,* 30 November 1987, 128.

23. "Can the World Survive Economic Growth?" *Time,* 14 August 1972, 56.

24. This Paul Ehrlich should not be confused with the *real* Paul Ehrlich, who won the 1908 Nobel Prize for Medicine and whose life was portrayed in the film *Dr. Ehrlich's Magic Bullet* (1940), starring Edward G. Robinson.

25. Tierney, "Betting the Planet," 76.

26. Ibid., 81.

27. Thomas A. Mahoney, "Disaster Lobby Gets a Free Ride," *Air Conditioning, Heating, & Refrigeration News,* 16 October 1989, 26.

28. The Club of Rome, *The Limits to Growth* (New York: Universe Books, 1972).

29. Bailey and Ames, "Raining in their Hearts," 32.

30. Allan Mayer and William J. Cook, "Thinking Small," *Newsweek,* 2 June 1975, 56.

31. Ibid., 60.

32. In summer 1990, after Iraq invaded Kuwait and the world was preparing for the Gulf War, the price of oil quickly rose from approximately $20 to $40 a barrel. Most economists were predicting a return to the oil crisis of the 1970s, if and when war broke out in the gulf. In September 1990, I was interviewed on National Public Radio's *Marketplace* about when I thought the price of oil would reach $80. I made the then-startling prediction that the price of oil would halve, not double, when the shooting started, because then the uncertainty of a war would be over—and the world would again have to deal with the reality of an overabundance of petroleum. The war began on January 15, 1991, and the price of oil fell from $40 to $15 a barrel within one week.

33. All 1970 resource statistics from C. B. Reed, *Fuels, Minerals and Human Survival* (Ann Arbor: Ann Arbor Science Publishers, 1975). All 1987 oil and gas statistics from the National Energy Information Center in Washington, D.C. All other 1987 resource statistics from the *1990 World Almanac and Book of Facts.*

34. Office of Technology Assessment (OTA), Congress of the United States, *Technology and the American Economic Transition: Choices for the Future* (Washington: Government Printing Office, 1988), 3.

35. Tierney, "Betting the Planet," 78.

36. Ibid., 78.

37. Julian Simon, *The Ultimate Resource*.

38. Ed Rubenstein, "The More the Merrier," *National Review,* 17 December 1990, 42.

39. "Squeezing in the Next Five Billion," 19.

40. Tierney, "Betting the Planet," 80.

41. Ibid., 81.

42. Ibid.

43. Ibid.

44. John Maynard Keynes, *The General Theory of Employment, Interest, and Money,* Harvest/HBJ ed. (San Diego: Harcourt Brace Jovanovich, 1964), 383. Keynes's great work was first published in England in 1936.

45. Given that unemployment at the time was an incredible 25 percent, it can be argued that the Keynesian actions of the 1930s (which actually preceded the *General Theory* by several years) may actually have (politically) saved capitalism during the Great Depression.

46. "The fundamental psychological law upon which we are entitled to depend with great confidence . . . is that men are disposed, as a rule and on the average, to increase their consumption as their income increases, but not by as much as the increase in their income." Keynes, *General Theory,* 96.

47. Ibid., 97.

48. The highest federal personal marginal income tax rates were 91 percent and 70 percent in 1960 and 1980 respectively.

49. Corporations originally began paying for employees' health care as a means to increase their compensation without them having to pay up to 91 percent of their wage increases in income taxes. This caused the evolution of a health care system with little or no cost controls—since the person receiving the benefit was not individually paying for the provider of the service (and thus selecting the most cost-efficient provider or product). Moreover, a two-tiered health care system evolved in which corporate employees received health care that was up to 91 percent federally subsidized (by their not having to pay income taxes on the benefits), and unemployed persons (who most needed the benefits) received little or no health care at all.

50. The underground or "black market" economy in the United States

is estimated to exceed $500 billion per annum. For 1993, expenditures for elementary and secondary school education (public and private) are estimated at $195.9 million.

51. W. Carl Biven, *Who Killed John Maynard Keynes?* (Homewood, Ill.: Dow Jones–Irwin, 1989), 32.

52. Samuelson and Nordhaus, *Economics.*

53. "The Economy: 'We are All Keynesians Now,' " *Time,* 31 December 1985, 65.

54. The writer continued: "Prizes such as the Nobel are intended to encourage talented people to go into socially useful pursuits. But we do not need more economists. Indeed, we might be better off if some of the talented people who have become economists had become something else." Robert J. Samuelson, "Booby Prize: Cancel This Nobel, Please," *The New Republic,* 3 December 1990, 18.

55. Businesses were supposed to be granted tax incentives for purchasing *new* equipment, which stimulated economic growth. However, a "mistake" was made in the final drafting of the real estate tax rules, allowing these incentives to apply to *new* owners of *old* buildings—creating a massive real estate tax shelter industry with no corresponding economic benefits. This leakage is estimated to have reduced federal revenues up to $100 billion until it was corrected by the Tax Reform Act of 1986. Paul Zane Pilzer, "Why the Volume of Institutional Real Estate Sales Has Declined," *Real Estate Review,* Summer 1988.

Another type of leakage in federal tax receipts, which still continues today, involves the leveraged buyout business (LBO) that began in the early 1980s. In an LBO, corporate equity is swapped for corporate equity, so that the "owner" (now the debt holder) can receive dividends (now called interest) without first paying corporate income taxes.

56. From 1981 to 1989 annual federal spending for national defense increased $127 billion per year (from $158 billion to $285 billion) and annual federal spending for Social Security increased $80 billion per year (from $140 billion to $220 billion). *The Budget of the United States Government Fiscal Year 1989* (Washington: Government Printing Office, 1989), 6g32–6g35.

57. *Statistical Abstract of the United States: 1989,* 489, 688.

58. Savings as a percent of disposable income was 8.1 percent in 1970, 7.1 percent in 1980, and averaged 3.95 percent from 1986–1989. U.S. Department of Commerce, Bureau of the Census, *Statistical Abstract of*

the United States: 1991 (Washington: Government Printing Office, 1991), 708.

59. For example, suppose a business purchased a new piece of equipment for $1 million in 1981—borrowing the full $1 million cost. Under ERTA, the business would receive a 10 percent ($100,000) investment tax credit in 1981 plus the ability to depreciate the full $1 million cost over an accelerated three-year period. At a 48 percent business income tax rate, this $1 million income tax deduction was worth $480,000 in cash during the first three years—saving the business a total of $580,000 in income taxes, probably more than the equipment cost (from 1981 to 1984) in loan payments. And this analysis doesn't even assume any return in productivity from the new equipment—no wonder businesses rushed to retool their plants after 1981!

60. U.S. manufacturing employment fell from 20,285,000 in 1980 to 19,062,000 in 1989. Total sales of U.S. manufacturing firms rose from $1,897 billion in 1980 to $2,745 billion in 1989. *Statistical Abstract of the United States: 1991,* 667, 910.

61. Weekly at-home food costs from 1980 to 1989 rose at only 70 percent of inflation rate (which included at-home food costs). Ibid., 786, 772.

62. In 1991 the median tenure for employees in all U.S. industries was 6.5 years, ranging from 27.1 years for barbers to less than 1.5 years for food service personnel. U.S. Department of Commerce, Bureau of the Census, *Statistical Abstract of the United States: 1993* (Washington: Government Printing Office, 1993), 650.

Chapter 4: Economic Alchemy

1. Paracelsus, *Selected Writings,* ed. Jolande Jacobi, trans. Norbert Guterman, Bollingen Series XXVIII (Princeton University Press, 1951).

2. While Bacon is often credited with the discovery of saltpeter and gunpowder, it is now recognized that these and many of his other inventions "undoubtedly were derived from the study of Arab scientists." "Bacon, Roger," and "Alchemy," Microsoft *Encarta,* 1993.

3. "Alchemy," Microsoft *Encarta.*

4. Janice Castro, "Goodbye Beta," *Time,* 25 January 1988, 52.

5. Andrew Tanzer, "Sharing," *Forbes,* 20 January 1992, 82.

6. The original Apple II design actually was open-architecture, but

Apple closed the door to outside hardware developers with its introduction of the Macintosh in 1984.

7. "Shaking the Beanstalk," *The Economist,* 24 September 1988, 88.

8. For example, Hercules Inc., a company recognized for its aggressive stance on technology, had over three thousand PCs in North America in 1988 but fewer than one hundred IBM PS/2 machines. Boudette, Neal, "Waiting for the Right Bus; IBM and the clonemakers create a quandary for customers," *Industry Week,* 17 October 1988, 77.

9. Synthetic rubber was originally developed by Germany during the First World War, when it was denied access to Asian natural rubber. However, interest in nonnatural rubber evaporated until World War Two. By 1945, U.S. plants were producing 1 million tons of synthetic rubber a year. "Rubber," *Grolier Electronic Encyclopedia,* 1990.

10. In a letter to Robert Hooke, 5 February, 1675/6, quoted in *The Concise Oxford Dictionary of Quotations,* new ed. (London: Oxford University Press, 1986), 176.

11. While today we may think of writing mainly in terms of personal and artistic expression, the fact is that most of the earliest examples of writing we have, such as the clay tablets on which are etched the cuneiform script of the ancient Sumerians and Babylonians, are either business receipts, government records, or explanations of agricultural techniques.

12. While printing originally began in eighth-century China, it was Gutenberg's printing press and method of casting type that made it widely available.

13. The first electrically powered washing machine was invented in 1910 by Alva J. Fisher, but the product did not become widely available until the invention of an electrically powered agitator-type washer by Howard Snyder in 1922.

14. The story of how businesspeople originally misused the telephone was told to me by the greatest "alchemist" in my life, my cousin, Charles Jay Pilzer. His influence and love is felt in everything I do.

15. John Kenneth Galbraith, *The Affluent Society,* 4th revised ed. (New York: New American Library, 1958), 226.

16. Television-ownership statistics for 1960 from *World Almanac and Book of Facts,* 1973 ed. (New York: Pharos Books, 1973), 1032. Statistics for 1988 from *World Almanac and Book of Facts,* 1989 ed. (New York: Pharos Books, 1989), 356.

17. U.S. Department of Commerce, Bureau of the Census, *Statistical Abstract of the United States: 1991* (Washington: Government Printing Office, 1991), 1272, 1275.

18. By the mid-1980s more than half of all U.S. households could boast at least two cars. *Statistical Abstract of the United States: 1989,* 709.

19. Compare, for example, a $350 seventeen-cubic-foot refrigerator of 1971 with its 1989 counterpart; not only is the modern unit nearly a third cheaper in real terms; it is also 27 percent more energy efficient and offers a variety of luxury features (such as an automatic ice maker) that its predecessor lacked. Or compare a typical 1971-model sub-compact car (say, a $2,700 Datsun 510) with its 1989 "equivalent" (say, a $7,500 Ford Escort). Adjusted for inflation, the two cars cost roughly the same. But in terms of amenities, reliability, fuel efficiency, and performance, the 1989 Ford is far superior to the 1972 Datsun.

Chapter 5: What's Happening to Our Jobs

1. New International Version.

2. Steven N. S. Cheung, "Ronald Harry Coase," *The New Palgrave: A Dictionary of Economics* (Macmillan Press Limited, London, 1987), 455.

3. Although Coase won the Nobel Prize for economics in 1991, Coase is actually a professor of law who eschews mathematical analysis by so-called economists.

4. While Coase's work in the 1930s is generally credited with founding the transaction-cost approach to economic organization, he did not use the actual term "transaction cost," which only came into widespread use during the 1960s. Cheung, "Ronald Harry Coase," 456.

5. Theoretically, a communist nation has the lowest transaction costs between individual workers and entities, because everyone works for the same "company," but the highest inefficiencies of waste and erroneous decisions, because individuals have the lowest individual incentives to work.

6. Employees receiving a 7 to 10 percent raise each year see their salary double in as little as seven years.

7. Charlotte Erickson, *American Industry and the European Immigrant: 1860–1885* (Cambridge: Harvard University Press, 1957), 21–25.

8. Ibid., 21.

9. Ibid., 25.

10. James Howard Bridge, *The Inside History of the Carnegie Steel Company* (New York: Arno Press, 1972), 81. Originally published in 1903 as *The History of the Carnegie Steel Company*.

11. Strouse, Jean, "How Economic Empires Are Born," *The New York Times,* 25 February 1992, A15.

12. Leonard Dinnerstein and David Reimers, *Ethnic Americans: A History of Immigration and Assimilation* (New York: New York University Press, 1977), 40–42.

13. Ibid., 37.

14. The 1921 immigration act, which was originally vetoed by outgoing President Wilson but was signed by President Harding, restricted immigration from Africa and Asia combined to about three thousand immigrants per year. See Vernon M. Briggs, *Immigration Policy and the American Labor Force* (Baltimore: Johns Hopkins University Press, 1984), 43.

15. Ibid., 45.

16. The Japanese exclusion provisions were not repealed until 1952. Ibid., 45.

17. *Business Week,* 17 October 1988.

18. Jeane MacIntosh, "Penney's Profits Increase in 4th Quarter and Year," *Women's Wear Daily,* 16 February 1990, 15.

19. Kenneth R. Sheets, "Building Up to One Great Big Letdown," *U.S. News & World Report,* 8 January 1990, 56.

20. Paul Glastris, "A Season of Hope for Sears," *U.S. News & World Report,* 11 December 1989, 52.

21. The founder of Durant Motors, William Crapo Durant, was also the earlier founder of General Motors in 1908. It was Durant who bought control of the Buick Motor Company in 1904 and then spearheaded the acquisition of Cadillac and Oldsmobile. Durant subsequently lost control of General Motors and founded Durant Motors in 1921.

22. The conglomerate merger—the combining of two substantially unrelated businesses—became popular only in the late 1960s.

23. Paul Samuelson and William D. Nordhaus, *Economics,* 12th ed. (New York: McGraw-Hill, 1985), 540.

24. The number of imported passenger cars sold in the United States rose from 1,285,000 in 1970 to 2,398,000 in 1980, and the number of imported trucks rose from 166,000 in 1970 to 747,000 in 1980. U.S. Department of Commerce, Bureau of the Census, *Statistical Abstract of the*

United States: 1991 (Washington: Government Printing Office, 1991), 1034.

25. The term "junk bonds" is a carryover from the 1960s when a bond, by definition, meant a very secure, highly rated debt instrument—any debt instrument falling below this very high level of security was called "junk." These early high-yield bond issues weren't really junk at all, since they were at least as secure as the stocks which they replaced.

26. U.S. Department of Commerce, Bureau of the Census, *Statistical Abstract of the United States: 1993* (Washington: Government Printing Office, 1993), 652.

27. *Statistical Abstract of the United States: 1993,* 690.

28. Gross domestic product (GDP) was $2,708 in 1980. Even when we adjust all numbers into constant 1987 dollars, real GDP rose from $3,776 in 1980 (1987 dollars) to $4,923 in 1992 (1987 dollars)—a 30 percent "real" increase in economic output. *Statistical Abstract of the United States: 1993,* 690.

Note: Although inflation-adjusted numbers are here presented, the author disagrees with government inflation adjustment mechanisms because they do not account for a continually increasing definition of lifestyle (quantity and quality).

Chapter 6: The Workplace of the Twenty-First Century

1. This story was told to me by a cherished friend and great civic leader, the late Leon Rabin of Dallas, Texas.

2. "Economics," Microsoft *Encarta,* 1993.

3. The full title, *An Inquiry into the Nature and Causes of the Wealth of Nations,* consists of five books covering topics from the history of economic development in Europe since the fall of the Roman Empire to education in the Middle Ages to criticism of the colonial policies of European nations. Mark Blaug, *Great Economists Before Keynes* (Cambridge: Cambridge University Press, 1988), 232.

4. While Smith publicly applauded the role of government in providing what the private sector could not, Smith crusaded against interference with the invisible hand with a "crusading attack on existing economic policies—the vestiges of what he labeled the 'mercantile system.' " In doing so, Smith set a pattern of involvement for economics in political affairs that continues to this day. Ibid., p 233.

5. My mother, Miriam Pilzer, marched with the communist flag down Park Avenue in New York while she was a college student during the early 1930s. Later, as a teacher during the 1950s, she survived the purges of former communists by having changed her name after marriage.

6. *The Random House Unabridged Electronic Dictionary,* (Random House Inc., 1993).

7. *The Random House Unabridged Electronic Dictionary* defines "secular humanism" as "any set of beliefs that promotes human values without specific allusion to religious doctrines."

8. Nelson's Bible dictionary lists over 180 professions mentioned by name in the New and Old Testaments. *Nelson's Illustrated Bible Dictionary* (Thomas Nelson Publishers, 1986).

9. "Guild," Microsoft *Encarta,* 1993.

10. Pilzer, Paul Zane, *Other People's Money* (New York: Simon & Schuster, 1989), 18.

11. "In 1776 Anne Robert Jacques Turgot, controller general of finance for Louis XVI of France, abolished all but four of the craft guilds in order to permit workers freely to offer their services to employers, and during the French Revolution all guilds were abolished. Prussia and other German states abolished the German craft guilds at the beginning of the 19th century, and those craft guilds that still remained in Great Britain were abolished by acts of Parliament in 1814 and 1835." "Guild," Microsoft *Encarta,* 1993.

12. A third type of union, the Public Employee Union, emerged in the middle twentieth century.

13. Pilzer, *Other People's Money,* 31–33.

14. There is significant evidence that President Roosevelt, for political purposes, publicly supported legislation he was personally opposed to. For example, FDR was vehement in his opposition to national deposit insurance but became its most stalwart public supporter when he realized that the public, led by President Hoover on the right and Senator Huey Long on the left, was going to demand and get deposit insurance anyway. Ibid., 34–52.

15. "Labor union," *The Software Toolworks Multimedia Encyclopedia* (Grolier Electronic Publishing, Inc., 1992).

16. U.S. Department of Commerce, Bureau of the Census, *Statistical Abstract of the United States: 1993* (Washington: Government Printing Office, 1993), 689.

17. The American public saves $300 million per year by being able to purchase catsup at half the 1980 price. This represents $375,000 per year in consumer savings for each of the eight hundred jobs displaced ($300 million divided by eight hundred).

18. Author's estimate as the owner and manager of several thousand warehouse spaces.

In an 18,000-square-foot warehouse run by Parkland Hospital in Dallas, after waiting years for an inventory picking and control program to be added to the mainframe computer used to purchase and check in supplies, a savvy warehouseman finally brought in his own personal computer and programmed it himself. Each night an employee comes in to manually type the data from hundreds of daily invoices printed off the mainframe into his PC. Even with the needless waste of retyping already computerized data, this innovation saves Parkland Hospital the equivalent of four full-time warehouse employees.

19. Keller, Maryann, "The Risks of Reorganizing," *Automotive Industries,* January 1990, 11.

20. 2 Samuel 12: 5–7 (New International Version).

21. For example, assume five-year accelerated depreciation on a $1 million ten-year-life capital asset purchased in 1987. In 1992 the company would be carrying the asset on its books for $0, yet the asset would have a productive/liquidation value of $500,000—which could only be realized if the company sold the asset to a third party.

22. More accurately $506,705 less, since the $1,081,818 retirement figure should be reduced by approximately 30 percent for income taxes to $757,272 in order to make it comparable to the $250,567 figure. Distributions from pension plans are taxable as income when they are withdrawn.

23. *Statistical Abstract of the United States: 1993,* 650.

Chapter 7: Money

1. Although many people remember this story as having something to do with Jesus' anger at moneylenders (who aren't even mentioned), Jesus' anger appears to have been directed primarily at the commercialization of the temple area by the men who sold the sheep, doves, and cattle that the pilgrims exchanged for silver to support the temple. Jesus himself supported the temple tax, which he willingly paid (Matthew 17:24–27). The money changers served a valuable purpose in changing the offerings

pilgrims brought to the temple into silver—it was required by law for every person over twenty to make an annual offering of silver to the temple (Exodus 30:14).

2. While not directly related to the original cause of the Great Depression, the collapse of currency as a medium of exchange due to excessive hoarding surely prolonged it. Paul Zane Pilzer with Robert Dietz, *Other People's Money* (New York: Simon & Schuster, 1989), 32.

3. King Solomon paid for cypress trees needed to build the temple with wheat and olive oil (1 Kings 5:11). Silver was so commonly used as money that the Hebrew word for silver, *keceph,* came to mean money.

4. "Money of the Bible," *Nelson's Illustrated Bible Dictionary* (Thomas Nelson Publishers, 1986).

5. Paul Zane Pilzer, *Unlimited Wealth,* updated ed. (New York: Crown Publishers, Inc., 1994), 17.

6. "And Ishbi-Benob, one of the descendants of Rapha, whose bronze spearhead weighed three hundred shekels and who was armed with a new [sword], said he would kill David" (2 Samuel 21:16, NIV).

7. Excerpted and revised from the Preface and Chapter 1 of Pilzer, *Other People's Money—The Inside Story of the S&L Mess.*

8. Charles Dickens, "My Account with Her Majesty," *All the Year Round* 2 (5 March 1864): 79–83.

9. Ernest Russell, "Humanity as the Bank Clerk Sees It," *World Today* 14 (June 1908): 659.

10. Regulation Q typically allowed savings institutions to pay approximately $5\frac{1}{4}$ percent interest, approximately $\frac{1}{4}$ percent above the rate paid by commercial banks.

11. Commercial paper is today defined as a debt obligation issued by a nongovernmental entity with a maturity of less than 270 days.

12. The prime rate averaged 6.25 percent and commercial paper averaged 3.75 percent in 1992. U.S. Department of Commerce, Bureau of the Census, *Statistical Abstract of the United States: 1993* (Washington: Government Printing Office, 1993), 826.

13. In 1992, $547.5 billion of commercial paper was outstanding as contrasted with $536 billion of total commercial and industrial loans by commercial banks. *Statistical Abstract of the United States: 1993,* 824, 797.

14. Today, most automobile dealers readily admit that they make much more money from financing automobile purchases than from selling automobiles.

15. The Depository Institutions Reform Act of 1980, and the subsequent Garn-St. Germain Act of 1982, effectively lifted the interest rate ceilings on consumer deposits and the controls on what savings banks could do in investing them.

16. *Statistical Abstract of the United States: 1993,* 806.

17. Ibid., 793, 805.

18. "Udder People's Money," *The Economist,* 6 December 1993, 83.

19. *Statistical Abstract of the United States: 1993,* 826.

20. Ibid.

21. From its inception in 1913 until 1979, the Fed unsuccessfully attempted to control interest rates in the economy. Then, on October 6, 1979, in what came to be known as the "Saturday Night Special," Federal Reserve Chairman Paul Volcker announced that the Fed would no longer attempt to control inflation by artificially controlling interest rates—and instead would concentrate on limiting inflation by controlling the supply of money. The Fed proved as ineffectual in controlling the money supply in the 1980s as it was in controlling interest rates in the 1970s. More recent leaders of the Federal Reserve seem to be aware of their helplessness in manipulating free markets and have concentrated more on commentary than on attempting ineffectual action.

22. This recent phenomenon of zero or negative marginal product cost is causing an enormous paradigm shift in managerial practices that few companies yet realize. In my discussions with businesspeople on this subject it has become apparent that what is needed is a cohesive management theory or book entitled *Managing in a Zero Marginal Product Cost Environment.*

23. This increased use of existing plant capacity contributed in the 1980s to making Communism obsolete. In a communist, or state-planned, economy, manufacturing plants operate at close to 100 percent capacity and are typically efficient only when first opened—because only when they are new do they typically use the latest technology. In contrast, in a capitalist, or free-market, economy, manufacturing plants often operate at less than 50 percent capacity overall, but they are often twice as efficient over time because continual competition forces them to keep up with the latest technological advances.

This reality caused the economic growth rate of the former Soviet Union to surpass the United States in the postwar period, which led Premier Khrushchev to bang his shoe at the United Nations in 1961, resounding, "We will bury you." However, this reality also caused the demise of the former Soviet Union in the 1980s, when no amount of plant utilization could make up for an inability to keep up with rapidly advancing technology.

Now, with the increased use of excess plant capacity worldwide due to the recent development of our virtual economy, the capitalist system is enjoying the benefits of both systems—highly increased plant utilization and the incentive, fostered by competition, to rapidly implement new technological advances.

24. John Maynard Keynes, *The General Theory of Employment, Interest, and Money,* Harvest/HBJ ed. (San Diego: Harcourt Brace Jovanovich, 1964), 104.

25. In this hypothesis, lawyers and investment bankers have some of the lowest job satisfaction ratings because they are among the furthest removed from the end users who benefit from their labors. Teachers, entertainers, and some distributors have among the highest job satisfaction ratings since they continually see the real results of their efforts.

26. Although economists do not currently adjust economic data for changes in lifestyle over time, they do make certain adjustments for lifestyle when comparing economic data between countries. For example, on a monetary (e.g., currency conversion) basis, U.S. GNP per capita in 1990 was $21,863, contrasted with $23,558 in Japan. However, when purchasing power parities (PPPs) are taken into account—PPPs adjust for the cost differences between purchasing the same market basket of goods in each country—U.S. GDP per capita in 1990 was $21,449, contrasted with $17,634 in Japan. *Statistical Abstract of the United States: 1993,* 1387, 1392.

27. In 1970 housing expenditures were $94 billion of $646.5 billion total U.S. personal consumption, and in 1990 housing expenditures were $547.5 billion of $3748.4 billion total U.S. personal consumption. GDP was $1010.7 billion in 1970 and $5522.2 billion in 1990. *Statistical Abstract of the United States: 1993,* 699, 690.

28. The same percentage of total disposable income (15 percent) in 1990 versus 1970 purchased 51 percent more housing for only 22 percent more population—a net gain in the number of housing units per person of 24 percent. If the number of units grew 24 percent at the same total cost, the cost per unit fell approximately 20 percent, from 15 percent to 12 percent of disposable income.

29. Lest some pundit hypothesize that this increase was just from an

abundance of extra-large homes for the very rich, the median square footage also increased about the same percentage, from 1385 square feet to 1920 square feet. *Statistical Abstract of the United States: 1993,* 1223.

30. Ibid.

31. John Kenneth Galbraith, *The Affluent Society,* 4th rev. ed. (New York: New American Library, 1958), 226.

32. The Great Depression began early in England in 1925 when the then chancellor or the exchequer Winston Churchill disastrously put the British government back on the gold standard. Reflecting on this colossal mistake in managing the supply of money, Nobel laureate John Kenneth Galbraith writes: "Ten years before . . . Winston Churchill had initiated the military action at the Dardanelles, the most spectacular military error of World War I; now on economics and finance he had equally excelled. He would later and brilliantly recover. No politician of modern times has rivaled Churchill's ability to go back and forth from desolate error to major success." John Kenneth Galbraith, *A Journey Through Economic Time—A Firsthand View* (New York: Houghton Mifflin Company, 1994), 52–54.

33. The first central bank in the United States, the Bank of the United States, was established in 1791 despite the opposition of Thomas Jefferson, who felt that it was unconstitutional for the federal government to establish a central bank. It was terminated in 1811 when its charter expired. The second Bank of the United States was chartered in 1816 and terminated in 1836 by President Jackson, who also had severe doubts about the constitutionality of the United States to maintain a central bank.

34. Figures for 1992 from the board of governors of the Federal Reserve System. *Statistical Abstract of the United States: 1993,* 821.

35. Ibid., 817.

36. Technically, the Fed does have some limited control over banks that issue credit cards—in 1991 bank cards accounted for 221 million of 1,027 million cards outstanding—although the typical reserve requirements imposed on bank demand accounts do not apply to consumer credit. Ibid., 817.

37. Bryant, Adam, "From Frequent-Flier Miles, Currency for the Earthbound," *The New York Times,* 22 August 1994, 1.

38. Telephone interview on August 23, 1993, with Bob Meyer, editor and publisher of *Barter News* (Mission Viejo, California).

39. *The New York Times* quoted the Federal Reserve Bank of Los

Angeles as its source for a chart showing the number of each denomination in circulation. The entire U.S. population in 1992 was 255 million, the same year that the Fed reported $292 billion in currency in M_1. Calvin Sims, "In Recycling of Greenbacks, New Meaning for Old Money," *The New York Times,* National Section, 22 May 1994, 12.

40. *Statistical Abstract of the United States: 1993,* 621.

Chapter 8: Government

1. "Government," Microsoft *Encarta,* 1993.

2. "Appendix: U.S. Constitution," *ZCI Publishing Concise Encyclopedia* (Dallas, Texas, 1994).

3. Ibid.

4. Adapted from a senior thesis that I wrote in 1974 under the tutelage of Professors Joseph Brendan McFadden and (the late) Professor Robert Joseph Sullivan, Department of Journalism, Lehigh University. During the research for this thesis I also had the great pleasure of working directly with Robert Rodale, son of J. I. Rodale and chairman of Rodale Press. Robert Rodale was killed in 1990 in an automobile accident in Moscow, on a mission to bring the benefits of the work of his family to the Russian people. He is greatly missed by many who loved and respected him.

5. Witkower Press Inc. of Hartford, Connecticut, had published a book *Arthritis and Common Sense* and claimed in their advertisements that it would help arthritic and rheumatoid sufferers. In 1954 the FTC ordered the Witkower Press to "forthwith cease and desist from representing, directly or indirectly, that their book was adequate, effective, and reliable in giving relief to arthritic and rheumatoid sufferers." Witkower Press accepted the ruling and did not appeal the case. In a similar case against Prentice Hall, the large publisher agreed to the FTC action because they did not want to enter into costly litigation with the federal government. Paul Zane Pilzer, "Rodale Press versus The Federal Trade Commission: A Comprehensive Analysis," senior thesis, Lehigh University (Bethlehem, Pennyslvania), May 21, 1974.

6. FTC commissioner Philip Elman, a Kennedy appointee and former law clerk to Supreme Court Justice Felix Frankfurter, wrote in his dissenting opinion: "It is the glory of a free society that a man can write a book contending that the earth is flat, or that the moon is made of green cheese, or that God is dead, without having to 'substantiate' or 'prove' his

claims to the satisfaction of some public official or agency. . . . It is arrogance to presume that in any field of knowledge, whether dealing with health or otherwise, all the answers are now in." Ibid.

7. At the original hearing on this case before the FTC Examiner, dissenting FTC commissioner Elman foreshadowed the path that the FTC was about to take when he wrote: "Congress did not create this Commission to act as a censor of unorthodox ideas and theories in books, whether they deal with politics or health. We should not forget that, in both fields, today's heresy may become tomorrow's dogma." Ibid.

8. This was illustrated by the U.S. automobile industry during the 1970s, when the Big Three collectively refused to implement electronic fuel injector technology that was developed in the late 1960s. By being early adapters of such technology—I still own a 1970 Volvo with electronic fuel injection that gets thirty miles to the gallon—European and Japanese auto manufacturers captured a third of the U.S. auto market, forcing the Big Three to retool their entire operations during the 1980s to catch up. Today, thanks primarily to overseas competition, U.S. automobiles once again offer the international consumer the most for their money. Moreover, the "forced" conversion from carburetors to fuel injectors more than doubled fuel economy (and halved pollution), bringing an end to the powerful oil cartels of the 1970s.

9. According to Schumpeter, the economic strength of a capitalist society lies in its continual desire to "incessantly revolutionize" its methods of production because of the pressures of competition. As Schumpeter saw it, advancing technology continually produces new tools and better methods for every step of the production process at an ever-increasing pace. Even if a company has just designed and implemented a new tool, or even a whole manufacturing plant, competition in the capitalist system forces "creative destruction" of the just-built plant when, due to advancing technology, there is a better method available to produce a superior product.

10. The final amendment in the Bill of Rights states that "The powers not delegated to the United States by the Constitution, nor prohibited by it to the states, are reserved to the states respectively, or to the people."

11. This is clearly evidenced by the two different theories or ways U.S. states currently record mortgages. In title-theory states, the title of mortgaged property is split into "legal title," held by the lender, and "equitable title," held by the borrower. The borrower gains full title to the

property ("the deed") upon retiring mortgage debt, and the lender is granted more immediate cure to a default than in lien-theory states. In lien-theory states, the lender receives a lien on the property to secure the debt, which must be foreclosed on in the event of default.

12. The real genius of Mikhael Gorbachev, which eventually led to the collapse of the Soviet empire, was his understanding that in perestroika (alchemic economic reform) the society first needed to have glasnost (the free exchange of information). Paul Zane Pilzer, *Unlimited Wealth*, updated ed. (New York: Crown Publishers, Inc., 1994), 19–20.

13. Isaiah 2:4 (King James Version).

14. After the director of ANT was arrested, I received a call from a senior U.S. State Department officer, who previously had been very helpful to our company in getting permission to fly Soviet pilots in and out of Los Angeles. He phoned to tell me that he and I had never "officially" met, and that the only time that he could see us "officially" meeting in the near future was when I was arrested and being tortured in a Soviet prison—as it would be his "official" job to negotiate my release. He then told me that "unofficially" he would do what he could to see that we would never meet "officially."

15. Poe, Richard, *How to Profit from the Coming Russian Boom* (New York: McGraw-Hill, 1993), 166–167.

16. The Constitution was finished on September 17, 1787, and went into effect on June 21, 1788, when it was ratified by nine states. It was ratified by the thirteenth state, Rhode Island, on May 29, 1790.

17. Beginning in 1989, in Texas and in at least twelve other states, the legislature has passed so-called Robin Hood bills, which confiscate education monies from wealthier districts and distribute such monies to poorer districts to equalize the amount spent per pupil statewide.

18. For example, in 1989 Utah spent the lowest amount per child on public education ($30,000 over twelve years) and New Jersey spent the highest ($90,000 over twelve years), but Utah had a higher percentage of high school graduation (80.6 versus 77.2) and the highest composite SAT scores (1034 versus 893 for New Jersey). Similarly, in the mid-1980s, several states doubled their spending per pupil on public education, while performance plummeted. Pilzer, *Unlimited Wealth*, 112–114.

19. U.S. Department of Commerce, Bureau of the Census, *Statistical Abstract of the United States: 1993* (Washington: Government Printing Office, 1993), 508.

20. Ibid.

21. Ibid., 493.

22. Ibid., 2, 621.

23. Even in the 1990s, when in many cases government employees earn more total compensation than the taxpayers who pay their salaries, this may not be so unfair. For many government workers, lifetime job security was one of the reasons they sought and obtained a government job in the first place.

24. "Cost of Crime: $674 Billion," *U.S. News & World Report,* 17 January 1994, 40–41.

25. *Statistical Abstract of the United States: 1993,* 312.

26. "Cost of Crime: $674 Billion," 40–41.

27. *Statistical Abstract of the United States: 1993,* 345, 347.

28. Ibid.

29. This statement comes from conversations with owners of collision repair shops, who often cannot find legitimate channels to purchase certain parts for body repair. In each state one could confirm this by comparing insurance claims paid for certain parts, say the rear bumper of a 1990 Cadillac Seville, with the number of additional bumpers actually manufactured and the number of stolen unrecovered 1990 Cadillac Sevilles.

30. In the 1960s, ignition systems were developed that locked the steering wheel when the key was removed, reducing the incidence of automobile theft for "joy rides."

Chapter 9: Leadership

1. "Economy," *Webster's New World Dictionary on PowerCD* (Dallas: Zane Publishing, 1995).

ACKNOWLEDGMENTS

"Tell us about the Cabala," the two soldiers asked the tsadik.[1]

"You're not ready to study the Cabala," the tsadik replied, interrupting the sipping of his tea after dinner. "Now your cousin Paul, he's almost ready."

The tsadik then explained the three requirements that must be met before studying the Cabala, the secret Jewish mysticism of the ancient rabbis. "First," he said, "you must be at least forty years old. Second, you must be very learned in all the books of the Torah, especially the Talmud. And third, you must never study the Cabala in a group larger than three (because you might be overheard), or smaller than two (because you might go mad if you study alone)."

The tsadik was my uncle, Charles Jay Pilzer, the wisest man I know. To everyone in the family he's always been *Uncle* Charlie, but he's actually my cousin, as we have a common great-grandfather. The soldiers were our Israeli cousins, teenagers, both on military leave from the army. They were visiting the United States and meeting the family's famous Uncle Charlie for the first time over dinner that night in Dallas, Texas.

As Charlie deflected the interest of our cousins to another subject, I felt a fifth presence at the table, the common ancestor to all four of us, a rabbi who had died in Poland around 1870. I could hardly wait until later that evening when Uncle Charlie and I would be alone.

"What do you mean that I'm almost ready to study the Cabala?" I

---

[1] Also spelled zaddick, "the spiritual leader of a Hasidic community," or "a righteous and just man."

"Zaddick," *Webster's New World Dictionary on PowerCD* (Zane Publishing and Simon & Schuster, 1995).

asked my uncle. "Compared to you I hardly know what the Talmud is, let alone anything about Jewish mysticism."

"Yes, you do," he replied, "and the best part is that you don't even know what you know." I could feel a presence of familial love almost too strong to have developed over just a single lifetime. Uncle Charlie continued.

"While I've always admired your economic success, your hubris and self-interest have often been a little hard to take. But I've known that one day you would use the gifts that God gave you for a much higher purpose. You've always been your father's physical duplicate, and watching you tonight *listening* to our young cousins, I can see that you are also becoming his spiritual double as well."

Charlie never did explain to me exactly what higher purpose he had in mind. It wasn't as if he didn't know the answer; Charlie *always* knows the answer. He just acted as if there were more things that I had to learn for myself before I was ready to hear the answer.

I'm hoping that my higher purpose has something to do with teaching people how to reconcile their material lives with their spiritual lives. In both areas, I've had some of the best teachers in modern times, and I relish the opportunity to put their knowledge to such good use.

My father lived vicariously through my academic career. Learning something new was always exciting for me because I could then teach it to my father. Many of those teaching sessions, however, ended in frustration when I found that I hadn't yet learned a subject well enough to explain it to him.

My father always consoled me by telling me that true knowledge is understanding how *little* you know. He taught me that the learning process is analogous to climbing mountains—each peak you climb becomes the foundation for another, previously unknown, higher range of mountains.

While conducting the research for this book, I reflected on those late-night sessions with my father when I tried to teach him the things I thought I had learned. I see now that he must have known many of the things he feigned misunderstanding. My father's incessant questioning was his way of ensuring that I had really learned what he knew I would need to succeed. More important, I realize now that the reason I love and miss him so much is not just because he was my father, but because he was my teacher.

I began teaching at New York University in 1979, just after he passed away. My students, hungry and always grateful for real knowledge that they can use, have replaced my father as my raison d'etre, the reason for my being. The more I try to teach them something, the more frustrated (and motivated) I become, trying to understand the subject better so that I might explain it better to them.

Similarly, I realize that some of my dearest friends also function as my best teachers. I acknowledge them here for their contributions to this book, and for their unrequited love and support. A few that stand out include Ed Ames, Michael Ashkin, Brad Bauer, Norman and Carol Beil, Reed Bilbray, Jenna Cramer, Catherine Crier, Philippa Feigen, John Grillos, John Hauge, Don and Jan Held, Richard Jaffe, Tony Meyer, Stanley and Elsie Pearle, Tony and Becky Robbins, George Stone, Dexter and Birdie Yager, and Caroline Zemmel.

Two years ago my mother had a nearly fatal automobile accident. During her recovery, I moved into her house—the house in which I was raised. I felt my late father's presence every day, especially when my brothers came to stay with us on weekends.

It was there, surrounded by my family and the memory of almost one thousand Sabbath dinners, that the proposal for this book was born. The proposal included the love and guidance of my mother, whose optimistic Panglossian view of life has served me throughout my life as a self-fulfilling prophecy. It included the love and guidance of my brother Steve and his wife, Donna, and of my brother Lee and his wife, Meryn. Lee has also been my best friend—and almost everything else of value—since we graduated together from Lehigh University in 1974.

No acknowledgments are complete without noting the contributions of my literary agent, Ms. Jan Miller. Jan is commonly known as "the dreammaker" to the many authors, including me, on whom she was the first one to take a chance. Now, after fifteen years, Jan's original role as just my trusted agent has taken a back seat to her role as my cherished friend. I love you, Jan, and will always be grateful for your support during the bad times as well as the good ones.

When I first broached with Jan the concept of a book on the theology of economics over dinner, she became so enthused that she phoned Bob Asahina of Simon & Schuster at home. Bob, who ultimately became my editor and the midwife for the proposal, was the first to see that the book could be more than just a review of the theology behind our economic system. He saw that it could have a much "higher purpose" in serving millions of people seeking to reconcile their material with their spiritual existence. I will have succeeded if this book lives up to just a few of his enormously high expectations.

My final and foremost acknowledgments are reserved for those of my readers who have taken the time to write me with their comments and individual concerns. Answering their mail has become, along with teaching my students, an important reason for my being.

In a world of numerous and exciting opportunities, I know what I want to do for the rest of my life—I want to teach. I am grateful to my students, and to the readers of this book, for giving me the opportunity. God bless you.

INDEX

About the Author

Paul Zane Pilzer completed college in three years and received his M.B.A. from Wharton Graduate Business School in fifteen months at age twenty-two. At age twenty-four, he was appointed a professor at New York University.

While employed as Citibank's youngest officer at age twenty-two and its youngest vice-president at twenty-five, Pilzer started several entrepreneurial businesses and earned his first million before age twenty-six.

He has been an appointed economic adviser in two presidential administrations. In 1985 he testified before Congress, warning that the S & L problem would grow to a $200 billion-dollar disaster. Congress didn't listen, and in 1989 Pilzer wrote *Other People's Money* (Simon & Schuster), which was critically acclaimed by *The New York Times, The Economist* magazine, and Nobel prizewinner John Kenneth Galbraith.

Pilzer's second book, *Unlimited Wealth* (Crown Publishers, Inc., 1991, 1994), explained how we live in a world of unlimited physical resources because of rapidly advancing technology. After reading *Unlimited Wealth,* the late Sam Walton, founder of Wal-Mart, said that he was "amazed at Pilzer's business capacity" and his "ability to put it into layman's terms." *Unlimited Wealth* has been published in Japan, Taiwan, and the Russian Republic.

But the greatest accolades have come for *God Wants You to Be Rich,* which appeared on *The New York Times* Business bestseller list, was featured on the cover of national magazines such as *Success,* and was the subject of a front-page story in *The Wall Street Journal.*

Today, Pilzer is a contributing editor to two economic journals, an adjunct professor at New York University, and the Founder and Publisher of Zane Publishing, Inc., a leading CD ROM educational publisher.

He has been a regular commentator on CNN and National Public Radio, and has appeared several times on the *Larry King Live!* television program.